T0235372

Lecture Notes in Computer Science 9695

Commenced Publication in 1973
Founding and Former Series Editors:
Gerhard Goos, Juris Hartmanis, and Jan van Leeuwen

More information about this series at http://www.springer.com/series/7408

Marko Bertogna · Luís Miguel Pinho
Eduardo Quiñones (Eds.)

Reliable Software Technologies – Ada-Europe 2016

21st Ada-Europe International Conference
on Reliable Software Technologies
Pisa, Italy, June 13–17, 2016
Proceedings

 Springer

Editors
Marko Bertogna
Università di Modena e Reggio Emilia
Modena
Italy

Eduardo Quiñones
Barcelona Supercomputing Center
Barcelona
Spain

Luís Miguel Pinho
CISTER/INESC-TEC, ISEP
Porto
Portugal

ISSN 0302-9743   ISSN 1611-3349 (electronic)
Lecture Notes in Computer Science
ISBN 978-3-319-39082-6   ISBN 978-3-319-39083-3 (eBook)
DOI 10.1007/978-3-319-39083-3

Library of Congress Control Number: 2016939061

LNCS Sublibrary: SL2 – Programming and Software Engineering

Printed on acid-free paper

This Springer imprint is published by Springer Nature
The registered company is Springer International Publishing AG Switzerland

Preface

The 21st edition of the International Conference on Reliable Software Technologies (Ada-Europe 2016) took place in the city of Pisa, hosted by Scuola Superiore Sant'Anna, an internationally renowned university school. This was the return of the conference to Italy, after Venice in 2008. Previous editions of the conference were held in Spain (Santander, 1999, Palma de Mallorca, 2004, Valencia, 2010, and Madrid, 2015), France (Toulouse, 2003, Brest, 2009, and Paris, 2014), the UK (London, 1997, York, 2005, and Edinburgh, 2011), Switzerland (Montreux, 1996, and Geneva, 2007), Sweden (Uppsala, 1998, and Stockholm 2012), Germany (Potsdam, 2000, and Berlin, 2013), Belgium (Leuven, 2001), Austria (Vienna, 2002), and Portugal (Porto, 2006). The conference series is run and sponsored by Ada-Europe, in collaboration with local organizations. This year Scuola Superiore Sant'Anna led the organization, with the support of a truly international team.

The conference took place during June 13–17, 2016, with a rich program on both the technical and social sides. The scientific part of the conference program featured 12 presentations selected among 28 peer-reviewed papers, which were grouped into four regular sessions spread out on the central days of the conference, on topics ranging from concurrency and parallelism to real-time systems via testing and verification and program correctness and robustness. The program also included eight industrial presentations, split across two industrial sessions. A session featuring presentations from students of the ITS EASY post-graduate school, which co-located its meeting with the conference, a poster session, and one vendor session with an accompanying vendor exhibition completed the core program. In addition to this rich set of contents, eight tutorials for the equivalent of 10 half-day sessions were scheduled on Monday and Friday. Also on Friday, the week featured the third edition of the Challenges and New Approaches for Dependable and Cyber-Physical Systems Engineering Workshop.

The submissions to scientific and industrial tracks of the conference program came from 25 countries and 96 distinct authors, from Europe, Asia, North and South America, and Africa. The final result was a truly international program with contributions from Australia, Austria, Canada, France, Germany, Italy, Portugal, Spain, Sweden, Tunisia, UK, and USA.

Each day of the core conference program opened with a keynote talk centered on topics of high interest within conference focus:

- "Why the Expressive Power of Languages Such as Ada Is Needed for Future Cyber Physical Systems." Alan Burns, from the University of York, UK, presented the challenges put forward to the developer of cyber physical systems to fully exploit the wealth of real-time systems theory, and how these are addressed with the high-level programming abstractions of Ada.
- "Challenges for the Automotive Platform of the Future." Valerio Giorgetta, from Magneti Marelli, Italy, presented how the concept of a car will be impacted by the

challenges put forward such as autonomous vehicles and functional safety and reliability.

- "The HiPEAC Vision." Marc Duranton, from CEA, France, presented an overview of the HiPEAC vision, a bi-annual document produced by the HiPEAC network of excellence, with the upcoming challenges in computing systems.

The proceedings contained in this volume cover the opening keynote talk and the full set of peer-reviewed papers. The remainder of the conference contributions are published, in successive instalments, in the *Ada User Journal*, the quarterly magazine of Ada-Europe.

The tutorial program covered a wide range of topics in the scope of the central themes of the conference, as follows:

- "A Semi-formal Approach to Software Development," William Bail, The MITRE Corporation, USA
- "Software Test and Verification Techniques for Dependable Systems," William Bail, The MITRE Corporation, USA
- "Embedded ARM Programming with Ada 2012," Patrick Rogers, AdaCore, USA
- "Ada 2012 (Sub)types and Subprogram Contracts in Practice," Jacob Sparre Andersen, JSA Research & Innovation, Denmark
- "Towards Energy Awareness and Predictability in the Linux Kernel," J. Lelli, ARM Ltd., Italy
- "Access Types and Memory Management in Ada 2012," J.P. Rosen, Adalog, France
- "Using Gnoga for Desktop/Mobile GUI and Web Development in Ada," J.P. Rosen, Adalog, France
- "Parallelism in Ada, C, Java and C#, Today and Tomorrow," Brad Moore, General Dynamics Canada, and Stephen Michell, Maurya Software, Canada

The industrial sessions featured eight presentations centered on various aspects of reliable software development:

- "What Has the ARG Been up to? — Recent and Future Changes to Ada 2012," Jeff Cousins, ARG Rapporteur, UK
- "Using Ada's Visibility Rules and Static Analysis to Enforce Segregation of Safety Critical Components," Jean-Pierre Rosen and Jean-Christophe Van-Den-Hende, Adalog and Alstom-Transport, France
- "Automated Testing of SPARK Ada Contracts (AUTOSAC)," Christopher Bryan, Rapita Systems, UK
- "Ada Usage in HMI for Onboard Safety Critical Applications," Clara Maria Arcones-Gabriel, Enrique Chicharro-Lopez and Ismael Lafoz-Pastor, Airbus Defence and Space, Spain
- "An Update on Programming Language Vulnerabilities," Stephen Michell, WG23 Convenor, Canada
- "Middleware for Distributed and Redundant Software," Vincent Monfort, Systerel, France

- "Model-Based Design and Schedulability Analysis for Avionic Applications on Multicore Platforms," Wenceslas Godard and Geoffrey Nelissen, Airbus Group SAS, France and CISTER/ISEP, Portugal
- "Fitting the CONCERTO Component Model Approach to AUTOSAR Development Flow," Andrea Russino, Stefano Puri and Alessandro Zovi, Intecs and Università di Padova, Italy

This edition of the conference featured a focused topic on "Safe and Predictable Parallel Software Technologies." Ada has been a language that has always excelled with its advanced high-level concurrency support. In the last 20 years, Ada has steadily extended its wealth of concurrency features and capabilities to a considerable extent, yet within the bounds of a sequential task reasoning. With the advances in processor architectures, and in particular the move into a parallel world, it is time to discuss how Ada should be evolved into supporting in the language the notion of fine-grained parallelism. The program included a special session on "Ada and Parallelism," which discussed the design choices and evolutions of the language to support fine-grained parallel programs. The session included both presentations from experts in the following topics as well as an open discussion to the floor:

- "Paraffin: A Parallelism Library for Ada," Brad Moore, Gran Dynamics, Canada
- "Ada Container Iterators for Parallelism and Map/Reduce," S. Tucker Taft, Ada-Core, USA

We would like to acknowledge the work of all the people who contributed, with various responsibilities and official functions, to the making of the conference program. First of all, the authors of the contributions, who were largely responsible for the success of the conference. Then the members of the Program and Industrial Committees, who worked hard to review and select a high-quality set of papers, both for the Springer LNCS volume in the case of peer-reviewed papers and the *Ada User Journal* in the case of the industrial presentations, the special session papers, and the workshop.

Finally, the group of organizers who made the conference program a reality: Giorgio Buttazzo (Conference Chair); Ettore Ricciardi (Local Chair); Marco Di Natale and Tullio Vardanega (Industrial Co-chairs); Jorge Real (Tutorial and Workshop Chair); Geoffrey Nelissen (Publication Chair); Mauro Marinoni and Dirk Craeynest (Publicity Co-chairs); Paolo Gai and Ahlan Marriott (Exhibition Chair). They all deserve our gratitude for their effort.

We hope that the attendees enjoyed the conference, both its technical and social program, as much as we did in organizing it.

June 2016   Marko Bertogna
                                                                Luís Miguel Pinho
                                                                Eduardo Quiñones

Organization

The 21st International Conference on Reliable Software Technologies, Ada-Europe 2016, was organized by Ada-Europe, in cooperation with ACM SIGAda, ACM SIGBED, ACM SIGPLAN, and Ada Resource Association.

Conference Chair

Giorgio Buttazzo   Scuola Superiore Sant'Anna, Italy

Program Co-chairs

Marko Bertogna   University of Modena and Reggio Emilia, Italy
Luís Miguel Pinho   CISTER/INESC-TEC, ISEP, Portugal

Special Session Chair

Eduardo Quiñones   Barcelona Supercomputing Center, Spain

Tutorial and Workshop Chair

Jorge Real   Universitat Politecnica de Valencia, Spain

Industrial Co-chairs

Marco Di Natale   Scuola Superiore Sant'Anna, Italy
Tullio Vardanega   Università di Padova, Italy

Publication Chair

Geoffrey Nelissen   CISTER/INESC-TEC, ISEP, Portugal

Exhibition Co-chairs

Paolo Gai   Evidence Srl, Italy
Ahlan Marriott   White Elephant GmbH, Switzerland

Publicity Co-chairs

Mauro Marinoni   Scuola Superiore Sant'Anna, Italy
Dirk Craeynest   Ada-Belgium and KU Leuven, Belgium

Local Chair

Ettore Ricciardi   ISTI-CNR, Pisa, Italy

Sponsoring Institutions

AdaCore
Esterel Technologies
Ellidiss Software, TNI Europe Ltd.
Vector Software
Rapita Systems Ltd.
PTC

Program Committee

Mario Aldea	University of Cantabria, Spain
Ted Baker	National Science Foundation, USA
Marko Bertogna	Università di Modena e Reggio Emilia, Italy
Johann Blieberger	TU Wien, Austria
Bernd Burgstaller	Yonsei University, Korea
Albert Cohen	Inria, France
Juan A. de La Puente	Universidad Politécnica de Madrid, Spain
Michael Gonzalez Harbour	Universidad de Cantabria, Spain
J. Javier Gutierrez	Universidad de Cantabria, Spain
Jerome Hugues	ISAE, France
Raimund Kirner	University of Hertfordshire, UK
Albert Llemosi	Universitat de les Illes Balears, Spain
Franco Mazzanti	ISTI-CNR, Italy
Stephen Michell	Maurya Software Inc., Canada
Jurgen Mottok	Regensburg University of Applied Sciences, Germany
Laurent Pautet	Telecom ParisTech, France
Luís Miguel Pinho	CISTER/INESC-TEC, ISEP, Portugal
Erhard Plodereder	University of Stuttgart, Germany
Eduardo Quinones	Barcelona Supercomputing Center, Spain
Jorge Real	Universitat Politècnica de València, Spain
Christine Rochange	IRIT - Université de Toulouse, France
Jose Ruiz	AdaCore, France
Sergio Saez	Universidad Politècnica de València, Spain
Martin Schoeberl	Technical University of Denmark, Denmark
Tucker Taft	AdaCore, USA
Theodor Tempelmeier	University of Applied Sciences Rosenheim, Germany
Elena Troubitsyna	Aabo Akademi University, Finland
Santiago Uruena	GMV, Spain
Tullio Vardanega	Università di Padua, Italy

Industrial Committee

Ian Broster	Rapita Systems, UK
Jorgen Bundgaard	Ramboll, Denmark
Dirk Craeynest	Ada-Belgium and KU Leuven, Belgium
Arne Hamann	Bosch, Germany
Ismael Lafoz	Airbus Defence & Space, Spain
Ahlan Marriott	White Elephant, Switzerland
Paolo Panaroni	Intecs, Italy
Paul Parkinson	Wind River, UK
Eric Perlade	AdaCore, France
Jean-Pierre Rosen	Adalog, France
Jacob Sparre Andersen	JSA Consulting, Denmark
Claus Stellwag	Elektrobit AG, Germany
Jean-Loup Terraillon	European Space Agency, The Netherlands
Sergey Tverdyshev	SysGO, Germany
Rod White	MBDA, UK

Additional Reviewers

Etienne Borde	Erjola Lalo	Erna Oklapi
Hugues Cassé	Tobias Langer	Lukas Osinski
Jorge Garrido Balaguer	Simon Maurer	Hector Perez
Hamza Hamza	Manel Medina	Pascal Sotin
Saverio Iacovelli	Patrick Meumeu Yomsi	

Contents

Real-Time Systems

Invited Paper

Why the Expressive Power of Programming Languages Such as Ada Is Needed for Future Cyber Physical Systems

Alan Burns[✉]

Department of Computer Science, University of York, York, UK
alan.burns@york.ac.uk

Abstract. If Cyber Physical Systems (CPS) are to be built with efficient resource utilisation it is imperative that they exploit the wealth of scheduling theory available. Many forms of real-time scheduling, and its associated analysis, are applicable to CPS, but it is not clear how the system developer/programmer can gain access to this theory when real CPS are being constructed. This short paper gives the background to the associated presentation where the facilities available in the Ada programming language are highlighted and reviewed. The aim of the presentation is to show that Ada provides most of the programming abstractions needed to deliver future CPS.

1 Introduction

The design and implementation of reliable and cost-effective Cyber-Physical Systems (CPS) incorporates many issues in both the hardware and software aspects of the system. For reliability (and for many CPS, safety), timing constraints such as deadlines must be satisfied, and in many applications evidence for such compliance must be provided (perhaps in a safety-case to be used during certification). For cost-effectiveness, resources must be used effectively and sparingly. Resources in this context being platform hardware and run-time energy consumption.

The branch of Computer Science that deals with resource usage in this context is real-time scheduling. Scheduling protocols promote efficient (and at times optimal) resource utilisation. And scheduling analysis provides the means of verifying that, even in the worst-case, deadlines will be met.

Over the last 50 years a considerable body of knowledge and volume of results in the field of real-time scheduling have been produced. These results can, potentially, have a significant impact on how further CPS are developed. But to realise this potential it must be possible for software developers to exploit this theory; they must be able to apply the scheduling protocols and to subject their software to the relevant forms of scheduling analysis.

The means of exploiting scheduling theory is via the programming languages (PLs) and operating systems (OSs) available to the developer. PLs provide abstractions, such as tasks with priorities and priority based processor scheduling, whilst OSs provide interfaces that can support, for example, threads, priorities and priority-based dispatching.

© Springer International Publishing Switzerland 2016
M. Bertogna et al. (Eds.): Ada-Europe 2016, LNCS 9695, pp. 3–11, 2016.
DOI: 10.1007/978-3-319-39083-3_1

In this paper and talk I want to give a somewhat high level, and necessarily brief, review of the many scheduling results that may be of utility to CPS development. I then want to see to what extent these results are available to developers via OSs and programming languages. I shall argue that for all but the most basic level of support, OSs (and certainly OS Standards) lack the expressive power required. However, programming language abstractions do exist that give access to many (but of course not all) forms of scheduling protocols and analysis. And the programming language that implements/supports most of these abstractions is Ada. Therefore the expressive power of the Ada programming language will form the main focus of this keynote.

2 Scheduling Results

Here some of the major results from scheduling theory, which could be employed in CPS development are outlined. Requirements are linked to applicable scheduling protocols. Of course not all requirements are needed for all CPS, but each one has the potential to be useful. We looks at this work under four headings, uniprocessor systems, multiprocessor systems, mixed criticality systems and then a *catch all* section.

2.1 Uniprocessor Theories

We start with some very basic requirements

- *Interactions with the parallel world* – requires concurrency (tasks, threads, processes etc.).
- *Safe Sharing between distinct software components* – synchronisation controls (semaphores, mutexes, monitors etc.).
- *Synchronisation with external real-time* – clock abstractions and delay primitives.
- *Synchronisation with external events* – interrupt handling.

Concurrency allows tasks to execute non-deterministically. Basic scheduling allows this freedom to be constrained so that the possibility of meeting timing requirements is optimised (and verified if the appropriate analysis is applied):

- *Predicable task ordering* – (static) priority attributes for tasks, priority ceilings for monitors.
- *Deadline aware task execution* – deadline attributes for tasks, protocols for effective sharing.
- *Deterministic execution order* – Non-preemptive scheduling (with static priorities).

Building upon these basic schemes there are a wealth of protocols that aim to improve resource utilisation, for example:

- Deferred preemption [18].
- Dual priorities [13].
- Dynamic priorities (which can be used to program a wide variety of protocols).

or support more general computational models:

- Logical Execution Time (LET) [20, 21, 27].
- Anytime or imprecise algorithms (where following the production of an adequate result, further processing will improve the result up to the point when the result must be output).
- Dynamic periods and deadlines (elastic task model) [16].
- N in M constraints (only N out of every M jobs need meet their deadlines) [6].
- Multiframe Tasks (tasks execute through a series of frames with different resource requirements) [28].
- Generalised Task Model (where tasks are related by DAG models) [5].
- Open Systems with admission control (dynamic task creation) [12, 24].

Many CPS have to demonstrate resilience as well as functional correctness; for this, fault tolerance behaviour needs to be supported. This takes the form of error recognition, firewall protection and various forms of adaptive resource management. For example,

- Deadline miss detection
- Budget monitoring
- Budget overrun detection
- Budget enforcement
- Watchdog timers
- Aborting rogue computation
- Budget management per task
- Budget management per group of tasks
- Early task termination identification

Aborting rogue computation is needed at the task/thread level and at the functional code level. It must be possible to undertake this abandonment without leaving shared data in an undefined state.

2.2   Multiprocessor Theories

Once the execution platform changes from uniprocessor to one with multiple processors (or cores) then other requirements have to be addressed by the scheduling theory. The basic features that must be supported are:

- Partitioned scheduling – managing the static assignment of tasks/threads to processors/cores.
- Global scheduling – managing the run-time migration of tasks/threads to follow the rules of the scheduling protocol.
- Semi-partitioned scheduling – managing the controlled migration of individual tasks/threads at run-time [9, 10, 22].

- Sharing – controlling the sharing of resources between potentially parallel executing tasks/threads (this is a major open problem, in that effective general purpose protocols are not yet available).

On top of these basic protocols there are more advanced schemes that again deliver more efficient execution or support more general models of computation:

- TkC, and DkC (global schemes with priority-based scheduling then non-preemptive) [2, 19].
- tasklets to model parallelism within a task/thread [25].
- barriers to efficiently synchronise tasks/threads on multiprocessor platforms.

Finally there is the need to support heterogeneous as well as homogeneous hardware platforms.

2.3   Mixed Criticality Theories

Mixed criticality system introduce new scheduling protocols that aim to increase the resilience of such systems but keep their resource usage as low as possible. Most of the proposed protocols involve forms of change management. For example:

- task/thread parameter modification (extend period and deadlines),
- suspending tasks/threads,
- modifying scheduling attributes: priorities and deadlines,
- resume tasks/threads.

Also important is the means of supporting partitioning; in particular the allocation of processor time – the overrun of one subsystem must not impact on the resources available to another subsystem. This is especially true if the subsystems are of different levels of criticality. However, the complete separation of subsystems can lead to the over provisioning of resources as the certification of safety-critical software requires very conservative resource-usage estimates. Mixed criticality research has focused on scheduling protocols that provide managed sharing as well as adequate separation [8].

2.4   Others Requirements and Scheduling Features

Here we note some other issues:

- Control of when tasks/threads that preform I/O execute (e.g. minimising input and output jitter).
- Control of memory used by tasks/threads.
- Control of power used by tasks/threads.
- Control over the speed of variable rate processors.
- Control over placement on FPGA type hardware

3   Required Abstractions and/or Interfaces

To satisfy the above extensive list of requirements and protocols, one can either provide a (large) set of high-level abstractions/models, or aim to support primitives from which these abstractions can be programmed. For example, the notion of a periodic task could be provided in a model-based development scheme. Such a concept would have a defined period and deadline; but to give an elastic task it will be necessary to allow period and deadline to change – will the abstraction allow this? Also when executed by a priority based dispatcher how are the priority changes managed? Alternatively, the more general notion of a task or event handler, supported by clocks, a delay statement and a dynamic priority routine will allow any form of time-triggered computation to be programmed. In general a high-level abstraction is easier to use if it is exactly what is required; but lacks the expressive power to allow variants to be derived. Lower-level abstractions, however, present the programmer with more challenges.

Another problem with high level abstractions come from composition. (e.g. how to obtain a periodic tasks with deadline overrun protection, budget enforcement and an N in M execution requirement). Will the three or four high level models work together? Yes programming the required behaviour from lower level abstractions is more effort (and hence is potentially more error prone). But it does allow the actual necessary semantics to be delivered as long as the low-level abstractions are adequate and themselves provide the necessary expressive power.

The interfaces provided by a modern Real-Time operating system, such as one based on POSIX or Linux, give a good level of support for the protocols defined above. Threads have priorities, there are mutexes and priority ceiling protocols, priorities can by modified, budgets can be monitored, signals sent from one thread to another, and mappings to processors can be managed at run-time via affinities. But not all the requirements can be satisfied by OS standards. And composition via library APIs is error-prone and lacks the usability one would hope to have in a programming environment. Programming languages can however embed the protocols within the syntax as well as provide standard library routines, and this allows programmers to directly address the needs of CPS. But of course the programming language must be up to this challenge. In the following section I will look at what Ada provides and argue that it does indeed have (mostly) the required expressive power. Ada is chosen as it provides more low-level abstractions than any other programming language.

4   Ada's Provisions

For those very familiar with Ada they will find nothing new in this brief overview, but for others I hope to at least remind you of what is now supported in the full Ada language. The Ravenscar profile is an important technology for simple real-time scheduling. But for the schemes likely to be needed in future CPS the expressive power of the full language is required. Again I will do this in the form of lists. So first basic concurrency, Ada supports

- Calendar and real-time clocks.
- Static and dynamic creation of tasks.
- Delay mechanisms.
- Priority assignment.
- Protected objects with requeue to give controlled sharing.
- Dynamic task priorities and dynamic priority ceilings.

The requeue facility allows the full expressive power of a monitor to be provided without the need for very low level condition variables.

By supporting dynamic priorities and flexible delay mechanisms many different forms of behaviour can be programmed (such as an elastic task that changes its period).

To support scheduling protocols directly Ada supports:

- Priority based dispatching with priority ceiling protocol.
- EDF scheduling with the Stack Resource Protcol (SRP) [3,4] (and possibly in the future the Deadline Floor Protocol, DFP [1,11]).
- Round Robin and non-preemptive dispatching.
- Hierarchical scheduling (for example, combined priority-based and EDF).
- Primitives to allow tasks to suspend themselves and other tasks.
- Timing events – code that executes at a specified time (can be used to control input and output jitter).
- Group budget monitoring and control that allows standard execution time servers such as the Periodic Server, Sporadic Server and Deferrable Server to be constructed [7,14,15,17,26].

To support more resilient software Ada supports:

- Budget clocks that monitor task execution time, and can signal when specified levels of usage have been reached.
- Task aborting, and the ability to abandon computation at the sub-task level (ATC – select then abort))
- Timing events – that are only execute in error conditions, i.e. programmed watchdog timers.
- Signaling when a task terminates (useful when the task should not!).

The ATC (Asynchronous Task Control) facility is not only of use in error handling for it also allows anytime algorithms to be easily programmed – set the ATC at a deadline, loop through some code to improve quality of computation, storing result in a protected object, abandon when deadline is reacted.

Timing events are another language feature with multiple usages. They can be used positively to control when I/O operations occur, but they can be 'not used' for watchdog timers. Here the 'alarm' is programmed to occur at some future event. The 'I'm alive' signal simple pushes the alarm time further into the future.

To support multiprocessor execution, Ada provides:

– Affinities that can control where a task executes; a task can be restricted to just one CPU, a groups of CPUs or be allowed to execute on any CPU.
– Dynamic affinities to allow semi-partitioned schemes to be programmed.

Other features that are potential important in CPS:

– Use of memory pools to control this important resource.

Having introduced a wide range of important features currently supported by Ada it is only fair to consider some that are missing:

– Support for parallel execution within a task – a plan for including the notion of tasklet into the language is currently under consideration [23].
– Support for energy aware programming – API to whatever is supported by the underlying hardware/run-time is the only current approach available – I would like to execute a loop within a bound determined by energy available.
– Support for an effective synchronisation scheme for multiprocessor execution – many schemes have been proposed in the literature but there is not yet consensus on which Ada can build.

To illustrate the expressive power of Ada a couple of illustrative examples will be included in the presentation.

5   Conclusions

A brief introduction to the scheduling requirements for future Cyber Physical Systems has been given. The list of requirements has been mapped against the provisions of the Ada programming language. In general, Ada provides a rich set of facilities from which higher level abstractions can be built.

The alternative to the use of a facilitating programming language is to rely upon the provisions of the operating systems upon which the software executes. Unfortunately the APIs provided by real-time operating systems (RTOSs) are not flexible enough to deal with the emerging approaches to scheduling resources that are being considered for cost-effective future systems.

Clearly Ada is not a static finished language, it has proved itself to be adaptable and to be able to embrace new ideas and programming styles. New challenges will continue to emerge, such as support for fine grain parallelism, and Ada must be as adaptable going forward as it has been in the past.

References

1. Aldea, M., Burns, A., Gutirrez, M., Harbour, M.G.: Incorporating the deadline floor protocol in Ada. ACM SIGAda Ada Lett. Proc. IRTAW 16 **XXXIII**(2), 49–58 (2013)
2. Andersson, B., Jonsson, J.: Fixed-priority preemptive multiprocessor scheduling: to partition or not to partition. In: Proceedings of the International Conference on Real-Time Computing Systems and Applications (2000)

3. Baker, T.P.: A stack-based resource allocation policy for realtime processes. In: Proceedings of IEEE Real-Time Systems Symposium (RTSS), pp. 191–200 (1990)
4. Baker, T.P.: Stack-based scheduling of realtime processes. J. Real-Time Syst. **3**(1), 37–99 (1991)
5. Baruah, S.K.: A general model for recurring real-time tasks. In: rtss, p. 114. IEEE (1998)
6. Bernat, G., Burns, A.: Combining (n m)-hard deadlines with dual priority scheduling. In: Proceedings of 18th IEEE Real-Time Systems Symposium, pp. 46–57 (1997)
7. Bernat, G., Burns, A.: New results on fixed priority aperiodic servers. In: Proceedings of 20th IEEE Real-Time Systems Symposium, pp. 68–78 (1999)
8. Burns, A., Davis, R.I.: Mixed criticality systems: a review. Technical report MCC-1(e). Department of Computer Science, University of York (2015). http://www-users.cs.york.ac.uk/burns/review.pdf
9. Burns, A., Davis, R.I., Wang, P., Zhang, F.: Partitioned EDF scheduling for multi-processors using a C=D scheme. In: Proceedings of 18th International Conference on Real-Time and Network Systems (RTNS), pp. 169–178 (2010)
10. Burns, A., Davis, R.I., Wang, P., Zhang, F.: Partitioned EDF scheduling for multiprocessors using a C=D task splitting scheme. Real-Time Syst. J. **48**(1), 3–33 (2012)
11. Burns, A., Gutierrez, M., Aldea, M., González Harbour, M.: A deadline-floor inheritance protocol for EDF scheduled embedded real-time systems with resource sharing. IEEE Trans. Comput. **64**(5), 1241–1253 (2015)
12. Burns, A., Prasad, D., Bondavalli, A., Di Giandomenico, F., Ramamritham, K., Stankovic, J., Stringini, L.: The meaning and role of value in scheduling flexible real-time systems. J. Syst. Archit. **46**, 305–325 (2000)
13. Burns, A., Wellings, A.J.: Dual priority scheduling in Ada 95 and real-time POSIX. In: Proceedings of the 21st IFAC/IFIP Workshop on Real-Time Programming, WRTP 1996, pp. 45–50 (1996)
14. Burns, A., Wellings, A.J.: Programming execution-time servers in Ada 2005. In: Proceedings of IEEE Real-Time Systems Symposium (RTSS), pp. 47–56 (2006)
15. Burns, A., Wellings, A.J.: Programming execution-time servers in Ada 2005. In: Proceedings of the 27th IEEE Real-Time Systems Symposium, pp. 47–56 (2006)
16. Buttazzo, G., Lipari, G., Abeni, L.: Elastic task model for adaptive rate control. In: IEEE Real-Time Systems Symposium, pp. 286–295 (1998)
17. Caccamo, M., Sha, L.: Aperiodic servers with resource constraints. In: Proceedings of the IEEE Real-Time Systems Symposium, December 2001
18. Davis, R.I., Bertogna, M.: Optimal fixed priority scheduling with deferred pre-emption. In: Proceedings of IEEE Real-Time Systems Symposium, pp. 39–50 (2012)
19. Davis, R.I., Burns, A.: Priority assignment for global fixed priority pre-emptive scheduling in multiprocessor real-time systems. In: Proceedings of IEEE Real-Time Systems Symposium (RTSS), pp. 398–409 (2009)
20. Hagenauer, H., Martinek, N., Pohlmann, W.: Ada meets Giotto. In: Llamosí, A., Strohmeier, A. (eds.) Ada-Europe 2004. LNCS, vol. 3063, pp. 237–248. Springer, Heidelberg (2004)
21. Henzinger, T.A., Horowitz, B., Kirsch, C.M.: Giotto: a time-triggered language for embedded programming. In: Henzinger, T.A., Kirsch, C.M. (eds.) EMSOFT 2001. LNCS, vol. 2211, p. 166. Springer, Heidelberg (2001)

22. Kato, S., Yamasaki, N.: Semi-partitioned fixed-priority scheduling on multiprocessors. In: IEEE Real-Time and Embedded Technology and Applications Symposium, pp. 23–32 (2009)
23. Michell, S., Moore, B., Pinho, L.M.: Tasklettes – a fine grained parallelism for Ada on multicores. In: Keller, H.B., Plödereder, E., Dencker, P., Klenk, H. (eds.) Ada-Europe 2013. LNCS, vol. 7896, pp. 17–34. Springer, Heidelberg (2013)
24. Prasad, D., Burns, A., Atkin, M.: The measurement and usage of utility in adaptive real-time systems. J. Real-Time Syst. 25(2/3), 277–296 (2003)
25. Saifullah, A., Li, J., Agrawal, K., Lu, C., Gill, C.: Multi-core real-time scheduling for generalized parallel task models. Real-Time Syst. 49(4), 404–435 (2013)
26. Sprunt, B., Sha, L., Lehoczky, J.P.: Aperiodic task scheduling for hard real-time systems. J. Real-Time Syst. 1, 27–69 (1989)
27. Wellings, A., Burns, A.: The evolution of real-time programming revisited: programming the Giotto model in Ada 2005. In: Real, J., Vardanega, T. (eds.) Ada-Europe 2010. LNCS, vol. 6106, pp. 196–207. Springer, Heidelberg (2010)
28. Zuhily, A., Burns, A.: Exact scheduling analysis of non-accumulatively monotonic multiframe tasks. Real-Time Syst. J. 43, 119–146 (2009)

Concurrency and Parallelism

Modeling and Analysis of Data Flow Graphs Using the Digraph Real-Time Task Model

Morteza Mohaqeqi$^{(\boxtimes)}$, Jakaria Abdullah, and Wang Yi

Uppsala University, Uppsala, Sweden
morteza.mohaqeqi@it.uu.se

Abstract. Data flow graphs are widely used for modeling and analysis of real-time streaming applications in which having a predictable and reliable implementation is an essential requirement. In this paper, we consider scheduling a set of data flow graphs such that liveness and boundedness properties are guaranteed, which leads to a predictable and correct behavior of the application. A formal translation method is proposed to map a given set of data flow graphs to a set of graph-based real-time tasks. Additionally, sufficient conditions are derived under which the obtained task set provides a semantically correct implementation of the given data flow graphs. It is shown that the proposed approach provides a higher level of design flexibility compared to the existing methods which use a simpler, i.e. periodic, task model.

Keywords: Data flow graphs · Real-time task models · Buffer boundedness · Schedulability analysis

1 Introduction

During the past decades, data flow graphs [1,2] have been extensively used for modeling and analysis of real-time streaming and signal processing applications. A number of prominent measures of these applications, including throughput, timeliness, liveness, and processing latency have been analyzed based on this formalism. Such analyses help the designers to have a predictable and reliable implementation of the mentioned applications.

Recently, increasing attention has been paid to study data flow graphs from a real-time scheduling point of view [3–8]. A popular approach is mapping each actor in a given data flow graph to an independent real-time task. Then, the problem is to specify the real-time tasks parameters such that the timing behavior of the data flow is correctly reflected by the task set. The advantage of this approach is that it makes it possible to *reuse* the existing analysis frameworks developed for real-time systems in the scheduling of a set of data flow graphs. For instance, using this approach, the interfering effect of different data flow applications on each other can be analyzed based on the existing theory of real-time task models.

In spite of the relatively extensive studies in this context, only a limited number of real-time task models have been explored by the researchers. In particular,

© Springer International Publishing Switzerland 2016
M. Bertogna et al. (Eds.): Ada-Europe 2016, LNCS 9695, pp. 15–29, 2016.
DOI: 10.1007/978-3-319-39083-3_2

the work has been mainly focused on the periodic task model. Nonetheless, more expressive models can provide more flexibility to the designers which can lead to better solutions.

In this paper, we propose to use one of the most expressive yet efficiently analyzable real-time task models, namely the Digraph Real-Time (DRT) model [9], to specify data flow graphs. We present a translation method and discuss the potential benefits and the restrictions of this approach. The proposed method guarantees both boundedness and liveness properties of a data flow graph.

The rest of this paper is organized as follows: Sect. 2 describes the system model by presenting a brief review on the syntax and semantics of a data flow graph. The Digraph Real-Time task model is reviewed in Sect. 3. We present our translation method in Sect. 4. The proposed method is evaluated through the model of an MP3 playback application in Sect. 5. The work related to the current study is reviewed in Sect. 6. The paper is concluded in Sect. 7.

2   System and Application Model

In this paper, we consider a uniprocessor system which runs a number of applications modeled as a set of static data flow graphs. Formally, a static data flow is a directed graph (V, E), where V and E represent the set of vertices and edges, respectively. Each vertex represents an *actor*. Each edge denotes a FIFO channel (also called a buffer), connecting the input port and the output port of two (not necessarily different) actors. A channel c may contain an initial number of tokens, denoted by $\bar{c}$, at the system start time. Further, each channel c has a maximum capacity of $\tilde{c}$. This means that the number of tokens existing in c should never exceed $\tilde{c}$.

Any release of one instance (job) of an actor is called a firing. An actor can be fired only when the required number of tokens are available on its input ports. During its execution, an actor consumes the required tokens from the input ports, and generates some tokens to its output ports. The number of tokens which are produced (consumed) at each firing of an actor is called the production (consumption) rate. Static data flows are classified according to the variability of an actor behavior and its production/consumption rate in different firings. In the following, three major classes, namely synchronous, homogeneous, and cyclo-static data flows [2], are reviewed.

- Synchronous Data Flow (SDF): In an SDF, the execution time as well as the production/consumption rate of each actor is fixed.
- Homogeneous Synchronous Data Flow (HSDF): An SDF is homogeneous if all production/consumption rates are equal to one.
- Cyclo-Static Data Flow (CSDF): The cyclo-static data flow (CSDF) model is a generalization of SDF, in which each actor a has a sequence of different behaviors, affecting its execution time and the production/consumption rates, which repeats cyclically [3]. Let n_a be the length of this sequence.

Then, $[f_a(1), f_a(2), \ldots, f_a(n_a)]$ represents the execution sequence of an actor $a \in V$. This means that in its ith firing, the actor execution time is given by

$$f_a \left(((i-1) \bmod n_a) + 1 \right). \tag{1}$$

Similarly, the production and consumption rates are specified by sequences of length n_a. More specifically, for an actor a, and considering a specific buffer,
- $[g_a(1), g_a(2), \ldots, g_a(n_a)]$ denotes the sequence of production rates;
- $[h_a(1), h_a(2), \ldots, h_a(n_a)]$ denotes the sequence of consumption rates.

In the current work, our focus is on the CSDF model.

Example 1. Figure 1 shows the CSDF graph of an MP3 playback application [10]. This application consists of four tasks, including MP3, Sample Rate Converter (SRC), Audio Post-Processing (APP), and Digital to Analogue Converter (DAC).

Fig. 1. A CSDF graph for the MP3 playback application [10]. Production and consumption rates are shown on the edges.

An implementation of a data flow graph is supposed to provide *liveness* and *boundedness* properties. Intuitively, liveness means that each actor will be executed infinitely many times. In contrast, boundedness necessitates the existence of a bound on the maximum size of each buffer which is never exceeded by the writing actors during the system execution.

3   Digraph Real-Time Task Model

In this section, we review the digraph real-time (DRT) task model [9]. This task model will be used in the next section for modeling CSDF graphs.

A DRT task T is specified by a directed graph $G(T) = (V(T), E(T))$, where $V(T)$ and $E(T)$ denote the graph vertices and edges, respectively. Each vertex of the graph represents a *job type*. A vertex $v \in V(T)$ is labeled by a pair $\langle e(v), d(v) \rangle$, where $e(v)$ and $d(v)$ denote the worst-case execution time (WCET) and relative deadline of the corresponding job, respectively. Further, each edge $(u, v) \in E(T)$ is labeled with a positive number, $p(u, v)$, denoting the inter-release time between the two jobs u and v[1].

Each path in the graph denotes a possible sequence of jobs which may be generated by the respective task. If the outgoing degree of each vertex in a

---

[1] In the original definition of DRT, an edge label determines the *minimum* inter-release time. Nonetheless, the DRT schedulability analyses [9, 11] are valid for the modified version which we use here.

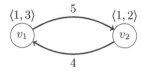

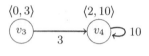

(a) A DRT task with two job types

(b) A periodic task with an initial phase of 3 modeled as a DRT task

Fig. 2. Two sample DRT tasks.

task graph is restricted by one, that is, no branching is allowed, then the model reduces to the Generalized Multiframe task model [12].

The focus of this paper is on the *constrained* deadline DRT tasks. Hence, given a DRT task T, it is assumed that for each $u \in V(T)$, we have $d(u) \leq p(u, v)$ for all $(u, v) \in E(T)$.

Example 2. A sample DRT task with two job types with inter-release times of 5 and 4 is shown in Fig. 2a. Further, Fig. 2b depicts a DRT task which models a periodic task with an initial phase.

The inherent capability of the DRT model to represent non-fixed and non-periodic behavior of a component makes it suitable for modeling CSDF graphs. In the next section, we present our method for representing CSDF graphs using set of DRT tasks.

4   Translation Method

In this section, we describe our translation method for transforming a given data flow graph to a set of DRT tasks. The method maps each actor to a real-time task. In the following, the details of the translation method and the criteria for determining the real-time task set parameters are provided.

Consider two actors a and b in a given CSDF graph. In addition, let c be a FIFO channel between them with an initial number of tokens of $\bar{c}$ and a maximum capacity of $\tilde{c}$. Let n_a be the size of the sequence which specifies the cyclically variable behavior of the actor a (as defined in the previous section). We associate a DRT task with $n_a + 1$ vertices, $v_0, \ldots, v_{n_a}$, to a. The starting vertex denotes a job type with the WCET of zero, which is used to enforce a phase (an initial phase before the release time of the first job) in the task. Additionally, for each i, $0 \leq i < n_a$, an edge is added from v_i to v_{i+1}. Also, we consider an edge from v_{n_a} to v_1. This set of edges enforce the cyclically repeating pattern of the given actor's behavior. The WCET associated with each vertex v_i, $0 < i \leq n_a$, is set to be the WCET of the ith firing of the actor, which is specified by $f_a(i)$.

As described, the DRT task corresponding to an actor a contains $n_a + 1$ vertices and $n_a + 1$ edges. Edge (v_0, v_1), which represents the phase of the task, is labeled by ϕ_a. Further, let the label of the other edges (v_i, v_{i+1}), $1 \leq i < n_a$,

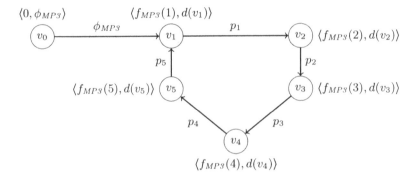

Fig. 3. DRT task for the actor MP3 of the CSDF graph presented in Fig. 1.

be denoted by $p_i{}^2$ (also, the edge (v_{n_a}, v_1) is labeled by p_{n_a}). The edge labels are parameters which should be determined such that the liveness and boundedness properties are achieved.

Example 3. Consider the data flow graph of the MP3 player application shown in Fig. 1. According to the specified translation method, the first actor (MP3) will be modeled as a DRT task with six vertices, as shown in Fig. 3. Given a sequence of execution times $[f_{MP3}(1), \ldots, f_{MP3}(5)]$ for this actor, we can assign the WCET of the job types of the DRT task as $e(v_i) = f_{MP3}(i)$, for $1 \leq i \leq 5$. Additionally, the other actors will be represented by a DRT task expressing a periodic behavior, in a similar way as shown in Fig. 2b.

For a complete translation, we need to determine the timing parameters of the DRT tasks. These parameters include the relative deadline of each job type, and the edge labels which represent the inter-release time between the jobs. The timing parameters should be assigned in such a way that the correctness conditions of the implementation are satisfied.

We use the correctness criteria in terms of the Kahn semantics [13] for a Kahn process network. As shown in [10], these criteria imply a *live* and *bounded* behavior of the system specified by a data flow graph. For this purpose, it must be guaranteed that the system never leads to a buffer overflow or buffer underflow. An overflow happens when writing to a buffer exceeds its maximum capacity. In turn, an underflow occurs whenever an actor tries to read from an empty buffer. In the following, we formalize these correctness requirements. To this end, we first need to determine the number of released and finished instances of each job (actor) up to each time instant.

---

² Please notice that, p_i is an actor-specific parameter. However, for brevity reasons, it is not explicitly indicated in the notation.

4.1   Number of Released/Finished Jobs

For an actor a, define $Rel_a(v, t)$ and $Fin_a(v, t)$ as follows:

$Rel_a(v, t) \equiv$ the number of instances of job type v released up to and
including time t,

$Fin_a(v, t) \equiv$ the number of instances of job type v finished up to and
including time t.

According to the translation model, the release and completion of a job corresponding to an actor firing are governed by the associated DRT tasks. As a result, $Rel_a(v, t)$ and $Fin_a(v, t)$ depend on the timing parameters of the derived DRT tasks. Here, we formally specify the relation between function $Rel_a(v, t)$ (also $Fin_a(v, t)$) and these parameters. First, it is noted that, for $t < \phi$, we have $Rel_a(v, t) = 0$ and $Fin_a(v, t) = 0$. Thus, in the following, we assume that $t \geq \phi$.

According to the defined notations, we can specify $Rel_a(v, t)$ as

$$Rel_a(v_i, t) = 1 + \left\lfloor \frac{t - \phi_a - \sum_{j=1}^{i-1} p_j}{\pi_a} \right\rfloor. \tag{2}$$

where $\pi_a = \sum_{j=1}^{n_a} p_j$ is the *super-period* of the DRT task. In words, π_a denotes the amount of time that it takes for the DRT to have a complete cycle, through which, each job (except the first job which represents the initial phase) is released exactly once. Also, a lower bound for $Fin_a(v, t)$ can be obtained by

$$Fin_a(v_i, t) \geq 1 + \left\lfloor \frac{t - \phi_a - \sum_{j=1}^{i-1} p_j - d(v_i)}{\pi_a} \right\rfloor. \tag{3}$$

It is worth noting that the equality does not necessarily hold. This is because that, depending on the scheduling approach, a job may be completed before its deadline, leading to a possibly higher number of finished jobs up to time t compared to the case in which the job finishes exactly at its deadline.

4.2   Underflow Analysis

Based on the semantics of a data flow graph, an actor may produce (consume) the output (input) tokens at any time during its execution. As a result, for the underflow analysis, we employ a pessimistic approach [10], in which, we consider the minimum possible number of tokens that may be buffered at each instant. Based on this approach, it is assumed that each actor writes to the output buffer(s) as late as possible. In other words, the tokens are assumed to be written to the buffer when the actor completes its execution. On the other hand, we suppose that each actor reads from its input buffer(s) as soon as possible, namely at its release instant.

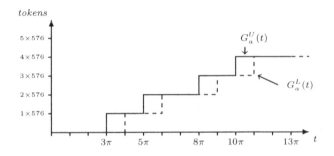

Fig. 4. Upper and lower bound on the number of produced tokens for the MP3 actor.

Regarding the abovementioned pessimistic assumptions, a lower bound for the total number of tokens written to the channel c by an actor a up to (and including) time t can be calculated as

$$G_a^L(t) = \sum_{i=1}^{n_a} g_a(i) \times Fin_a(v_i, t).$$ (4)

As an example, the dashed line in Fig. 4 depicts the function $G_a^L(t)$ for the MP3 actor of the CSDF graph specified in Example 1. In this example, it is assumed that any two successive firings are identically separated by a time interval of length π. Further, an implicit deadline has been considered (i.e. $d(v_i) = \pi$).

In addition, an upper bound for the total number of tokens read from a channel c by an other actor b up to and including time t is given by

$$H_b^U(t) = \sum_{i=1}^{n_b} h_b(i) \times Rel_b(v_i, t).$$ (5)

According to these relations, a sufficient condition for the underflow avoidance of channel c is formulated by

$$\forall t \geq 0 : \bar{c} + G_a^L(t) - H_b^U(t) \geq 0,$$ (6)

where $\bar{c}$ denotes the initial number of tokens of c.

4.3   Overflow Analysis

Based on an approach similar to the one presented for the underflow, we can specify a sufficient condition for overflow avoidance. In this case, the pessimistic assumptions are stated as follows:

- Each actor writes to the output buffer(s) as soon as possible (namely at its release time);
- Each actor reads from its input buffer(s) as late as possible (namely at its finish time).

Consequently, the maximum number of tokens written to a buffer c by an actor a up to time t can be specified as

$$G_a^U(t) = \sum_{i=1}^{n_a} g_a(i) \times Rel_a(v_i, t). \tag{7}$$

Figure 4 partly shows the variation of $G_a^U(t)$ for the MP3 CSDF graph, under the previously mentioned assumptions.

Additionally, the minimum number of tokens read from a buffer c by an actor b up to time t is given by

$$H_b^L(t) = \sum_{i=1}^{n_b} h_b(i) \times Fin_b(v_i, t). \tag{8}$$

Regarding the defined notations, no overflow happens if the following condition holds (recall that $\tilde{c}$ denotes the maximum buffer capacity)

$$\forall t \geq 0 : \bar{c} + G_a^U(t) - H_b^L(t) \leq \tilde{c}. \tag{9}$$

4.4   Design Space Exploration

Relations (6) and (9) provide sufficient conditions for the correctness of an implementation of a data flow graph. Then, the problem is to assign suitable values to the DRT tasks parameters, namely their inter-release times, p_i, and relative deadlines, $d(v_i)$, such that, while the mentioned conditions are satisfied, some design objective, e.g. the application throughput, is optimized. Furthermore, from a schedulability point of view, these values must be selected such that the obtained task set is schedulable, i.e., each job can complete its execution no later than its deadline. This can be checked using efficient methods proposed in [9, 11] for static-priority and dynamic-priority schedulability analysis of DRT task sets.

Here, we discuss a simplifying technique for improving the efficiency of the state-space exploration. First, it is observed that the correctness criteria derived in the previous sections are independent of the worst-case execution time of the actors. In other words, they deal only with the release times and completion times. As a result, the problem of finding an appropriate value assignment to the timing parameters can be first solved irrespective of the schedulability concerns. Afterwards, we have to consider the schedulability of the system. If the system with the derived value assignments is not schedulable, one can easily scale up the timing parameters such that the obtained task set becomes schedulable.

It is worth noting that scaling up all the parameters by the same amount does not affect the correctness of the system, i.e. the validity of (6) and (9). This is because that, in this situation, the numerator and denominator of the respective fractions in (2) and (3) are scaled with the same factor, and the value of the fraction remains unchanged. It should be noted that a similar approach, called abstraction-refinement, has been previously used for the periodic task model [6] to overcome the complexity of the problem. In addition to this technique, another simplification can be made by a linear approximation, which is specified in the following.

Linear Approximation: Based on Relations (2) and (3), it is observed that the functions $Rel_a(v_i, t)$ and $Fin_a(v_i, t)$, respectively, can be over-approximated and under-approximated by some linear functions. These approximations are constructed on the basis of the inequality $x < 1 + \lfloor x \rfloor \leq 1 + x$, which holds for any real number x [14]. Using this, we specify an overapproximation for the function $Rel_a(v_i, t)$ as

$$Rel_a^{UApp}(v_i, t) = 1 + \frac{t - \phi_a - \sum_{j=1}^{i-1} p_j}{\pi_a}. \tag{10}$$

In fact, for any $t \geq 0$, we have $Rel_a(v_i, t) \leq Rel_a^{UApp}(v_i, t)$. In addition, we can obtain an under-approximation for the function $Fin_a(v_i, t)$ as

$$Fin_a^{LApp}(v_i, t) = \frac{t - \phi_a - \sum_{j=1}^{i-1} p_j - d(v_i)}{\pi_a}. \tag{11}$$

These approximate functions can be used in calculating $G_a^L(t)$, $H_b^U(t)$, $G_a^U(t)$, and $H_b^L(t)$, defined in Eqs. (4), (5), (7), and (8). Then, we can rewrite the underflow and overflow avoidance conditions, presented in (6) and (9), based on these approximations. In the following, we elaborate the underflow condition; the procedure for the overflow condition can be done in a similar manner.

Using the provided approximations, we can rewrite the underflow avoidance condition as

$$\forall t \geq 0 : \bar{c} + \sum_{i=1}^{n_a} g_a(i) \times Fin_a^{LApp}(v_i, t) - \sum_{i=1}^{n_b} h_b(i) \times Rel_b^{UApp}(v_i, t) \geq 0.$$

Moreover, by replacing $Fin_a^{LApp}(v_i, t)$ and $Rel_a^{UApp}(v_i, t)$ from (11) and (10), we will get

$$\forall t \geq 0 : \tag{12}$$

$$\bar{c} + \sum_{i=1}^{n_a} g_a(i) \left(\frac{t - \phi_a - \sum_{j=1}^{i-1} p_j - d(v_i)}{\pi_a} \right) - \sum_{i=1}^{n_b} h_b(i) \left(1 + \frac{t - \phi_b - \sum_{j=1}^{i-1} p_j}{\pi_b} \right) \geq 0$$

From [10], it is known that, as a necessary condition for overflow and underflow avoidance, the average production rate for any buffer must be equal to its average consumption rate, namely

$$\frac{\sum_{i=1}^{n_a} g_a(i)}{\pi_a} = \frac{\sum_{i=1}^{n_b} h_b(i)}{\pi_b}. \tag{13}$$

Based on this fact, we can simplify the inequality specified in (12) as

$$\forall t \geq 0 :$$

$$\bar{c} + \sum_{i=1}^{n_a} g_a(i) \left(\frac{-\phi_a - \sum_{j=1}^{i-1} p_j - d(v_i)}{\pi_a} \right) - \sum_{i=1}^{n_b} h_b(i) \left(1 + \frac{-\phi_b - \sum_{j=1}^{i-1} p_j}{\pi_b} \right) \geq 0.$$

Also, from (13), we can write π_b as a linear function of π_a, that is, $\pi_b = \gamma \pi_a$ for some constant γ. Hence, we have

$$\forall t \geq 0 :$$

$$\bar{c}\pi_a + \sum_{i=1}^{n_a} g_a(i)\left(-\phi_a - \sum_{j=1}^{i-1} p_j - d(v_i)\right) - \sum_{i=1}^{n_b} h_b(i)\left(\pi_a + \frac{-\phi_b - \sum_{j=1}^{i-1} p_j}{\gamma}\right) \geq 0.$$

As seen, the obtained relation specifies a *linear* constraint on the problem parameters, which significantly reduces the complexity of the problem.

5   Evaluation

In this section, we evaluate the effectiveness of the proposed approach compared to a previously proposed method which employs a periodic task model for the analysis of CSDF graphs [6, 10]. We compare the two methods in terms of the throughput [15] and the buffer size requirements [16]. The throughput of a dataflow graph measures how often the application is executed in a unit of time. We assume the preemptive EDF algorithm for scheduling the obtained real-time tasks.

For the evaluation purpose, we apply the mentioned methods to the MP3 playback application shown in Fig. 1. According to [10], the execution time of the MP3 actor is specified as the sequence $f_{MP3}(.) = [670, 2700, 720, 2700, 720]\,\mu s$. Further, the execution time of SRC, APP, and DAC are specified as $2500\,\mu s$, $22\,\mu s$, and $22\,\mu s$, respectively.

The primary objective is to specify the timing parameters of the task set so as to minimize the total required buffer sizes, while the correctness criteria specified in (6) and (9) are respected and the task set is EDF-schedulable. As well, it is desired to increase the application throughput. In the following, we first present the obtained task sets for each approach. Then, the buffer requirement and the throughput achieved by each method are reported and discussed.

5.1   Obtained Task Sets

In this section, we first specify the periodic task set obtained in [10] for the MP3 playback application. Next, the corresponding DRT task set is described.

Periodic Task Model: According to the approach utilized in [10], a periodic task is considered for each actor. In order to have a safe analysis, one needs to consider the maximum execution time of each actor as the WCET of the corresponding periodic task. As a result, a WCET of $\max\{670, 2700, 720, 2700, 720\} = 2700\,\mu s$ is considered for the task associated to the MP3 actor. As the other actors have a fixed execution time, WCET of the respective tasks are simply set to those fixed values. The periods and phases assigned to the tasks according to this method are shown in Table 1 [10]. This parameter assignment leads to the system utilization of 99.96 %, which reveals the schedulability of the task set.

DRT Task Model: As pointed out before, the MP3 application can be modeled by four DRT tasks. When constructing the tasks, in order to decrease the number

Table 1. Task set parameters obtained for the periodic tasks [10]

	Period (μs)	Phase (μs)
MP3	13219.416	0
SRC	27540.45	66647.889
APP	62.45	121760.014
DAC	62.45	121916.139

of design parameters, we assume that the relative deadline of each job type is set to be equal to the inter-release time between that job and the next one. As noted in Example 3, for the actors SRC, APP, and DAC we can use the DRT task structure which models a periodic task with a specific phase. This is because these actors have a periodically repeating behavior. On the other hand, the MP3 actor is modeled by a DRT task with six different job types, as shown in Fig. 3. It is worth noting that, here, as opposed to the periodic task model, we can consider the actual pattern of the execution times for the MP3 actor, instead of using one conservative maximum value. The goal is to assign the relative deadline of each job such that the problem objective is optimized.

Initially, we use the same values reported in Table 1 for the DRT tasks associated to SRC, APP, and DAC. Additionally, for the DRT task related to MP3, we assume that the inter-release times, in the average, are equal to the period specified for the corresponding periodic task. As a result, the super-period of this task is $\pi_{MP3} = 5 \times 13219.416$. Now, we attempt to determine the concrete value of the inter-release times for each pair of job types of this task. In order to decrease the utilization of the task (and hence, increase the schedulability of the task set), we assign the relative deadline of each job (or equivalently, the inter-release time between that job and the next one) in proportion to its execution time. Since in the DRT task, we can consider the actual pattern of execution times instead of a fixed and pessimistic value (which is done in the periodic task model), the total utilization is lower than that of the periodic task. As a result, we can scale down the timing parameters, namely the phases and inter-release times, so as to increase the application throughput, while the task set is still schedulable. The results of this approach are shown in Table 2 and Fig. 5.

Table 2. Task set parameters for the DRT tasks (μs)

	Period	Phase
SRC	25061.809	60649.578
APP	56.829	110801.612
DAC	56.829	110943.686

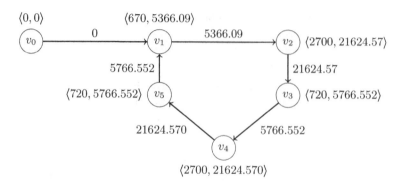

Fig. 5. Parameters for the DRT task which models the MP3 actor (μs).

5.2 Evaluation Results

The total buffer requirement and the throughput which is achieved by the two approaches are reported in Table 3. As seen, the DRT-based method outperforms the other one in terms of both the buffer requirement and the application throughput.

Table 3. Total buffer requirement and throughput for each method

	Buffer requirement	Throughput (s^{-1})
Periodic task set	2273	16013
DRT task set	2155	17596
Improvement	5%	9.8%

As a conclusion, it is seen that the DRT-based approach provides a higher degree of flexibility in the design of data flow graphs which can lead to better solutions. Of course, this advantage is achieved at the cost of treating more parameters, which means a larger state-space which must be explored.

6   Related Work

Synchronous Data Flow (SDF) [1] and Cyclo-Static Data Flow (CSDF) [2] are two very basic data flow models. In the past, several variants of these models have been proposed to provide more expressiveness and flexibility in the design of streaming applications. For instance, the *parametric* extensions of the SDF have been developed [17–19] which allow the data flow graph properties, such as the production and consumption rates, to be changed at runtime. In particular, Boolean Parametric Data Flow (BPDF) [18] is a parametric model in which the graph topology can be changed as well as the production and consumption rates of the actors. In this model, an edge can be labeled with a boolean expression which is modified by some actor. At runtime, according to the actual value of the boolean expression, an edge may be enabled or disabled, determining whether the edge should be considered in the firing of the actors at that moment. An assumption made in the related stuies, such as [18–20], is that each actor runs in a dedicated core. Hence, when analyzing the data flow graph, one does not need to take into account the interference of the actors (caused by resource contention) on each other. While this approach provides a high degree of predictability for a single data flow, it is not easily extendible to incorporate the impact of multiple data flows on each other when they are running on the same processing platform with possible resource contention.

Meanwhile, due to the increasing use of real-time operating systems in complex embedded systems which work in dynamic environments, using dynamic scheduling policies, such as rate-monotonic and earliest-deadline first (EDF), for SDFs has been considered recent studies. The advantage of this approach is that the already existing analyses for different scheduling algorithms can be used in this context. This provides the possibility of running multiple applications on the same processing resource, while the interfering effects is considered. One approach to utilize this facility is to use a set of independent real-time tasks to reflect the timing behavior of data flow graphs. One of the basic studies which use periodic real-time task model for data flow graphs is presented by Bmakhra and Stefanov [3]. They explore that how the execution of actors can be parallelized to achieve a maximum throughput. In the same realm, Ali et al. [8] consider the problem of assigning parameters of periodic tasks modeling an HSDF. They suppose a given set of applications each one modeled as an HSDF graph. Each application exhibits two kinds of requirements: a minimum throughput, which is the minimum output data rate (or iteration rate of the whole graph); and one or multiple *latency* constraints put on a number of pairs of actors. A latency constraint is a timing constraint between firing of two actors located on a path. While they consider more constraints compared to the model considered in this paper, their work is specific to HSDF, which is less expressive compared to the CSDF.

Moreover, Bouakaz et al. considered a more general category of data flow graphs. They extended the CSDF model by introducing ultimately periodic CSDF [10] in which the system behavior becomes repetitive after a finite interval, but it is not needed to be periodic from the beginning. They define the affine firing relation which specifies the condition under which a data flow implementation can satisfy the correctness criteria. They investigate the correctness of the implementation based on the periodic task model. In their work, the correctness conditions of an implementation, including boundedness, completeness, and soundness, are obtained based on the Kahn process network semantics [13].

The work presented in [6] can be regarded as one of the most related work to the current study. They consider a CSDF model with a set of buffer size constraints. The goal is to construct a set of periodic tasks reflecting the execution of the given SDFs. The main difference of that work compared to our approach is that we use a more expressive real-time task model, which suggests more flexibility, and thus, a higher degree of schedulability. This, in turn, allows to look for more efficient solutions.

7   Conclusion

In this paper, we proposed a formal translation method for converting a given set of data flow graphs to a graph-based real-time task model. We focused on cyclo-static data flow graphs in which an actor behavior, including its worst-case execution time, consumption rate, and production rate, is not necessarily fixed in different firings. We presented sufficient conditions for a correct translation in terms of liveness and boundedness of data flow graphs. The proposed method provides the opportunity of exploring a larger state-space for finding optimal or near optimal solutions for the design of corresponding applications. Based on the translated task model, one can easily perform analyses such as schedulability tests, while taking into account the interfering of the applications running on the same processing core.

The proposed approach can be extended by employing efficient optimization methods for finding task set parameters such that, while the design constraints are met, design objectives like the total buffer size or the application throughput are optimized. In addition, when the DRT tasks exhibit a restricted structure in which only a single cycle is contained, they can be modeled as a set of Generalized Multiframe (GMF) Tasks [12]. In this case, one may employ more efficient analysis methods specific to this task model for schedulability test of the translated tasks.

References

1. Lee, E.A., Messerschmitt, D.G.: Synchronous data flow. Proc. IEEE **75**(9), 1235–1245 (1987)
2. Bilsen, G., Engels, M., Lauwereins, R., Peperstraete, J.: Cycle-static dataflow. IEEE Trans. Sig. Process. **44**(2), 397–408 (1981)
3. Bamakhrama, M., Stefanov, T.: Hard-real-time scheduling of data-dependent tasks in embedded streaming applications. In: International Conference on Embedded Software, pp. 195–204 (2011)
4. Dkhil, A., Do, X.K., Dubrulle, P., Louise, S., Rochange, C.: Self-timed periodic scheduling for a cyclo-static dataflow model. In: International Conference on Computational Science, pp. 1134–1145 (2014)
5. Lele, A., Moreira, O., Bastos, J., Almeida, R., Pedreiras, P., van Berkel, K.: Analyzing preemptive fixed priority scheduling of data flow graphs. In: 12th Symposium on Embedded Systems for Real-time Multimedia, pp. 50–59 (2014)
6. Bouakaz, A., Gautier, T.: An abstraction-refinement framework for priority-driven scheduling of static dataflow graphs. In: 12th ACM/IEEE International Conference on Formal Methods and Models for Codesign, pp. 2–11 (2014)
7. Do, X.K., Dkhil, A., Louise, S.: Self-timed periodic scheduling of data-dependent tasks in embedded streaming applications. In: Wang, G., Zomaya, A., Martinez Perez, G., Li, K. (eds.) ICA3PP 2015. LNCS, vol. 9529, pp. 458–478. Springer, Heidelberg (2015). doi:10.1007/978-3-319-27122-4_32
8. Ali, H.I., Akesson, B., Pinho, L.M.: Generalized extraction of real-time parameters for homogeneous synchronous dataow graphs. In: 23rd Euromicro International Conference on Parallel, Distributed and Network-Based Processing, pp. 701–710 (2015)

9. Stigge, M., Ekberg, P., Guan, N., Yi, W.: The digraph real-time task model. In: Real-Time and Embedded Technology and Applications Symposium, pp. 71–80 (2011)
10. Bouakaz, A., Talpin, J.P., Vitek, J.: Affine data-flow graphs for the synthesis of hard real-time applications. In: 12th International Conference on Application of Concurrency to System Design, pp. 183–192 (2012)
11. Stigge, M., Yi, W.: Combinatorial abstraction refinement for feasibility analysis. In: 34th IEEE Real-Time Systems Symposium, pp. 340–349 (2013)
12. Baruah, S., Chen, D., Gorinsky, S., Mok, A.: Generalized multiframe tasks. J. Real-Time Syst. **17**(1), 5–22 (1999)
13. Geilen, M., Basten, T.: Requirements on the execution of Kahn process networks. In: Degano, P. (ed.) ESOP 2003. LNCS, vol. 2618, pp. 319–334. Springer, Heidelberg (2003)
14. Graham, R.L., Knuth, D.E., Patashnik, O.: Concrete Mathematics - A Foundation for Computer Science. Addison-Wesley, Reading (1989)
15. Ghamarian, A.H., Geilen, M.C.W., Stuijk, S., Basten, T., Theelen, B.D., Mousavi, M.R., Moonen, A.J.M., Bekooij, M.J.G.: Throughput analysis of synchronous data flow graphs. In: 6th International Conference on Application of Concurrency to System Design, pp. 25–36 (2006)
16. Benazouz, M., Marchetti, O., Munier-Kordon, A., Michel, T.: A new method for minimizing buffer sizes for cyclo-static dataflow graphs. In: 8th IEEE Workshop on Embedded Systems for Real-Time Multimedia, pp. 11–20 (2010)
17. Fradet, P., Girault, A., Poplavko, P.: SPDF: a schedulable parametric data-flow MoC. In: Design, Automation and Test in Europe Conference and Exhibition, pp. 769–774 (2012)
18. Bebelis, V., Fradet, P., Girault, A., Lavigueur, B.: BPDF: a statically analyzable dataflow model with integer and boolean parameters. In: International Conference on Embedded Software, pp. 3:1–3:10 (2013)
19. Bouakaz, A., Fradet, P., Girault, A.: Symbolic analysis of dataflow graphs (extended version). Doctoral dissertation, Inria-Research Centre Grenoble-Alpes (2016)
20. Bebelis, V., Fradet, P., Girault, A.: A framework to schedule parametric dataflow applications on many-core platforms. In: Conference on Languages, Compilers and Tools for Embedded Systems, pp. 125–134 (2014)

Eliminating Data Race Warnings Using CSP

Martin Wittiger[(✉)]

Institute of Software Technology, University of Stuttgart,
Universitätsstraße 38, 70569 Stuttgart, Germany
martin.wittiger@informatik.uni-stuttgart.de

Abstract. Embedded systems commonly use state to synchronize concurrent programs. This state-based synchronization avoids serious errors like data races and can supersede other means of synchronization like locks and global disabling of interrupts. However, it makes reasoning difficult and static analysis tools struggle to comprehend it. In this paper we explain how we model C programs conservatively using static analysis and then use CSP refinement checkers to analyse synchronization. This paper demonstrates how this process aids program understanding and leads to the dismissal of data race warnings in industrial systems. We examine real-world synchronisation schemes and explain how and why they work.

Keywords: Data race · Race condition · Static analysis · Embedded systems · CSP · Refinement checker · Software verification

1 Introduction

Data races form a major class of errors in concurrent programs. A program is said to contain a data race if two concurrently running threads access the same variable (or piece of memory), one of the accesses is a write, and there is no synchronization that guarantees the accesses are not simultaneous. This is a common definition of a data race [5,10,12].

In most languages, programs that contain data races have undefined behaviour. It is therefore of utmost importance for safety-critical embedded systems to be free of data races.

Even thorough testing can miss data races because the erroneous behaviour may occur only sporadically under rare timing conditions. Data races can, however, cause errors that lead to catastrophic failures of software components or expensive recalls.

The development of tools that can help find data races and thereby mitigate their risks is thus a long-standing research problem. Vaziri et al. [12] (also Raza et al. [9] and others) have proposed using static analysis to find data races.

This work was funded in part within the project ARAMiS by the German Federal Ministry for Education and Research with the funding ID 01IS11035. The responsibility for the content remains with the author.

M. Bertogna et al. (Eds.): Ada-Europe 2016, LNCS 9695, pp. 30–43, 2016.
DOI: 10.1007/978-3-319-39083-3_3

The data race problem is generally undecidable. So analysis tools must choose between being optimistic (missing some actual races) or conservative (producing some false positive warnings).

Savage et al. [10] have built an optimistic tool. The Bauhaus data race detection tool developed by our research group errs on the conservative side. We believe conservative tools are more appropriate in the realm of safety-critical systems because of their ability to prove the absence of such synchronization errors.

Attemps have been made to help software engineers cope with the sometimes vast numbers of false positive warnings conservative tools suffer from. Keul [6] was able to reduce their number. Degiorgi and Wittiger [1] prioritize warnings based on heuristics and Koutsopoulos et al. [7] visualize data race situations.

Concurrent systems employ different types of synchronization when accessing shared resources. Commercial desktop software mostly relies on mutexes and monitors while embedded systems avoid these two patterns. Almost all embedded systems we have encountered use global disabling of interrupts to achieve synchronization of concurrent tasks. Additionally, state-based synchronization is used. It is often hand-crafted to fit a specific system and typically relies heavily on scheduling properties such as task priorities.

When using state-based synchronization concurrent tasks verify the system is in a specific state before they access shared resources. This works well, when the task's predicates on state are mutually exclusive and state cannot change spontaneously. State-based synchronization is commonly implemented in the form of explicit state machines.

Static analysis tools can handle disable interrupt patterns easily and efficiently. State-based synchronization, on the other hand, is generally more difficult.

Keul [6] performs an analysis step called a simple path exclusion that recognizes state machines used for synchronization. Schwarz et al. [11] use the term flag-based synchronization to denote essentially the same idea. Both approaches only recognize state machines that follow simple, syntactic patterns. They have very strong requirements on variables storing state. Both models forbid the assignment of non-constant values to state variables and they either exclude variables that have their address taken altogether or capitulate when they are assigned through dereferencing a pointer.

Building upon previously described ideas [13], we substantially reduced the requirements on state variables. This enables us to find, not only simple and obviously correct synchronization patterns, but also complex and unintuitive ones.

For the approach presented in this paper we automatically extract a conservative model of the actual system from the source code through static analysis.

CSP (Communicating Sequential Processes) is a mathematical language to formally describe the behaviour of concurrent communicating processes. It was developed by Hoare [4]. We translate the model into CSP_M (machine-readable CSP), which is understood by CSP refinement checkers. Finally, we use those refinement checkers to test whether specific data race situations are reachable in the model—and if they are not, eliminate them from the list of warnings.

In doing this, we accept an increase in the computational complexity to reduce the number of false positive warnings whilst maintaining practicality for industry-sized systems. We were able to recognize a previously undetected, state-machine-like pattern in a real-world industrial embedded system and use it to dismiss data race warnings.

2   Integration of CSP into the Data Race Detector

Bauhaus is a collection of static analysis tools. The tools are written in Ada and analyse C, C++ and Java. This collection includes the data race detector we build upon. It parses C code to obtain an AST. It then performs static analysis to turn the AST into a concurrency-aware intermediate representation. Among the analyses performed are pointer analysis and control flow analysis. The latter relies on an extra input specifying tasks, start routines and scheduling-related information. Care is taken to use a pointer analysis that is correct in a concurrent setup and conservative—like all our methods.

Further analyses augment the intermediate representation. Escape analysis, for example, categorizes variables according to their reach as local, thread-local, or communicative[1] and helps to increase the precision of pointer analysis. Lockset analysis deals not only with mutexes (should they be used) but also with global disabling/enabling of interrupts.

2.1   Constant Propagation and Constant Folding

Data race analysis can function without information about integer values. Our new approach, however, depends upon integer constants as they form the basis of our model. To handle them efficiently we have implemented a combined constant propagation and constant folding analysis.

Aside from literals, the only true constants in C are macros that, when expanded, become literals. In Fig. 1, C is an example of this. The preprocessor of our C frontend expands these macro constants allowing us to treat them like literals.

Some systems we have encountered extensively use **const** to declare de facto constants (like D and E in Fig. 1). When a variable is declared **const**, but not **volatile** and is immediately initialized to a constant expression, we consider it—somewhat optimistically—a constant and propagate its value to its uses.

The third type of constant we recognize are enums. Our propagation algorithm treats them like other constants.

We found that many constant expressions exist in embedded systems, presumably due to configuration. Simple constant folding has therefore increased the number of expression resolved to constant values considerably: in one examined system by approximately 88 %.

---

[1] Actually, the analysis provides finer results with several grades in between those mentioned. We refer the reader to Keul [6] for more details.

```
#define C 1                          const int R;
const int D = 2;                         int S = 13;
const int E = C * 3;          volatile const int T = 15;
typedef enum {F = 4, G, H} ct;
```

Fig. 1. A section of C code declaring a true constant, de facto constants and an enum. Our constant propagation considers C–H constants with values 1–6, but not R–T.

Our analysis is context and flow-insensitive. We could add a copy propagation analysis with limited context sensitivity and flow sensitivity. While this would increase precision at moderate cost, we are content with our current analysis because it has worked well in our experiments.

2.2 Model Extraction

Our intermediate representation is a threaded call/control flow graph. This graph is disconnected because thread-sensitivity ensures control flow does not switch between threads. If a specific method is called in multiple threads, multiple copies show up in the intermediate representation. We avoid actual duplication in memory by using lean adaptors for the actual representation of program code.

Some methods are marked as entry points of tasks. One of those tasks is the main task, which does global initialization and calls the main method.

To create a model of our system, we first choose state variables. These state variables must satisfy the properties of atomicity and consistency.

The effects of an assignment to an atomic variable become visible in one indivisible step. No intermediate or partial assignments may ever be observable.

In C, atomicity can be achieved by declaring variables atomic. The compiler guarantees that reading and writing such a variable happens in a single CPU instruction. Just ensuring variables have memory bus size (typically `int`) is not quite enough. One can, however, achieve atomicity by additionally avoiding awkward alignment and disabling certain compiler optimizations.

A variable behaves consistently if a newly assigned value is visible by all future reads until another assignment occurs (sequential consistency). C programmers often declare variables `volatile` to achieve consistency. This is—strictly speaking—not covered by the C99 standard. In practice, however, compilers provide stronger promises than required by the C standard. System engineers from the embedded systems domain have assured us that with the compiler settings used for the systems examined, assignments to volatile variables will become visible to other tasks immediately and in a sequentially consistent manner.

When all the conditions listed above are met, we consider variables declared as `volatile int` to be suitable state variables for synchronization.

State variables are subject to race warnings themselves. Because system developers consider concurrent assignments to volatile ints to be safe, they do not typically surround them with protection and our general race detector will flag those accesses unless they are coincidentally protected by some mechanism.

Some heuristics should be applied when choosing state variables:

– Any state variable must be compared to a constant in a path predicate at least once. While variables can in principle help synchronization without appearing in path predicates, it is impossible in our conservative approximation for them to help us eliminate a warning.
– A variable that is never assigned a constant is probably of no use.
– A state variable should have an escape status greater than thread-local. We restrict ourselves to such variables because only communication variables contribute to synchronization directly.

Our tool lists variables that match those properties and fulfil the requirements for state variables. For typical real-world systems this list is too long. Therfore, we rely currently on a manual selection of one or more variables from that list.

Once a set of state variables is chosen, we project our intermediate representation on those variables. We retain the call graph and the control flow within methods but replace the statements in basic blocks and the flow predicates.

All expressions are examined for side effects such as function calls and assignments. If constant folding has not reduced them to a constant, they are considered to be of indeterminable value (written as IND). We assume a left-to-right evaluation order (see Fig. 2).

```
a = (x = 1);              x = 1; a = 1;
f(g(), a = 7);            g(); a = 7; f(IND, 7);
a = h(x++);               x = IND; h(IND); a = IND;
```

Fig. 2. This example shows how we model side effects. The left-hand side C fragment is modelled like the right-hand side shows. Variables are assigned constants or IND only.

Assignment statements are conservatively approximated. It follows from the approximation of expressions that the assigned value is either a known constant or indeterminable. In general, targets are not known with certainty and have to be approximated as well. Imprecision occurs, for instance, when assigning to dereferences of pointers (like *p = 7) or indexed arrays (like a[x] = 9). We distinguish three different cases for the targets of the assignment:

1. If it can be shown the assignment may not influence any state variable, it is simply omitted.
2. If the assignment targets a state variable (or even multiple ones) but may also write to other variables, we emit a weak update on the state variable. A weak update is an assignment that may change the value or leave its previous value in place.
3. If the assignment targets exactly one state variable, we emit a strong update. This is an assignment that will change the variable's value.

Note that a weak update with indeterminable value has the same effect as a strong update with indeterminable value: Both leave the variable in its least defined state. Strong updates are cheaper than weak updates. In Fig. 3, line 1, we could thus place a strong update to get better output.

Further improvement is possible: Placing two consecutive weak updates in line 2 is overly conservative. In this situation we ensure that either a or b is indeed assigned. We thus allow neither skipping both assignments nor assigning both variables.

Care has to be taken to ensure variables do not overlap. Casting an int variable to an array of char, for instance, and then assigning to the first index is different from assigning to the original variable. Similar issues arise with union types and structs (records).

C Code	⋆p	Assignments
⋆p = f (7);	a; x	a ← IND
⋆p = 3;	a; b	a ← 3 ⊓ b ← 3
⋆p = 2 + 3;	a	a ← 5
⋆p = 4;	x; y	—

Fig. 3. This table shows how assignments to dereferenced pointers are treated. Here, a and b are state variables, x and y are not. The middle column shows the points-to set of p.

Similar principles govern the translation of path predicates. In our intermediate representation, basic blocks either have an unconditional successor or they have a predicate, a then and an else successor. Unconditional successors stay as they are. We conservatively approximate conditions by leaving boolean operations intact and focussing on the atoms of those operations. These are either comparisons of state variables with constants, boolean constants (both of which can easily be modelled), or considered indeterminable (again written as IND). We thus allow partially determinable conditions. This, in essence, leads to separate conditions for then and else branches that may overlap. Figure 4 shows examples of how this works.

2.3 CSP_M Generation

We write the extracted model to a text file, which is used for debug purposes and the generation of CSP$_M$ output. It enables an (almost) line-for-line translation into CSP$_M$.

The world of CSP, put very briefly, consists of processes and signals. Processes send signals to their environment and follow a non-deterministic finite automaton-like specification where they move from state to state by emitting signals. In the CSP$_M$-definition "P = a -> Q |~| b -> R" P is a process that can send signal a to become process Q and send signal b to become process R.

Predicate	Model Predicate	Implied Conditions for	
		Then-Branch	Else-Branch
`a == 1`	`a == 1`	$a = 1$	$a \neq 1$
`b != 3`	`b != 3`	$b \neq 3$	$b = 3$
`a == 1 || 0 == b`	`a == 1 || b == 0`	$a = 1$ or $b = 0$	$a \neq 1$ and $b \neq 0$
`x == 7`	`IND`	true	true
`a == 2 && x == 7`	`a == 2 && IND`	$a = 2$	true
`x == 1 || b == 1`	`IND || b == 1`	true	$b \neq 1$
`7 + 2 == 1`	`false`	false	true

Fig. 4. This table shows predicates being translated into the model and the implied conditions for the then and else branch. Again, a and b are state variables, x is not. If a condition for a branch is true, it does not mean the branch will be taken. It simply means that it can be taken.

Processes are also allowed to change states quietly with so-called τ-transitions (Fig. 5, line 4) or successfully terminate (Fig. 5, line 6).

They can undergo sequential composition—meaning a second process springs into life as soon as the first process terminates successfully—and be synced—meaning they act in parallel but have to agree on some or all the signals they send.

```
void p (void) {          P  = B1
    a = 1;               B1 = a_to_1 -> B2
    while (a == 1)       B2 = a_is_1 -> B3  |~|  a_isnot_1 -> B5
        if (IND)         B3 = B4  |~|  B2
            a = 2;       B4 = a_to_2 -> B2
}                        B5 = SKIP
```

Fig. 5. Comparison of a C procedure and the CSP$_M$ output (interrupts omitted). In this Example a is a state variable and the condition of the if statement is considered indeterminable in the model. As required in CSP$_M$ signals have lower-case and processes upper-case identifiers.

With these instruments we build processes that realize the behaviour of our model. These processes send signals setting variables to values and checking whether variables are at certain values.

Each variable is also translated to a process. These variable processes are then synced with the other processes. This ensures that variable-related signals occur only in semantically reasonable order.

In Fig. 5 we explore how a small C procedure is translated into CSP$_M$. Later we will see how refinement checkers process this output. Yields to preemptions are omitted in this figure. After each operation on a state variable visible to the environment, the process offers to yield to a preemption. A separate logic ensures only preemptions allowed by the scheduling actually take place.

This means tasks can only be preempted to run tasks with a higher priority whenever we use priority-based scheduling.

Lastly, we mark the position of accesses causing data race warnings and emit the question whether the data race situation is reachable. For this question a denotational CSP model must be chosen. We have chosen the traces model, which is typically used for safety concerns (showing nothing bad happens) and is the simplest and cheapest model. Other models available include stable failures typically used to show freedom from deadlock (something will always happen) and failures-divergences used to treat liveness concerns (showing eventually progress will be made). We create a separate file for each data race warning under consideration.

2.4   CSP Refinement Checker

There are several refinement checkers available for CSP_M. FDR2 [2], developed at the University of Oxford, has been used by many projects. Recently, a new version was released called FDR3 [3]. The University of Düsseldorf has presented a tool called ProB [8]. It works with CSP_M as well as B and LTL models and can even mix specifications written in different languages.

During the work on this project we have used all three refinement checkers. We found ProB to be suitable for smaller specifications but preferred FDR2 for larger systems. The creators of FDR3 plan to make use of parallel computations and we deem it likely that FDR3 will become an interesting option in the future.

The way FDR3 (and FDR2) tackle CSP_M is quite instructive. They evaluate CSP_M expressions into generalised labelled transition systems (GLTS) resembling non-deterministic finite automata.

Figure 6(a) shows the GLTS derived from the output shown in Fig. 5. While semantically correct, this transition system is unnecessarily large. FDR3 can apply compression functions that reduce or even minimise the size of transition systems. Normalization is a strong compression function yielding transition systems free of τ-transitions. Figure 6(b) shows its result, which inescapably allows for exactly the same traces as the original.

Some of the traces of P are incongruous with variable semantics. The system in Fig. 6(b) clearly allows a_isnot_1 to immediately follow a_to_1 and a_isnot_1 to follow a_is_1 without an assignment in between. To force the adherence to variable semantics we sync P with the process A. The result (in normalised form) is shown in Fig. 6(c).

2.5   CSP Preprocessing

The generated output can be fed directly into the refinement checkers—and this is what we do for small examples. For larger systems two different issues arise.

FDR2's as well as FDR3's manuals forbid empty μ-statements (a set of mutually recursive processes that cannot perform any visible signals). While they are usually unproblematic, their presence sometimes causes irregular behaviour of the refinement checkers.

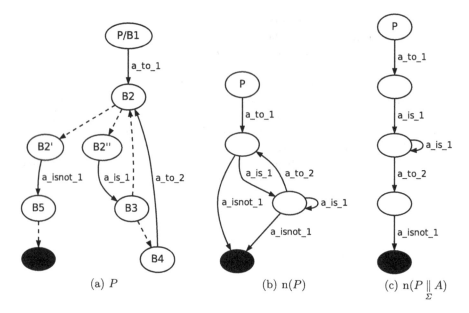

Fig. 6. GLTS produced by FDR3 for the CSP_M-code from Fig. 5. The unlabelled dashed edges are silent τ-transitions; the black nodes can successfully terminate. From left to right: The system generated from P. The compressed, minimally sized system for P. The compressed system resulting from syncing P with A.

Our automatically generated CSP_M code is rather verbose. It significantly differs from handwritten code. All refinement checkers we have used have trouble parsing it—in part just because of its sheer size.

Preprocessing the CSP_M output solves both problems for us. This preprocessing is done by parsing the original file and then applying sound transformations to enhance the suitability for the refinement checkers. This includes elimination of unused/unreachable definitions, shortening of identifiers, and algebraic transformations. This shrinks the CSP_M-code to about 2 % of its original size.

3   Illustrative Examples

We will now explore how our implementation behaves in practice. Our first example is shown in Fig. 7. It features a system with two tasks and three global variables. Our data race detector prints warnings for both x and y. The variable state fulfils the requirements for state variables: So, can our new implementation rule out those warnings?

First, let us consider x. It seems as if the low-priority task (task_low) will only access x when the system is in STARTUP state, whereas the high-priority task (task_high) will only access x when the system is in any other state.

To our surprise, the refinement checker refuses to rule out this warning, and this trace shows why: Just after task_low has set state to STARTUP,

```
typedef enum {STARTUP, RUN, SHUTDOWN} State;
int x, y;
volatile State state;
void task_high (void) {                 void task_low (void) {
    if (state != STARTUP)                   state = STARTUP;
        x++;                                x = 1;
    if (state != SHUTDOWN)                  state = RUN;
        y++;                                while (true)
    if (IND)                                    if (state == RUN)
        state = SHUTDOWN;                           work ();
}                                               else
                                                    y++; }
```

Fig. 7. A small example system with data race warnings on x and y.

it is interrupted by **task_high**. y is incremented, and then the indeterminable condition from the last if statement is assumed to be true, and state is thus set to SHUTDOWN. When the low-priority task resumes its work and initializes x to 1, the system is no longer in STARTUP state and a second interruption by the high-priority task leads to the data race situation.

Now we consider y. A first examination shows that the low-priority task accesses y only when the system is not in RUN state. The high-priority task accesses y only when the system is not in SHUTDOWN state. These two conditions can both be satisfied by putting the system in STARTUP state[2].

This, however, cannot happen since no such definition reaches the code position in question. FDR2 agrees with our finding and does indeed eliminate the warning.

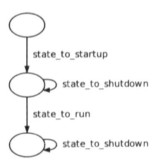

Fig. 8. The normalized GLTS. For this figure, we have restored the enum values, which are normally replaced by their implementation values.

---

[2] The variable **state** could also have an ill-defined value, like the one it has before initialization. Our approach is aware of such other values.

To further our inspection of this example, we will look at transition systems. FDR2 effortlessly plots the whole transition system of this example but the result is too large to be informative. CSP$_M$ allows the hiding of signals. This turns a normal, externally visible signal into an internal τ-transition. To obtain the graph shown in Fig. 8 we have hidden all signals of the system process except those modifying the variable `state`.

When examining the graph, we notice a few things. We see immediately that the system state can go from `STARTUP` to `SHUTDOWN` state and then back to `RUN` state—which is likely unwanted behaviour. In fact, the state variable itself is subject to a possible race condition that breaks the abstraction. We can also notice how normalisation blurs the lines between tasks. Lastly, we can spot that the system never terminates successfully. This is, of course, expected since the low-priority task enters an infinite loop and accordingly never terminates.

We observe how, even though the state-based synchronization pattern is broken, it can still be used to dismiss data race warnings on the variable y. Also, if this were a real system, one ought not to jump to the conclusion that it is broken. Maybe the indeterminable condition in the high-priority task can only be satisfied after the system has switched to `RUN` state. If this is the case, there is no data race and there are no suspicious changes of state.

```
void read() {
    x++;
    if (IND) state = 1;
    if (IND) state = 2;
}

void task_high (void) {
    while (state == 1)
        read();
    if (IND) state = 0;
}

void task_low (void) {
    if (IND) state = 2;
    switch (state) {
        case 0 :
            break;
        case 1 :
            if (IND) state = 2;
            break;
        case 2 :
            read();
    }  }
```

Fig. 9. Pattern observed in an industrial embedded system.

We will now look at a pattern observed in an actual industrial embedded system where our approach eliminates data race warnings (Fig. 9). We have changed identifier names and cut irrelevant portions of the original source code.

The system reads a message byte-by-byte that was previously received, presumably from a hardware bus. Two tasks call the method **read** and it accesses global variables, here represented by a single variable x, without disabling interrupts first. Our data race detector therefore prints warnings for the variable x.

There is also a state variable involved: A high-priority task does most of the reading while **state** is 1, and a low-priority task finishes the job after **state** is set to 2. The variable **state** can also be set to 0, which seems to cancel the current operation.

Using our implementation and FDR2 we have shown that the warning about a data race on x can be eliminated. We argue as follows: **task_high** will only call **read** if state is 1 when it starts to execute. **task_low** on the other hand will call **read** only after observing that **state** has the value 2. There are several statements changing the state. There is even one that assigns 1. But despite all that, there is no trace allowing for a sudden switch of **state** to 1.

Figure 10 confirms this reasoning. The transition system shows how the data race position (marked DRW) is only reached when the **state** is 1 and that the task method only terminates after having verified that **state** is not 1.

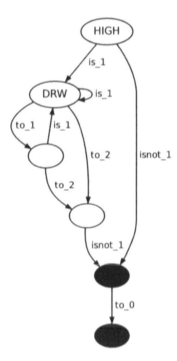

Fig. 10. The GLTS resulting from normalizing task_high.

When we examined the actual system we had to overcome two complications; there is a task of very high priority, which cancels the operation occasionally by setting state to 0. This sudden change of state is no cause for concern, at least not for the data race warning in question.

There are two more tasks with high priority, which seem to predicate some of their work on state being not 1 or state being not 2. Both tasks read state multiple times but do not write to it. This caused us problems: The complexity those reading accesses added to the system caused FDR2 to run for a long time without producing an answer. To solve this, we used FDR2 to verify the absence of writing accesses in a separate step and then removed those tasks from the CSP_M-file. Only then did FDR2 complete its run. The only manual steps required in the analysis of the system were this seperate removal and the choosing of state variables from a list of candidates. All other steps are automated.

The synchronization system we have discovered is convoluted. A tool looking for specific patterns would not take it into account. We do not know whether it was designed to be state-based synchronization. We only found it works for the variable x. In fact, at the source point where read accesses x, the original system touches several variables. We thus had a number of virtually identical CSP_M-files that all led to the exclusion of a data race warning.

4   Conclusion and Future Work

We have successfully implemented a tool that uses static analysis to extract a conservative model of state-based synchronization from industry-sized embedded systems. We demonstrated how, by translating this model into CSP_M, we can use refinement checkers to abstractly interpret the original system. Our description shows how this can provide a rigorous understanding of concurrent actions in a complex system and recognize not only simple but also complicated and obfuscated state based synchronization.

It is very difficult to reason correctly about concurrent systems. Our tool helps understand what may happen. The capability to provide traces that work as counter-examples for schemes that are broken adds to this understanding. Our work takes us further beyond obstacles such as indirect assignments, variable values, or even partial deviation from the state machine pattern.

Our approach scales to the size of real systems and we have been able to eliminate actual warnings.

There are two measures that may help to overcome manual selection of variables. Improving CSP_M generation could reduce the state space the refinement checkers have to cope with and enable them to either run faster or allow for more variables to be used in each file.

Changing and improving heuristics would allow us to focus on the most important state variables.

We plan to address both issues in the future. Our vision is to build a system that automatically screens all data race warnings and eliminates some of them, thereby reducing the number of false positive warnings.

References

1. Degiorgi, S., Wittiger, M.: Rating the results of conservative static data race analyses (dt.: Ergebnisbewertung konservativer statischer Data-Race-Analysen). In: Workshop for Software-Reengineering WSR 2013 (2013)
2. Formal Systems (Europe), Oxford University: Failures-Divergence Refinement: FDR2 User Manual (2010)
3. Gibson-Robinson, T., Armstrong, P., Boulgakov, A., Roscoe, A.W.: FDR3 — a modern refinement checker for CSP. In: Ábrahám, E., Havelund, K. (eds.) TACAS 2014 (ETAPS). LNCS, vol. 8413, pp. 187–201. Springer, Heidelberg (2014)
4. Hoare, C.A.R.: Communicating Sequential Processes. Prentice Hall International, Englewood Cliffs (2004)
5. ISO/IEC: Standard for Programming Language C++ (2011)
6. Keul, S.: Tuning static data race analysis for automotive control software. In: 11th IEEE International Working Conference on Source Code Analysis and Manipulation (SCAM), pp. 45–54 (2011). http://dx.doi.org/10.1109/SCAM.2011.16
7. Koutsopoulos, N., Northover, M., Felden, T., Wittiger, M.: Advancing data race investigation and classification through visualization. In: 2015 IEEE 3rd Working Conference on Software Visualization (VISSOFT), pp. 200–204 (2015). http://dx.doi.org/10.1109/VISSOFT.2015.7332437
8. Leuschel, M., Fontaine, M.: Probing the depths of CSP-M: a new FDR-compliant validation tool. In: Liu, S., Maibaum, T., Araki, K. (eds.) ICFEM 2008. LNCS, vol. 5256, pp. 278–297. Springer, Heidelberg (2008)
9. Raza, A., Vogel, G., Plödereder, E.: Bauhaus – a tool suite for program analysis and reverse engineering. In: Pinho, L.M., González Harbour, M. (eds.) Ada-Europe 2006. LNCS, vol. 4006, pp. 71–82. Springer, Heidelberg (2006)
10. Savage, S., Burrows, M., Nelson, G., Sobalvarro, P., Anderson, T.: Eraser: a dynamic data race detector for multithreaded programs. ACM Trans. Comput. Syst. **15**(4), 391–411 (1997). http://dx.doi.org/10.1145/265924.265927
11. Schwarz, M.D., Seidl, H., Vojdani, V., Apinis, K.: Precise analysis of value-dependent synchronization in priority scheduled programs. In: McMillan, K.L., Rival, X. (eds.) VMCAI 2014. LNCS, vol. 8318, pp. 21–38. Springer, Heidelberg (2014)
12. Vaziri, M., Tip, F., Dolby, J.: Associating synchronization constraints with data in an object-oriented language. In: Conference Record of the 33rd ACM SIGPLAN-SIGACT Symposium on Principles of Programming Languages, pp. 334–345. ACM (2006). http://dx.doi.org/10.1145/1111037.1111067
13. Wittiger, M., Felden, T.: Recognition of real-world state-based synchronization. In: Proceedings of the 17th Workshop Software-Reengineering and Evolution (WSRE), pp. 9–10 (2015)

Real-Time Stream Processing in Java

HaiTao Mei(✉), Ian Gray(✉), and Andy Wellings(✉)

University of York, York, UK
{hm857,Ian.Gray,Andy.Wellings}@york.ac.uk

Abstract. This paper presents a streaming data framework for the Real-Time Specification for Java, with the goal of levering as much as possible the Java 8 Stream processing framework whilst delivering bounded latency. Our approach is to buffer the incoming streaming data into micro batches which are then converted to collections for processing by the Java 8 infrastructure which is configured with a real-time ForkJoin thread pool. Deferrable servers are used to limit the impact of stream processing activity on hard real-time activities.

1 Introduction

A stream processing system consists of a collection of modules that compute in parallel and communicate via channels [16]. Modules can be either *source capturing* (that pass data from a source into the system), *filters* (that perform atomic operations on the data) and *sinks* (that either consume the data or pass it out of the system). Real-time stream processing systems are stream processing systems that have time constraints associated with the processing of data as it flows through the system from its source to its sink. Typically, the sources of streaming data may originate from an embedded system (for example, the Large Hadron Collider can output a raw data stream of approximately 1PB/s [17]) or from a variety of internet locations (e.g., Twitter's global stream of Tweet data). In the context of this work, we assume stream processing is computationally intensive and is a soft real-time activity. Hence, we are interested in the latency of processing each element in the stream and bounding the impact that stream processing has on other hard real-time activities that might be sharing the same computing platform.

The most recent version of Java (Java 8) has introduced Streams and lambda expressions to support the efficient processing of in-memory stream sources (e.g., a Java Collection) in parallel, with functional-style code. One of the primary goals is "to accelerate operations upon large amounts of data by dividing the task between multiple threads (processors)" [5]. The parallel implementation builds upon the `java.util.concurrent` ForkJoin framework introduced in Java 7. The Java 8 Stream processing infrastructure is based on three assumptions: its data source has been populated into memory before processing, the size of data source will not change, and the goal is to *process the data as fast as possible using all of the available processors*. Hence it is targeted at batched streams.

© Springer International Publishing Switzerland 2016
M. Bertogna et al. (Eds.): Ada-Europe 2016, LNCS 9695, pp. 44–57, 2016.
DOI: 10.1007/978-3-319-39083-3_4

Previously we have evaluated the efficacy of Java 8 Streams as a framework for processing real-time batched streams and have found it inadequate [14] even when used in conjunction with the Real-Time Specification for Java (RTSJ). The essence of the problem is that using the ForkJoin framework introduces priority inversions, as it is not possible to construct the worker threads as real-time threads. (By definition, all standard Java threads have a lower priority than all real-time Java threads.) We have suggested changes to JSR 282[1] to circumvent this problem, which have now been adopted. We have also presented a real-time stream processing framework for batched data, which includes a real-time ForkJoin pool [14]. In this paper, we consider how real-time *streaming* data sources can be handled, and propose an extended framework. We assume the presence of a multicore platform hosting version 2.0 of the RTSJ. Our goal is to, where possible, use the proposed Java 8 Streams and evaluate their adequacy for a real-time environment.

The paper is structured as follows. Section 2 introduces Java 8 Streams. Related work is considered in Sect. 3. In Sect. 4, our overall approach is discussed. This is followed in Sect. 5 by a description of our implementation. Section 6 then evaluates our approach by comparing its performance against the regular Java concurrency framework. Finally we present our conclusions.

2   Java 8 Streams

Streams and Lambda expressions are the most notable features that have been added in Java SE 8. The Stream API and lambda expressions are designed to facilitate simple and efficient processing of data sources (such as from Java collections) in a way which can be easily pipelined and parallelised.

A lambda expression is an anonymous method, which consists of arguments and corresponding processing statements for these arguments. For example, `(a,b)->a+b` defines a Lambda expression that sums two arguments. Lambda expressions make code more concise, and extend Java with functional programming languages concepts. Internally, a lambda expression will be compiled into a *functional interface* by the Java compiler. Functional interfaces were introduced by Java 8, and are interfaces which contain only one method, which cannot have a default implementation.

A sequence of operations with a data source forms a pipeline. Streams make use of lambda expressions to enable passing different methods into each operation in the pipeline if required. A pipeline consists of a source, zero or more intermediate operations, and a terminal operation. An intermediate operation always returns a new stream, rather than perform methods on the data source. One example of intermediate operations is `map`, which maps each data elements in the stream into a new element in the new stream. A terminal operation forces the evaluation of the pipeline, consumes the stream, and returns a result. Thus, streams are lazily evaluated. An example of terminal operations is `reduce`, which

---

[1] The JCP Expert Group are due to release a new version of the RTSJ (Version 2.0) in early 2016. This version will be compatible with Java 8.

performs a reduction on the data elements using an accumulation function. A simple word count example can be described by the following code using the Stream API and Lambda Expressions:

```
Collection<String> dataToProcess = WordsToCount;
Map<Object, Long> result = dataToProcess.parallelStream()
  .flatMap(line->Stream.of(Pattern.compile("\\s+").split(line)))
  .collect(Collectors.groupingBy(
          w -> w,TreeMap::new,Collectors.counting()));
```

One of the main advantages of streams is that they can be either sequentially evaluated, or evaluated in parallel. Sequential evaluation is carried out by performing all the operations in the pipeline on each data element sequentially by the thread which invoked the terminal operation of the stream. When a stream is evaluated in parallel, it uses a special kind of iterator called a *Spliterator* to partition the processing, and all the created parts will be evaluated in parallel with the help of a ForkJoin thread pool. Efficiency is achieved by the work stealing algorithm that is used by the ForkJoin pool.

3   Related Work

The StreamIt [7] language is specifically designed for processing data streams on platforms ranging from embedded systems to large scale and high performance system. StreamIt defines several data flow abstractions for stream processing, such as `filter` (similar to the `filter()` method in Java 8 Streams), and a Java-like high-level API to access these abstractions. StreamIt uses the synchronous data-flow model and allows thus very aggressive compiler optimisations. Borealis [8] focuses on distributed stream processing, and defines a set of stream operations, e.g., `map`, `join` etc., written in the Java API. Neither StreamIt nor Borealis provide real-time support.

Storm [3], Heron [11], and Samza [2] are distributed stream processing frameworks. Computation graphs (typically directed acyclic graphs) can be constructed to represents the stream processing logic, where edges represent data flow and vertexes represent computation. A data push model is employed for stream dispatching. Spark Streaming [6] is a distributed stream processing library that is built on top of Spark [1]. Spark Streaming periodically groups the received data in streams into a micro batch, and processes it with the Spark engine. However, none of the above are integrated into a real-time environment.

Inspired by StreamIt and the RTSJ, StreamFlex [15] is a stream processing framework which provides bounded latency. StreamFlex provides a set of classes, such as `filters`, which are used to construct computation graphs for stream processing. The processing latency is bounded by changing the virtual machine to support real-time periodic execution of threads, computational activities isolation, and a memory model that avoids the use of garbage collectors. However as a result, StreamFlex is a very different programming model to more standard languages and is not compatible with Java 8 Streams. Also it does not support priority assignment to limit the impact of soft real-time streaming work on hard real-time activities.

AdaStreams [10] is a stream processing library with a run-time system that targets at multiprocessor platforms. Filter that is similar to the one in StreamIt, Splitter and Joiner are created as stream processing abstracts, and a processing graph can be constructed by connecting them together. However, it does not support real-time constraints.

Mattheis [13] proposed a framework that uses work-stealing algorithms in parallel stream processing in soft real-time systems. This work investigated the variance of latency when using work stealing algorithms with different strategies. It determined that latency is reduced by using FIFO ordering when stealing from the global queue, and when using LIFO ordering for stealing from the local queue. This is the approach adopted by Java 8, which we use unchanged.

Extending Storm to provide real-time support is proposed in [9], which defines a real-time processing stack including a real-time OS, a real-time JavaVM, and real-time versions of Storm's classes. Two core concepts in Storm: the Spout (source of streams) and the Bolt (computation logic in the data flow graph) are extended to be sporadic activities, so that these activities can be configured with minimum interval times, computation times, and priorities. In addition, a fixed-priority scheduler is provided. A drawback of Storm is that it uses an eager computation model which does not provide all of the optimisation opportunities of the lazy model of Java 8.

4   A RTSJ-Based Real-Time Stream Processing Framework

The overall goal of the work is to leverage as much as possible the Java 8 Stream processing framework within an RTSJ environment. The fundamental problem that must be addressed is how to map a *streaming* data source into *batched data* so that it can be processed with our current real-time stream processing framework. The proposed approach is to group the streaming data into *micro batches*, each of which can be treated as a static data source. Then a stream can be created to process each micro batch. The overview of this approach is shown in Fig. 1.

The size of each micro batch is determined by two factors: the *input data volume* – incoming data is buffered up to an application-defined maximum amount and once the buffer is full the batch is processed; and *time* – individual data elements of the input data stream have an application-defined maximum latency for their processing, so a micro batch must be released early if the processing time of the batch is such that a data item may miss its deadline. Figure 2 illustrates the approach. The handler turns the buffer into a collection, which can then be processed using the stream processing framework. Note that, when the batch is processed in the case of a full buffer, the next timeout will be reset to be $time_{now} + timeout$. The micro batch will be processed using the real-time

Fig. 1. The overview of real-time processing streaming data.

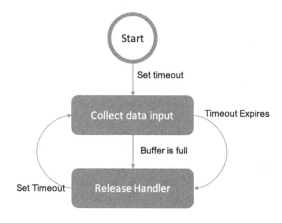

Fig. 2. The Real-Time Micro Batching approach.

stream processing framework, and the underlying work is performed by a real-time ForkJoin thread pool at a desired priority. The approach is described using the Real-Time Specification for Java (RTSJ). Three classes are defined:

`Receiver`: Maintains a dedicated real-time thread which is used to receive data from a source, e.g., a TCP/IP socket. It also maintains a buffer that stores the received data, and when enough data has arrived it notifies the `Handler`. Users can define their own receivers; for example, to receive data from different data flow sources.

`Timer`: Manages when the next timeout occurs. When fired, the next fire time is automatically reset.

`Handler`: Contains the user-defined processing logic for each micro batch using Java 8 Streams. Once notified, it retrieves data from the receiver as a Collection and performs the processing logic.

4.1 The Real-Time Micro Batching Stream API

The approach described above is implemented in a new framework called `BatchedStreams`. `BatchedStreams` adopts the described micro batching approach to provide real-time behaviour.

This overall approach is quite straightforward and allows the data flow behaviour to be captured well. However, the micro batching approach is difficult to implement in a way which allows user code to be as concise as when using standard Java 8 Streams. This is because a Java 8 Stream pipeline (e.g., `.map().filter().forEach()`) cannot be created outside of the context of a Stream, and a Stream can only have a single source of input data.

To address this problem, defined as part of `BatchedStreams` are `ReusableStreams`. `ReusableStreams` implement the standard Java Streams API, but also allow their processing pipeline to be reused over different input Collections (i.e., to apply to multiple batches) once its terminal operation has been invoked. `ReusableStreams` also allow more concise code through the use of Java 8 lambda expressions to specify the processing logic, as detailed in the follow sections.

`ReusableReferencePipeline` implements the `ReusableStream` interface, and represents a reusable stream of Java objects. In addition, we have implemented the equivalent classes for Java's primitive types.

The Structure of BatchedStream `BatchedStreams` maintain instances of `Receiver`, `Timer` and `Handler`. The instance of `ReusableStream` that is used to represent processing logic is also maintained by the `BatchedStream`. The `BatchedStream` starts the timer and the receiver, and sets their handler. Once a micro batch is released, the handler processes it using the `ReusableStream`, and optionally, using the `BatchedStreamCallback` to further process (e.g., to accumulate) the result. The `BatchedStreamCallback` is a functional interface, the method of which is invoked by the `ReusableStream` once its terminal operation returns, and acquires the returned result. The reusable pipeline must be initialised before processing any micro batch. A reusable pipeline can either be initialised then passed to the constructor of the `BatchedStream`, or be initialised by a functional interface named `ReferencePipelineInitialiser`, which is required by the constructor. Functional interfaces enable the `BatchedStream` to take the advantage of Java's lambda expressions to make code more concise. An example, which calculates how many words have been received from a TCP/IP socket, is described as follows:

```
long count = 0;
BatchedStream<String> textStreaming = new BatchedStream<>(
    new StringSocketRealtimeReceiver(...),
    p -> p.flatMap(line -> Stream.of(line.split("\\W+"))).count());
textStreaming.setCallback( r -> count += (long) r );
textStreaming.start();
```

The pipeline here counts how many words are within a micro batch, and is the same as it would be with normal Java 8 Streams. The pipeline is initialised using a lambda, and the callback that accumulates all the local results is set.

The `BatchedStream` cannot extend the `ReusableReferencePipeline` class because several terminal operations that are defined in the `Stream` interface are required to return a result. Applying terminal operations, such as `reduce`, on a `BatchedStream` represents a reduction of all the data elements from the data source. However, the `BatchedStream` generates one local result for every micro batch release.

Stream Processing in Real-Time To evaluate a Stream under real-time constraints requires the use of a real-time ForkJoin thread pool. The standard Java thread pool is insufficient because all standard Java 8 Streams execute using the same system-wide ForkJoin pool. This pool consists of standard Java threads which do not support real-time properties [14]. Furthermore, standard Java streams are defined to have a lower priority than all real-time (RTSJ) threads.

The real-time constraints are met by BatchedStreams that submit each micro batch and its corresponding reusable pipeline to a real-time ForkJoin thread pool [14]. This is a pool in which each worker thread is an aperiodic real-time thread and the priority of each worker thread is assigned when the pool is created.

Bounding the Impact of BatchedStream Typically stream data processing is computationally-intensive, and the unpredictability of data flows makes the corresponding CPU demand unpredictable. In an RTSJ runtime environment, we assume that stream processing occurs within a soft real-time task. With all such soft real-time activities, there is tension between achieving a short response time without jeopardising any hard real-time activities. Running stream data processing at the lowest priority in the system will not give good response times, but running it at too high a priority might cause critical activities to miss their deadlines. Hence, an appropriate priority level must be found, and any spare CPU capacity that becomes available must be made available as soon as practical.

The impact of stream data processing can be bounded by associating servers that are described in [14] with real-time thread pools. Performing the previous example with real-time constraints requires the server and the priority to be configured. A real-time ForkJoin thread pool with the desired priority associated is created to process each micro batch using the given pipeline.

```
long count = 0;
BatchedStream<String> textStreaming = new BatchedStream<>(
    new StringSocketRealtimeReceiver(...), new PriorityParameters(26),
    new DeferrableServer(...),
    p -> p.flatMap(line -> Stream.of(line.split("\\W+"))).count());
textStreaming.setCallback( r -> count += (long) r );
textStreaming.start();
```

5   Implementation

The real-time stream processing framework is implemented in the RTSJ. The RTSJ execution environment used in this work was JamaicaVM [4]. JamaicaVM provides support for multiprocessor applications including affinity sets. Timers are implemented using the RTSJ's PeriodicTimer class. Handlers are implemented using the RTSJ AsyncEventHandler, which submits a micro batch to be processed when either the event buffer is full or the next timeout occurs. The processing infrastructure uses our real-time ForkJoin thread pool, which is described in [14]. Repeatedly applying the same pipeline on each micro batch is achieved by using our ReusableStream framework, described below.

5.1   The ReusableStream Pipeline

Recall that the purpose of ReusableStreams is to create a pipeline of operations which may be repeatedly applied to different data collections. In addition, the ReusableStream must remain compatible with the existing Java Stream API.

ReusableStreams were defined as an interface that extends the Java Stream interface. They define a method named processData which takes a reference to a data source (Java Collection) to be processed, and optionally a callback which is called to present the result.

In a ReusableStream, operation pipelining uses a linked list. Each node maintains one intermediate operation and its arguments, and each intermediate operation returns a new node that will be appended to the tail of the linked list. When the terminal operation is invoked, the execution thread travels through the pipeline, and performs each operation on each data element. In order to make a pipeline reusable, the terminal operation is added to the linked list as well, rather than forcing stream evaluation. This is the only difference between the use of standard Java streams and ReusableStreams.

5.2   Real-Time Stream Processing

The stream is processed using BatchedStreams at different priority levels by submitting the ReusableStream that is used to process each micro batch to a real-time ForkJoin pool at the desired priority. In a globally scheduled system, each worker thread within the real-time ForkJoin thread pool can execute on, or migrate to any available processor. No CPU affinity is applied. In a fully-partitioned system, each worker thread within the real-time ForkJoin thread pool is constrained to execute on one processor, and task migration is forbidden using CPU affinity. The implementation uses javax.realtime.AffinitySet to pin each worker thread within a real-time ForkJoin pool to different processors. A semi-partitioned system is a mix of these two schemes. The semi-partitioned system extends the fully partitioned system, so that a certain number of tasks can migrate to a set of allowed processors. In a semi-partitioned system, different worker threads are allocated with different affinity sets, which determine the set of processors the task can migrate to.

6   Evaluation

The main goal of the evaluation is to determine the latency of stream processing and its impact on other real-time activities. First, we compare the latency of processing each data element in a stream using BatchedStream and the real-time stream processing framework (described in Sect. 4.1) with the standard Java 8 Stream processing framework. The experiments were performed on a 3.7 GHz Intel Core i7 processor (with 4 physical cores) platform, running Debian 7 Linux with a 3.2.0-4-rt-amd64 real-time kernel. Three physical cores were selected to be used by experiments using the Linux "taskset" shell command, and hyper-threading was turned off. The RTSJ VM uses the aicas JamaicaVM version 6.5.

6.1   Latency of Stream Processing

This experiment considers stream processing activities using a `BatchedStream` running on one processor (Processor 2). The same processor also hosts three periodic real-time threads at the same time. The experiment demonstrates that bounded latency can be provided when using `BatchedStreams` to process streaming data.

The underlying real-time stream processing framework that is used by `BatchedStreams` and the real-time thread employed by the receiver have medium priority. The experimental data flow is simulated using a real-time thread running on Processor 1 which sends one pre-generated string text per random interval at a low rate (minimum inter-arrival time (MIT) = 200 ms, maximum inter-arrival time (MAT) = 400 ms). The execution time for processing each string is set to 34 ms, and the deadline is 60 ms, thereby illustrating the computationally intensive nature of the processing required. We set the period of micro batching in the `BatchedStream` to be 10 ms. These values have been chosen to highlight the impact of a varying data arrival rate on our framework. In addition, the buffer size of the receiver is set to be 1024 elements, which ensures that storing all the elements within the data flow in this experiment will not trigger the early release of the micro batch. The other real-time threads have the real-time characteristics shown in Table 1, all times are in milliseconds.

Table 1. Periodic Real-time Threads Characteristics

Name	Priority	WCET	First Release	Period	Deadline	Processor ID
T1	Low	28	0	100	100	2
T2	Low	28	130	200	200	2
T3	Low	28	50	400	400	2

We start the stream processing at time 0, and real-time threads according to their release characteristics. The thread's first release times are offset to ensure a more balanced background load. The data flow starts 400 ms after the stream processing and generates 100 strings. The latency of each data element is measured, and illustrated in Fig. 3. As we can see, the latency of each data element in the data flow varies significantly when using the Java Stream framework as the processing infrastructure. As a consequence, some of data elements miss their deadlines. This is because the processing suffers from priority inversion on Processor 2, where all the periodic real-time threads will pre-empt the worker threads in the standard Java ForkJoin pool. The variance of the latency is notably reduced when using the real-time stream processing framework, as shown by the black line in Fig. 3. Priority inversion is avoided, and all data elements meet their deadlines. Note that, the variance of the latency when using the real-time stream processing framework is due to the variation of the time waiting in the buffer, as data can arrive at any time within the micro batching interval.

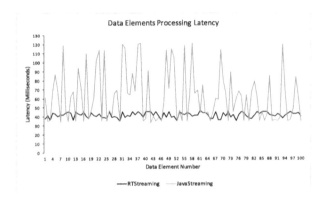

Fig. 3. The Latency of Data Elements In Data Streams.

We repeat each experiment 30 times and with different intervals of micro batching (10, 20, 40, and 60 ms). The distribution of latency of using the different frameworks are illustrated in Fig. 4a. This shows that the latency is well bounded when employing the `BatchedStream` with the help of the real-time stream processing infrastructure. As expected, the larger the micro batching interval, the larger the variance in the latency. With standard Java, the pattern is the same, only with much larger variance in the response times.

6.2   Different Data Rates

The experiments presented in Sect. 6.1 had an inter-arrival time between strings in the range of 200–400 ms. This represents a low load on the system. The experiments reported in this section consider the impact of varying this arrival rate to represent medium (M), high (H) and overload (O) workloads. The experiments and the streams investigated and their underlying processing frameworks are described in Table 2. The configuration of processors, and interference from real-time threads are the same as the previous experiment. The buffer size is 1024 elements, and the interval of micro batching is 100 ms. Each stream under this experiment contains 100 data elements, and the sequence of arrival times of each data element was generated before the experiment.

Again, each experiment was repeated 30 times, and the results are shown in Fig. 4b. The latency of streams at the medium and high rate is well bounded by employing `BatchedStreams` with the real-time processing framework. However, there are few deadline misses when the stream is bursty, and there are many deadline misses when the rate is very high (and therefore results in system overload). These issues are discussed in the following sections, and proposed solutions will be given. For all the cases, the latency of using standard Java frameworks cannot be guaranteed to meet the deadline because of the priority inversion issue.

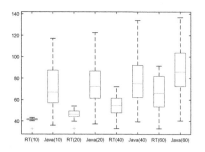

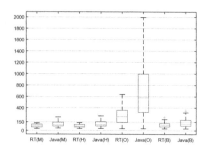

(a) The Latency of Data Elements in Streams with Different Intervals.

(b) Latency Distribution of Processing Different Rate Streams.

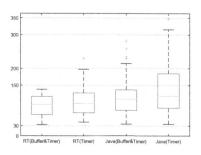

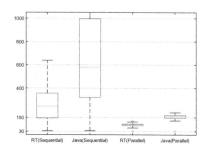

(c) Using Suitable Buffer Size To Handle Bursts.

(d) Latency Distribution of Parallel Stream Processing.

Fig. 4. Latency Distribution Experiment Results.

Table 2. Streams And Their Processing Frameworks, MIT and MAT Represents The Minimum and Maximum Interval. Times Are In Milliseconds.

Name	Processing Framework	MIT	MAT	Burst Size	WCET	Deadline
RT(M)	Real-Time	100	200	0	28	150
Java(M)	Java	100	200	0	28	150
RT(H)	Real-Time	50	100	0	28	150
Java(H)	Java	50	100	0	28	150
RT(O)	Real-Time	20	40	0	28	150
Java(O)	Java	20	40	0	28	150
RT(B)	Real-Time	200	400	4	28	150
Java(B)	Java	200	400	4	28	150

6.3   Burst Handling

With a bursty stream, there were deadline misses when releases of each micro batch within the `BatchedStream` was purely triggered by timeouts. The reason is that the waiting time of a data element can result in deadline misses.

For example, consider 4 data elements (d_1, d_2, d_3, d_4) that arrive in the system at time t when a burst occurs, while the next timeout is $t + 90$, thus, the latency of the last data element $Latency_{d_4} = 90 + ResponseTime_{d_4}$.

The minimum latency of d_4 in this case is determined when the response time of each data element equals their execution time (28 ms) and when there is no preemption or blocking.

$$Min(Latency_{d_4}) = 90 + WCET_{d_1} + WCET_{d_2} + WCET_{d_3} + WCET_{d_4}$$

Thus, the best-case latency of d_4 in this case is 202 ms, therefore missing its deadline.

One possible solution to this problem is to reduce the interval of micro batching, i.e., the timeout, so that the latency is within the deadline even when bursts occur. In this experiment, the maximum interval is $deadline - (WCET_{d_1} + WCET_{d_2} + WCET_{d_3} + WCET_{d_4})$, i.e., $150 - (28 + 28 + 28 + 28) = 38$ ms. However, as the stream rate in this experiment is generally slow, bursts only occur infrequently. Hence, using this interval to handle this stream is not efficient, because this introduces many releases of the handler where there is no data in the buffer.

An alternative approach, and the one we adopt, is to vary the buffer size to enable data to be processed immediately when bursts occur. The waiting time will be reduced, and therefore, the data within bursts can meet their deadlines. In this experiment, the buffer size of the BatchedStream is configured to be 4 elements, i.e., the burst size. Redoing the experiments for the bursty stream, the results are illustrated in Fig. 4c. The latency is reduced so that all the data elements now meet their deadlines, which is shown in the first plot in Fig. 4c. The second and the forth plots are taken from from the last experiment for easy comparison. The third plot represents the latency distribution of employing standard Java framework.

The interval of micro batching, i.e., the timeout, the maximum count of data arrived during this interval, and the execution time of each data determine the maximum latency of a stream. For example, assuming the maximum data arrival during the interval is N, the maximum latency can be represented by the following formula when there is no preemption from higher priority activity.

$$Max(Latency) = Interval + \sum_{i=1}^{N} WCET_{d_i}$$

When the maximum latency equals the deadline, N can be calculated. Thus, in the bursty case where the burst size is unknown, the buffer size should be configured to be at most N in order to provide bounded latency for bursts. Note that, this is based on the assumption that there are always enough computation resources so that even a very large burst can be processed within the deadline.

6.4   Parallel Stream Processing

With the experiments presented in Sect. 6.2, a stream whose MIT is 20 and MAT is 40 ms cannot be guaranteed to meet the deadline because the system is overloaded. The computation of each data element may require more time than the data arriving interval (minimum interval is 20 ms, but the execution time is 28 ms). The experiment reported in the section investigates the latency of parallel stream processing, by allocating another processor (Processor 3) to the `BatchedStream`'s underlying processing infrastructure, for both the real-time and standard Java versions. The rest of the configuration remains unchanged. The results are illustrated in Fig. 4d, where the first two plots are taken from the original experiment (see Sect. 6.2). The last two plots represent the latency distributions for the stream that was processed in parallel using the real-time and standard Java infrastructure. Each data element in the stream meets its deadline when using the parallel real-time processing infrastructure. Deadline misses still occur when using standard Java infrastructure because of the priority inversion occurring on Processor 2.

7   Conclusion and Future Work

This work has proposed an efficient general purpose real-time stream processing framework, based on a standard programming language which targets shared memory, multiprocessor platforms. The `BatchedStream` API, that uses the Java 8 Streams framework has been defined. With the help of `ReusableStreams`, `BatchedStreams` enable a real-time stream processing job to be defined with concise code. `BatchedStreams` provide bounded latency, using a real-time micro-batching model in conjunction with an underlying processing infrastructure that utilises a real-time ForkJoin thread pool to avoid priority inversion issues. Configuring the affinity sets of worker threads in a real-time ForkJoin thread pool allows different scheduling schemes, including global, fully partitioned, and semi-partitioned, to be supported.

Whilst `BatchedStreams` provide real-time stream processing facilities, its latency analysis for multiprocessors is subject to future work. Maia et al. [12] have proposed an approach for response time analysis of a `BatchedStream`-like processing model, i.e., ForkJoin pool, on a fixed priority global scheduling system. We will use this approach as a starting point for the analysis of the waiting time of each data element in a stream.

`BatchedStreams` currently only provide pipeline-style stream processing. Our current work is addressing how `BatchedStreams` can provides DAG-style computation logic when processing streams in real-time. This requires the current pipeline evaluation model to be augmented with extra operations (such as `shuffle`, and `collect`).

References

1. Apache Spark - Lightning-Fast Cluster Computing. http://spark.apache.org/. Accessed 5 Dec 2015
2. Apache Samza. http://samza.apache.org. Accessed 5 Dec 2015
3. Apache Storm. http://storm.apache.org/. Accessed 5 Dec 2015

4. JamaicaVM — aicas.com. https://www.aicas.com/cms/en/JamaicaVM. Accessed 1 Dec 2015
5. JEP 107: Bulk Data Operations for Collections. http://openjdk.java.net/jeps/107. Accessed 5 Dec 2015
6. Spark Streaming — Apache Spark. http://spark.apache.org/streaming/. Accessed 5 Dec 2015
7. StreamIt-Research. http://groups.csail.mit.edu/cag/streamit/shtml/research. shtml. Accessed 5 Dec 2015
8. Abadi, D.J., Ahmad, Y., Balazinska, M., Cetintemel, U., Cherniack, M., Hwang, J.-H., Lindner, W., Maskey, A., Rasin, A., Ryvkina, E., et al.: The design of the borealis stream processing engine. CIDR **5**, 277–289 (2005)
9. Basanta-Val, P., Fernández-García, N., Wellings, A., Audsley, N.: Improving the predictability of distributed stream processors. Future. Gener. Comput. Syst. **52**(C), 22–36 (2015)
10. Hong, G., Hong, K., Burgstaller, B., Blieberger, J.: Adastreams: a type-based programming extension for stream-parallelism with Ada. In: Proceedings of Reliable Software Technologiey - Ada-Europpe 2010, 15th Ada-Europe International Conference on Reliable Software Technologies, Valencia, Spain, 14–18 June 2010, pp. 208–221 (2005)
11. Kulkarni, S., Bhagat, N., Fu, M., Kedigehalli, V., Kellogg, C., Mittal, S., Patel, J.M., Ramasamy, K., Taneja, S.: Twitter heron: Stream processing at scale. In: Proceedings of the ACM SIGMOD International Conference on Management of Data, SIGMOD 2015, pp. 239–250. ACM, New York, NY, USA (2015)
12. Maia, C., Nogueira, L.M., Pinho, L.M., Bertogna, M.: Response-time analysis of fork/join tasks in multiprocessor systems. In: 25th Euromicro Conference on Real-Time Systems (2013)
13. Mattheis, S., Schuele, T., Raabe, A., Henties, T., Gleim, U.: Work stealing strategies for parallel stream processing in soft real-time systems. In: Herkersdorf, A., Römer, K., Brinkschulte, U. (eds.) ARCS 2012. LNCS, vol. 7179, pp. 172–183. Springer, Heidelberg (2012)
14. Mei, H.T., Gray, I., Wellings, A.: Integrating Java 8 streams with the real-time specification for java. In: Proceedings of the 13th International Workshop on Java Technologies for Real-time and Embedded Systems, p. 10. ACM (2015)
15. Spring, J.H., Privat, J., Guerraoui, R., Vitek, J.: Streamflex: high-throughput stream programming in Java. ACM SIGPLAN Notices **42**(10), 211–228 (2007)
16. Stephens, R.: A survey of stream processing. Acta Inform. **34**, 491–541 (1997)
17. Vidal, X., Manzano, R.: Taking a closer look at LHC. http://www.lhc-closer.es/ 1/3/12/

Testing and Verification

Addressing the Regression Test Problem with Change Impact Analysis for Ada

Andrew V. Jones[(✉)]

Vector Software, Inc., London, UK
andrew.jones@vectorcast.com

Abstract. The *regression test selection problem*—selecting a subset of a test-suite given a change—has been studied widely over the past two decades. However, the problem has seen little attention when constrained to high-criticality developments and where a "safe" selection of tests need to be chosen. Further, no practical approaches have been presented for the programming language Ada. In this paper, we introduce an approach to solving the selection problem given a combination of both static and dynamic data for a program and a change-set. We present a *change impact analysis* for Ada that selects the safe set of tests that need to be re-executed to ensure no regressions. We have implemented the approach in the commercial, unit-testing tool VectorCAST, and validated it on a number of open-source examples. On an example of a fully-functioning Ada implementation of a DNS server (IRONSIDES), the experimental results show a 97% reduction in test-case execution.

Keywords: Ada · Change impact analysis · Regression testing · Unit testing · Test-case selection · Code coverage · Change-based testing · Safety-critical software

1 Introduction

In their seminal work of 1988 [5], Harrold and Soffa introduced a dataflow-based approach for minimising the regression test effort in the context of Pascal. Since then, the problem of regression test execution has seen considerable attention [3, 12, 22].

Furthermore, and given the recent emergence of agile processes [24], which promote test-driven development as well as continuous integration [9], there is now a desire from developers to be able to re-test modified software rapidly. However, in the context of Ada, there are few articles (to the best of our knowledge, there only exists one paper [13] from 1997 that investigates change impact analysis for Ada) discussing how to solve the problem, without reverting to "retest all" [17].

Consequently, this paper considers the *test-case selection problem* [3]:

> "*determine which test-cases need to be re-executed [. . .] in order to verify the behaviour of modified software*"

© Springer International Publishing Switzerland 2016
M. Bertogna et al. (Eds.): Ada-Europe 2016, LNCS 9695, pp. 61–77, 2016.
DOI: 10.1007/978-3-319-39083-3_5

when applied to systems developed using Ada. It follows that we aim to investigate the plausibility of applying change impact analysis to regression testing of Ada source code. To this end, we seek to minimise the number of tests a developer needs to re-execute to determine if the behaviour of their software has been affected after making a change.

Our approach for *change-based testing* (CBT) of Ada is as follows. We begin by assuming the existence of a test baseline T of regression tests associated with a set of Ada source files, as well as access to both the original and modified source code. The analysis then proceeds as follows:

1. The difference between the original and modified source code is assessed to construct a *change-set* $\mathcal{A}$. This change-set encapsulates changes at the interface, package and subprogram[1] levels.
2. An intermediate representation of the program is constructed, based on both static data (derived without executing the program) and dynamic data (collected by executing the existing test baseline T). This intermediate representation forms the basis of a dependency graph of the Ada source code.
3. Given the change-set $\mathcal{A}$ and the intermediate representation, we determine a set of tests $T' \subseteq T$ that is affected by the changes in $\mathcal{A}$. We use the internals of the test automation tool VectorCAST to calculate the correspondence between changes in $\mathcal{A}$ and the dependency graph.

In Step 1, we are concerned with the calculation of the subset of packages and subprograms that were modified by a given change-set. Step 2 is focused on establishing the set of interdependencies in the software. Finally, Step 3 is concerned with the identification of those tests whose behaviour was affected from the data in Step 1. As we demonstrate later, we consider the locality (i.e., specification vs. body vs. subprogram) of the change to allow us to accurately understand its change-impact.

To-date, approaches to performing a change impact analysis for object-oriented languages either consider a static or a dynamic-derived dependency graph [3,12,22]. Uniquely, we consider a hybrid approach, using data from both static and dynamic analyses. Our change impact analysis calculates three types of dependency:

- Statically:
    1. Type and Ada specification dependencies – where Package A depends on Package B as part of A's specification
    2. Uses and Ada body dependencies – where Package A depends on Package B as part of A's body
- Dynamically:
    3. Subprogram invocation and coupling – where a subprogram Foo in Package A calls a subprogram Bar in Package B

---

[1] In this paper, we use the term "subprogram", without introducing ambiguity, to refer to either a function or a procedure inside of an Ada package.

Considering dependency data that is derived both statically and dynamically results in a technique that is not exclusively tied to subprogram-level analysis [16]. That is, we can consider the change impact at different levels of the software architecture. For example, it can support changes that occur at package-scope or to the object hierarchy.

Approaches based on static slicing [10] of the program are often overly-conservative, while maintaining "safety" [11]. When developing safety-critical systems, it can be accepted that this conservatism is of benefit, as it accounts for all possible behaviours of the system. However, this can lead to a change impact analysis that results in the (undesirable) "retest all" answer, which can be of little use to developers wishing to verify their day-to-day work.

Conversely, dynamic slicing (e.g., an analysis based on collected code coverage), considers only the behaviours and impacts that have been observed as part of previous system executions. An analysis based purely on dynamic data will potentially lead to "unsafe" conclusions [11].

We describe our approach as *safe* – by this, we mean that any test contained within "impact set" is *at least necessary* to exercise all of the impacts of the changes in a given change-set. Our work also aims for *minimality*, but not the *minimal* test-case set. Minimality cannot be achieved without a heavier approach to the change-impact process. For example, a finer-grained analysis could be based on modifications to the *def-use chains* [7] for package-level variables, and subsequently only execute those tests that depend on those variables.

We note that, basing the analysis (partly) on code coverage allows us to avoid complications when it comes to Ada 83 features such as generics, or Ada 95 features such as dynamic binding [1]. If the internals of a subprogram change invoke another (late-bound) subprogram, this would be detected as a subprogram-level change. Consequently, all tests executing that subprogram would be re-executed, invoking the newly added dynamic call. As such, there is no need to adopt a heavier approach that needs to consider polymorphism [17]. We discuss this further in Sect. 3.5.

Structure of the Paper. The rest of the paper is structured as follows. In the immediate subsection (Sect. 1.1), we provide an overview of the relevant literature to the regression test problem. The subsequent section (Sect. 2) provides a brief introduction to software change impact analysis and VectorCAST. In Sect. 3, we introduce our approach to impact analysis for Ada. We then provide an experimental evaluation (Sect. 4), based on a selection of open-source examples. In the final section (Sect. 5), we conclude.

1.1 Related Work

In 1988, Harrold and Saffa [5] introduced an *incremental testing* methodology for Pascal. To achieve this, they associated a test with the path taken through a module. The "incremental tester" would then try to re-use test-cases by identifying the tests that exercise the changes, or those which had their execution path modified by the change.

Loyall *et al.* [13], implemented a prototype impact analyser that presents the static dependency graph in a hyperlinked form to allow for easy navigation. While their tool does support Ada, it does not actually calculate the impact of a change in the source code – it is designed to support a "what if" approach to potential changes. A user can select an entity that might be modified, and then see the effects of this modification.

In [20], Ren *et al.* introduce the tool *Chianti*, which is able to calculate the set of affecting changes in a Java program that can lead to the behaviour of a test being modified. They consider two approaches: one based on static call graphs, and one based on dynamic call graphs. However, they do not consider the combination of static and dynamic data for a more precise analysis.

The theoretical underpinnings of *Chianti* were presented in [21], where the classification of *types* of (atomic) changes in Java programs was introduced. An approach was then designed to calculate the impact on other areas of the system, given a collection of atomic changes.

Law and Rothermel [11] consider the application of dynamic program slicing to the change impact process. Their approach is focused on the affect of program modifications on other parts of the program, rather than the test-case minimisation problem. They present the algorithm *PathImpact* that decides if a change in procedure p of a program P has a potential impact on other procedures reachable from p in the call graph G of P. *PathImpact* then calculates a forward and backwards slice through the program, as well as tracking function calls and returns, such that a backwards analysis is accurately scoped. In [15], Orso *et al.* present the *CoverageImpact* algorithm, which walks the execution data in combination with a forward slice of the variables in the program to calculate the impacted set. This set is then used to identify the tests that should be re-executed.

2   Background

We briefly introduce *change impact analysis* (Sect. 2.1) and VectorCAST (Sect. 2.2).

2.1   Software Change Impact Analysis

Simply put, software change impact analysis [19] is a family of techniques for determining the effects and outcomes of a source code modification, and for improving developer productivity in the context of such a change. We refer the interested reader to [3, 12].

We illustrate the outcome of a potential change in Fig. 1. For example, consider a change to Package C in the source tree shown. We will have two types of impact:

Upstream changes – this is where Package A calls into Package C. A modification to either the internal behaviour or external interface to Package C can cause a potential change in Package A.

Downstream changes – this is where Package C calls into Package F. While the internal behaviour of Package F cannot be affected by this change (Package F can be oblivious to Package C), Package F may now be used in a different way.

In the context of this paper, we are interested in identifying the set of tests that must be re-run in the presence of a change to Package C. To elucidate, any tests that execute directly on C would have to be re-run (depending on the scope of the change) and any tests associated with units (e.g., A) that have code coverage on the modified parts of C should also be re-run. We exclude re-executing the tests for Package F, as the tests on Package C, which collect coverage on F already, will validate this modified use of F.

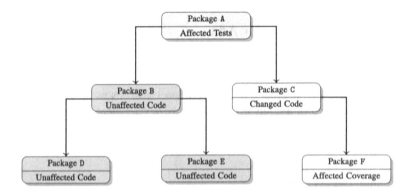

Fig. 1. How changes can propagate through the source tree

2.2 VectorCAST

VectorCAST/Ada[2] is a commercial, dynamic unit testing and code coverage tool for Ada. To construct automatically unit testing environments for Ada source code, VectorCAST parses the provided Ada program, extracts the relevant Ada types/packages, and then presents a "test-case designer" that allows a user to specify tests without the need to write tests in Ada directly. Crucially, VectorCAST is also able to instrument the source code to obtain code coverage from test case execution.

Following [18], we note that unit testing environments can be constructed in two ways:

- A "unit test" mode, where testing is performed on an individual unit, where all of its external dependants have been automatically mocked [18].

---

[2] www.vectorcast.com; in what follows, we write VectorCAST to mean VectorCAST/Ada.

- An "integration test" mode, where testing can be performed across multiple units, and where the external dependants have been brought into VectorCAST and can be instrumented for code coverage. In this mode, the behaviour of the external interfaces (via expected call and return values) can also be tested.

With the exception of a change to a dependant specification, change-based testing in unit testing mode is limited to selecting the tests to re-run inside of a single unit. Change impact analysis is more complex when you consider integration-style tests, as there will be dependencies between the units contained inside the testing project. The test selection problem is then to minimise the re-test effort, in the context of changes in any dependants.

3   Change-Based Testing for Ada

We now present our approach for performing impact analysis and solving the test-case selection problem for Ada.

We consider a "safe" approach to change impact analysis at the expense of false negatives: in the context of a safety-critical software development, we consider it more appropriate to have an overzealous change impact, rather than exclude a test erroneously (false positives).

3.1   Dynamic Impact Analysis

The high-level of a typical *dynamic-only* impact analysis [12] is shown in Fig. 2. In this figure, we see that the "core" of a dynamic impact analysis approach is the ability to map test data to run-time data, therefore allowing us to calculate those tests effected. To support processing the change set into an impact set, we assumed that the relationship between this data is stored internally in the tool: the *intermediate representation*.

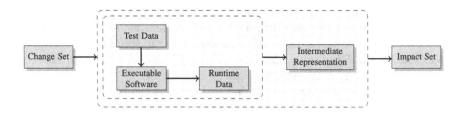

Fig. 2. Strictly dynamic change impact analysis

The intermediate representation can take a number of forms when considering a dynamic analysis. When considering code coverage-based analyses with information derived from test execution, such information can be stored as a dynamic dependency

```
 1   package body Peano is
 2
 3      function One return Integer is
 4      begin
 5         return Succ(Zero);
 6      end One;
 7
 8      function Zero return Integer is
 9      begin
10         return 0;
11      end Zero;
12
13      function Succ (Val : in Integer)
14         return Integer is
15      begin
16         return Val + 1;
17      end Succ;
18
19   end Peano;
```

(a) A trivial Ada program

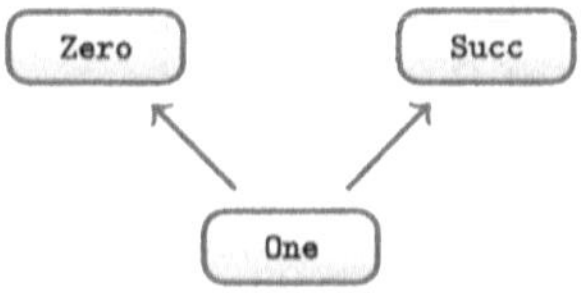

(b) Dynamic dependencies

Fig. 3. Example dependencies.

tree. For the Ada program shown in Fig. 3a, we exemplify its dynamic-only dependency tree in Fig. 3b. A change in either `Zero` or `Succ` may affect the behaviour of `One`.

We presume the existence of an original program P and a modified program P', which has been derived from P. Furthermore, it is also assumed that both P and P' are both syntactically and semantically correct (i.e., compilable). The analysis places no restriction beyond these on the nature of the changes.

In the context of what follows, we assume that the intermediate representation contains both static and dynamic data, and the availability of information about the packages (specifications and bodies) and subprograms that have been altered.

3.2   Intermediate Representation for Ada

We now introduce the data structures used to construct our analysis for Ada. As we are developing a hybrid approach using both static and dynamic data, we introduce both separately.

Static Data. For the data we wish to extract statically from the Ada program, we consider the following data-types:

$$Contains : Package \rightarrow Subprogram^*$$
$$Uses : Package \times \{Body, Spec\} \rightarrow Package^*$$

The data structure *Contains* is used to map Ada *Packages* to zero-or-more *Subprograms* contained within that *Package*. Similarly, *Uses* creates a dependency map between *Package* body and specifications, to the package specifications that they "with".

We use the relation *Contains* to find all affected subprograms given either a specification or a package body-level change; *Uses* allows us to track when a dependant has been modified (e.g., if Package A with B, and if B changes, we know that we need to re-execute any test covering Package A).

For the presentation that follows, we assume that it is possible to compute the inverse of *Contains* and *Uses*.

Dynamic Data. We now consider the dynamic data we require for our analysis:

$$Covers : Test \rightarrow Subprogram^*$$

which maps test-cases in the test baseline, $\mathcal{T}$, to the subprograms covered when a given test is executed. We note that, unlike [11,16], we are not concerned with the ordering of subprogram calls/returns for a given test.

It is clear that, when combining these tree-like data structures, it is possible to construct a combined, static/dynamic dependency tree. Such a tree could be unfolded to construct a directed, acyclic dependency graph of the program. This is because dependency relationships between entities are transitive. That is, if A depends on B and B depends on C in one or more dependency relationships, then A depends on C.

3.3 Example

Before presenting the approach to solve the test-case selection problem, we exemplify the technique when applied to Ada source code. We illustrate the process using the small Ada program shown in Fig. 4.

In this example, we have two Packages (A and B), each containing a single function. In the body of Package A, we have an external dependency on the specification of B, via the use of the "with" directive. It is clear that there is an implicit dependency between each package and its specification (i.e., that the body of A depends on the specification of A). It follows that we have A × *Body* → B in *Uses*, and A → Foo in *Contains*.

For the Ada example illustrated in Fig. 4, we show the *static-only dependencies* (i.e., those excluding subprogram calls) in Fig. 5a. As we can see, when we do not consider subprogram invocations between packages, there is no statically-determined dependency between A's package body and B's package body.

We now consider that a test-case t has been created that exercises the subprogram Foo. In this instance, dynamically executing a test-case for the function Foo will then obtain code coverage on both Foo and Bar. After t has executed, we can see that there is a (dynamic) dependency between Foo and Bar (Fig. 5b). That is, we have $t \rightarrow \{Foo, Bar\}$ in *Covers*.

Finally, the combined dependencies are show in Fig. 5c. As we can see, this is the union of the dependencies from the static and the dynamic data. As shown in Fig. 5c, there now exists an *implied* dependency between Foo and the body of B (the dashed

```
1    with B;
2
3    package body A is
4
5        Qux : Integer;
6
7        function Foo return Integer is
8        begin
9            return Qux + B.Bar;
10       end;
11
12   begin
13
14       Qux := 0;
15
16   end A;
```

(b) Package Body for A

```
1    package A is
2
3        function Foo
4            return Integer;
5
6    end A;
```

(a) Package Specification for A

```
1    package body B is
2
3        Narf : Integer;
4
5        function Bar return Integer is
6        begin
7            return Narf;
8        end;
9
10   begin
11
12       Narf := 0;
13
14   end B;
```

(d) Package Body for B

```
1    package B is
2
3        function Bar
4            return Integer;
5
6    end B;
```

(c) Package Specification for B

Fig. 4. An exemplary Ada program

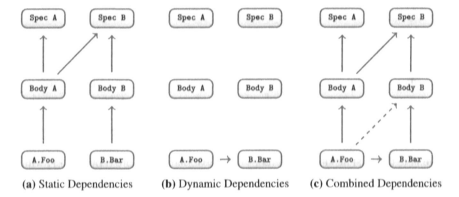

(a) Static Dependencies   **(b)** Dynamic Dependencies   **(c)** Combined Dependencies

Fig. 5. Types of dependency

arrow between Foo and B). This is because we have a traversal through the dependency graph of:

$$Foo \rightarrow Bar \rightarrow B$$

Consequently, it can be calculated[3] that a change the body of B will impact test-cases that are associated with the subprogram Foo.

3.4   Calculating the Selection

To solve the test-case selection problem, we introduce an ancillary algorithm AFFECT-EDSUBPROGRAMS (Algorithm 1). The algorithm is a classic *work-list* algorithm, used to calculate the transitive closure of the dependency tree. For ease, we use *entity* to refer to a specification, body or subprogram.

Algorithm 1. AFFECTEDSUBPROGRAMS

Input: *change* : *entity*   # *change entity*
Input: *static_dependencies* : *entity* → *entity**   # *static dependencies*
Output: *impacted_subprograms*   # *set of affected subprograms*

1: *impacted_subprograms* ← ∅
2: *found* ← ∅
3: *new* ← {*change*}
4: **while** *new* ≠ ∅ **do**
5:     *next* ← *new*.pop()   # *pops and removes*
6:     *found* ← *found* ∪ {*next*}
7:     **if** *next* is *subprogram* **then**
8:         *impacted_subprograms* ← *impacted_subprograms* ∪ {*next*}
9:     **end if**
10:    *successors* ← *static_dependencies* (*next*)
11:    *unprocessed* ← *successors* \ *found*
12:    *new* ← *new* ∪ *unprocessed*
13: **end while**
14: **return** *impacted_subprograms*

Our algorithm for solving the test-case selection problem is shown in Algorithm 2. The algorithm takes a given Ada program P, a baseline set of tests T, the data stored in *Covers* and changed entity c, and returns the set of tests to be re-executed. Once the set of affected subprograms has been computed by AFFECTEDSUBPROGRAMS, AFFECTEDTESTS iterates over these subprograms and selects all tests covering them. These selected tests represent our solution to the test-case selection problem.

We note that AFFECTEDTESTS relies on an external procedure STATICDEP, which calculates the transitive closure of *Contains* and *Uses*.

---

[3] where "*impact*" is the inverse relation of dependency.

Algorithm 2. AFFECTEDTESTS

Input: P	# an Ada program
Input: $\mathcal{T}$	# a set of tests
Input: $Covers : \mathcal{T} \rightarrow Subprograms^*$	# test coverage
Input: c : entity	# a change in P
Output: $impacted\_tests \subseteq \mathcal{T}$	# set of affected tests

---

```
 1: impacted_tests ← ∅
 2: impacted_subprograms ← AFFECTEDSUBPROGRAMS (c, STATICDEP (P))
 3: for all t ∈ T do
 4:     for all m ∈ impacted_subprograms do
 5:         if m ∈ Covers (t) then
 6:             impacted_tests ← impacted_tests ∪ {t}
 7:             break
 8:         end if
 9:     end for
10: end for
11: return impacted_tests
```

Given a change-set comprising of a number of modifications to the program (e.g., multiple package body or subprogram changes), it is possible to encapsulate AFFECTEDTESTS in a higher-level procedure that iterates over each change and collects the aggregate set of affected tests (c.f., *ImpactAnalysis* in [15]).

3.5   On Change Impact for Polymorphic Programs

There has been a lot of consideration in literature [6, 19, 21] applied to the intricacies of change impact pertaining to object oriented programming. However, in the context of the framework presented, the use of object oriented techniques within Ada does not introduce any further difficulties.

For example, consider a change C that affects the dynamic call tree in a given program P. We will consider the addition or removal of a specialised subprogram in a derived package. If a specialised subprogram is added/removed from a derived package, then the derived specification (upon which P depends) will change, leading to all tests for P, which have code coverage on the derived package, to be re-executed.

If a package body member is changed in the base package, then this will invalidate all tests that have associated code coverage on the derived package, if the derived package has any static/dynamic calls to its parent. If there are no tests that generate any coverage on the base package via calls from the derived package, then a modification to the package global in the base package will have no effect on the derived package's behaviour, and so no tests will be impacted.

Example. Consider two packages `Base` and `Derived`, where the specification of `Base` has two subprograms `Alpha` and `Beta`, and that `Derived` only specialises the subprogram `Alpha`. We further assume a program *P*, and associated test, that calls `Derived.Alpha`, and `Derived.Alpha` calls `Base.Beta`. This will create a combined dependency tree as shown in Fig. 6 (we use a dashed line to show dynamic dependencies).

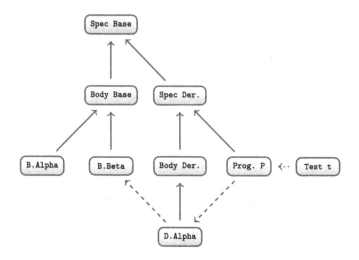

Fig. 6. A polymorphic dependency tree

If we now extended `Derived` such that it contains a specialised version of `Beta`, this would then cause a change in the specification and body of `Derived`, and so we would re-execute any tests that have coverage on the subprogram `Alpha`.

Alternatively, consider a change to a package body member in `Base`. Via the dependency tree from Fig. 6, this would then cause any tests with coverage on `Base.Alpha` and `Base.Beta` to be invalidated. Consequently, our test on `Derived.Alpha` would therefore be affected, as per the dynamic coverage collected.

4   Experimental Evaluation

To validate the effectiveness of the technique presented in reducing the number of test-cases to be re-executed, we performed an empirical evaluation comparing VectorCAST with and without change impact analysis.

4.1   Experimental Setup

We considered examples from two sources: "Malaise" and IRONSIDES; we summarise these below. A high-level overview of the packages selected is shown in Table 1.

Table 1. Example specifics

Metric	Malaise	IRONSIDES
Number of files	9	9
Number of lines (incl. comments/whitespace)	654	4,745
Number of non-empty Ada lines	468	3,441
Number of subprograms	46	97
Aggregate complexity metric [25]	94	492
Total number of tests	228	573
Coverage (statement/branch)	68%/68%	47%/36%

Malaise. We considered a selection of 9 files taken from [14] – a copy-left reposi-tory of Unix-based utilities written in Ada. Some of the packages selected included: ada_words.adb, which provides "basic Ada parsing of delimiters, separators and reserved words"; conditions.adb that supports "several tasks to wait until unblocked all together or one by one"; and forker.adb, an "API to a standalone forker process".

IRONSIDES. The Internet Domain Name System—or DNS—is an infrastructure whose responsibility it is to translate domain names (e.g., www.vectorcast.com) into their corresponding IP addresses (e.g., 67.225.168.102). IRONSIDES [4], an open-source and freely-available DNS server implemented in SPARK Ada. Via the use of SPARK, the code of IRONSIDES is mathematically proven to be free of defects via the use of formal methods. For the purposes of this evaluation, we consider a subset of 9 files taken from the IRONSIDES "authoritative" (2015-04-15) branch [2].

Testing Methodology. To support the empirical evaluation of the presented change-based testing approach, we used VectorCAST to generate automatically three types of test:

- "empty tests" – these are default test-cases generated by VectorCAST that provide empty parameter values to every function;
- "min-mid-max tests" – these call each test with the min, mid and maximum value for each parameter;
- "basis path tests" – we used VectorCAST's ability to generate automatically basis path tests according to McCabe's complexity metric [25].

For Malaise, we generated all three types of test; however, to produce a manageable test-suite size, we only generated empty and basis path tests for IRONSIDES (i.e., we did not consider min-mid-max tests). The size of the test-suite and the coverage attained from its execution are presented in Table 1.

For each of the examples, we used VectorCAST to capture the initial state of the software, and then applied modifications to each of the files: namely, we added a "null;" statement to the beginning of a number of subprograms, such that

VectorCAST would detect a subprogram-level change. An example of an automated change—highlighted with a box—to the package Ada_Words from Malaise is shown in Listing 1.1.

Listing 1.1. An example modification in the package Ada_Words

```
 1  function Is_Delimiter (C : Character) return Boolean is
 2  begin
 3      null;
 4      case C is
 5          when '&' | ''' | '(' | ')' | '*' | '+' |
 6               ',' | '-' | '.' | '/' | ':' | ';' |
 7               '<' | '=' | '>' | '|' =>
 8              return True;
 9          when others =>
10              return False;
11      end case;
12  end Is_Delimiter;
```

After applying each change, we then performed an "incremental build and execute" inside of VectorCAST, to analyse the code-base and then only re-test the code that changed. To validate the effectiveness of the proposed approach, we executed the same process but without passing the incremental flag to VectorCAST. The version of Vector-CAST used for both the incremental and non-incremental runs was the official release of 6.4d (released 2016-02-29).

All of the Ada sources for both of the examples (reproduced under a copy-left licence from both [14] and [2]), the VectorCAST artefacts (e.g., the auto-generated tests) and an "evaluation runner" script are available from [8].

4.2 Results

We performed our evaluation on a 32-bit Linux machine running Fedora 21, with 8 GiB of RAM and a 6-core Intel Xeon clocked at 2.50GHz. The compiler used was "GNAT 4.9.2 20150212 (Red Hat 4.9.2-6)".

Table 2. Experimental results

Example	Mode	Units changed	Subprograms changed	# Tests executed	Build + exec. time (s)
Malaise	Without CBT	9	21	4,788	1,002.48
	With CBT			165	165.85
IRONSIDES	Without CBT	9	93	53,289	6,986.17
	With CBT			1,347	1,147.14

The results of our evaluation can be seen in Table 2. The column "# Tests Executed" represents the total number of tests re-executed after performing the individual subprogram change, with each change processed separately. Similarly, "Build + Exec. Time" is the total time (in seconds) that VectorCAST took to re-build the test environment, incorporating the current change-set, and to re-run the affected tests.

As we can see, using the change impact analysis presented in this paper, the total number of tests needing to be executed for Malaise was reduced from 4,788 (running all 228 test-cases for each of the 21 changes) to only 165 (re-running only the impacted tests). Similarly, for IRONSIDES, the number of tests required to be re-executed to ensure that no regressions were introduced in the software was reduced by 97%.

We observe that the final column (time) does not scale accordingly, as the auto-generated tests are quick to execute, compared to the higher-cost environment construction. Nonetheless, across both examples, we see an 84% reduction in time to re-test.

Given the size and real-world applicability of IRONSIDES (with its higher performance than commercial DNS servers [4]), we feel that the results obtained would be representative of the benefits achievable in an industrial Ada project.

5   Conclusions

In this paper, we have introduced the first practical approach to applying change impact analysis to the test-case selection problem for Ada. To the best of our knowledge (c.f., [3, 12]), ours is the first approach that explicitly uses a combination of both statically derived data and dynamic data from test execution. In safety-critical markets (see, e.g., DO-178C [23] for aeronautics), it is commonplace for there to be a requirement to demonstrate "test completeness" via a code coverage mandate. Consequently, linking a change-impact analysis to data that engineers will already be collecting is advantageous.

We also considered the affect of object oriented techniques when identifying those tests to be re-executed. Considering exclusively static data has previously been investigated [21] and lead to a number of "heavy-weight" frameworks [20]. While simplistic, our approach can also handle changes introduced in the polymorphic hierarchy.

We performed an empirical evaluation of our technique as part of an experimental extension to VectorCAST. Our results on a modest-sized example are promising, but further evaluation is needed.

5.1   Further Work

We have identified a number of additional avenues that could improve on the test-case selection process (at the expense of a heavier technique). The most immediate area to tackle is on the change impact process at a lower level than just subprograms. For example, if the change is constrained to a particular branch of a conditional, then it would be plausible, without a loss of safety, to select only those tests that previously entered the same block.

Our presentation of *AffectedSubprograms*, and calculating the transitive closure of *StaticDep* (Sect. 3.4), leads us to invalidate all tests when the change is associated to a package specification or a body. When we consider a body-level change that, e.g., changes or introduced a new body-level member variable, this leads us to re-execute more tests than necessary. If we considered only those subprograms that referred to each member variable, we could then be more selective with those that we invalidate.

We leave consideration of how to efficiently handle type modifications at the specification level for further work.

5.2   Closing Remarks

In this paper, we presented, to the best of our knowledge, the first approach for considering change impact analysis for Ada applied to regression testing (outside of [13], which did not consider the test case selection problem). As highlighted above, there are a number of improvements to this technique to further reduce the scope of selected changes. We position this work as the first footing in this direction, and are not discouraged by the modest framework presented.

References

1. AdaIC: Comments on Ada in Relation to C++, November 1998. http://archive.adaic.com/docs/present/engle/comments/index.html. Accessed 22 Mar 2016
2. Carlisle, M.C.: IRONSIDES homepage, April 2015. http://ironsides.martincarlisle.com. Accessed 22 Mar 2016
3. Engström, E., Runeson, P., Skoglund, M.: A systematic review on regression test selection techniques. Inf. Softw. Technol. **52**(1), 14–30 (2010)
4. Fagin, B., Carlisle, M.: Provably secure DNS: a case study in reliable software. In: Keller, H.B., Plödereder, E., Dencker, P., Klenk, H. (eds.) Ada-Europe 2013. LNCS, vol. 7896, pp. 81–93. Springer, Heidelberg (2013)
5. Harrold, M.J., Souffa, M.L.: An incremental approach to unit testing during maintenance. In: Proceedings of the Conference on Software Maintenance, pp. 362–367 (1988)
6. Huang, L., Song, Y.: Precise dynamic impact analysis with dependency analysis for object-oriented programs. In: Proceedings of the 5th International Conference on Software Engineering Research (SERA 2007), pp. 374–384. IEEE Computer Society (2007)
7. Hummel, J., Hendren, L.J., Nicolau, A.: A framework for data dependence testing in the presence of pointers. In: Proceedings of the 1994 International Conference on Parallel Processing, pp. 216–224. CRC Press (1994)
8. Jones, A.V.: CBT for Ada Examples, January 2016. https://github.com/andrewvaughanj/CBT_for_Ada_Examples. Accessed 22 Mar 2016
9. Kaisti, M., Rantala, V., Mujunen, T., Hyrynsalmi, S., Könnölä, K., Mäkilä, T., Lehtonen, T.: Agile methods for embedded systems development - a literature review and a mapping study. EURASIP J. Emb. Sys. **2013**(1), 1–16 (2013)
10. Larsen, L., Harrold, M.J.: Slicing object-oriented software. In: Proceedinigs of the 18th International Conference on Software Engineering (ICSE 1996), pp. 495–505. IEEE Computer Society (1996)

11. Law, J., Rothermel, G.: Whole program path-based dynamic impact analysis. In: Proceedings of the 25th International Conference on Software Engineering (ICSE 2003), pp. 308–318. IEEE Computer Society (2003)

12. Li, B., Sun, X., Leung, H., Zhang, S.: A survey of code-based change impact analysis techniques. Softw. Test., Verif. Reliab. **23**(8), 613–646 (2013)

13. Loyall, J.P., Mathisen, S.A., Satterthwaite, C.P.: Impact analysis and change management for avionics software. In: Proceedings of the 1997 National Conference on Aerospace and Electronics, pp. 740–747 (1997)

14. Malaise, P.: PMA's Ada contrib, January 2016. http://pmahome.cigecompta.fr/ada/html/REPOSIT_LIST.html. Accessed 22 Mar 2016

15. Orso, A., Apiwattanapong, T., Harrold, M.J.: Leveraging field data for impact analysis and regression testing. In: Proceedings of the 11th Symposium on Foundations of Software Engineering, pp. 128–137. ACM (2003)

16. Orso, A., Apiwattanapong, T., Law, J., Rothermel, G., Harrold, M.J.: An empirical comparison of dynamic impact analysis algorithms. In: Proceedings of the 26th International Conference on Software Engineering (ICSE 2004), pp. 491–500. IEEE Computer Society (2004)

17. Parsai, A., Soetens, Q.D., Murgia, A., Demeyer, S.: Considering polymorphism in change-based test suite reduction. In: Dingsøyr, T., Moe, N.B., Tonelli, R., Counsell, S., Gencel, C., Petersen, K. (eds.) XP 2014. LNBIP, vol. 199, pp. 166–181. Springer, Heidelberg (2014)

18. Pezzè, M., Young, M.: Software Testing And Analysis - Process, Principles And Techniques. Wiley, Hoboken (2007)

19. Ren, X., Shah, F., Tip, F., Ryder, B.G., Chesley, O.: Chianti: a tool for change impact analysis of java programs. In: Proceedings of the 19th International Conference on Object-Oriented Programming, Systems, Languages, and Applications, pp. 432–448. ACM (2004)

20. Ren, X., Ryder, B.G., Störzer, M., Tip, F.: Chianti: a change impact analysis tool for Java programs. In: Proceedings of the 27th International Conference on Software Engineering (ICSE 2005), pp. 664–665. ACM (2005)

21. Ryder, B.G., Tip, F.: Change impact analysis for object-oriented programs. In: Proceedings of the 2001 Workshop on Program Analysis for Software Tools and Engineering, pp. 46–53. ACM (2001)

22. Soetens, Q.D., Demeyer, S., Zaidman, A., Pérez, J.: Change-based test selection: an empirical evaluation. Empirical Softw. Eng. 1–43 (2015)

23. Special Committee 205 of RTCA: DO-178C, Software Considerations In Airborne Systems And Equipment Certification. Radio Technical Commission for Aeronautics (2011)

24. Stålhane, T., Hanssen, G.K., Myklebust, T., Haugset, B.: Agile change impact analysis of safety critical software. In: Bondavalli, A., Ceccarelli, A., Ortmeier, F. (eds.) SAFECOMP 2014. LNCS, vol. 8696, pp. 444–454. Springer, Heidelberg (2014)

25. Watson, A.H., McCabe, T.J., Wallace, D.R.: Structured testing: a software testing methodology using the cyclomatic complexity metric. Technical report Special Publication 500–235, U.S. Department of Commerce/National Institute of Standards and Technology, September 1996

Test Case Prioritization Using Online Fault Detection Information

Mohsen Laali, Huai Liu[(✉)], Margaret Hamilton, Maria Spichkova,
and Heinz W. Schmidt

RMIT University, Melbourne, Australia
{mohsen.laali,huai.liu,margaret.hamilton,maria.spichkova,
heinz.schmidt}@rmit.edu.au

Abstract. The rapid evolution of software necessitates effective fault detection within increasingly restricted execution times. To improve the effectiveness of the regression testing required for extensive fault detection, test cases have to be prioritized. The test cases with the higher chance of capturing faults are executed earlier in the series. This prioritization enables faster feedback for fixing more faults earlier. Various prioritization techniques have been proposed based on the information provided by offline (static) test execution history on previous versions of the software. In this paper, we propose a family of new test case prioritization techniques, which utilize online (dynamic) information about the locations of previously revealed faults in the detection of other faults. Our empirical studies demonstrate that the new techniques are more effective than the existing traditional test case prioritization techniques.

Keywords: Software testing · Regression testing · Test case prioritization · Online test prioritization

1 Introduction

Software testing is an essential part of the software development process, which can be challenging as well as time and cost consuming in its own right. Myers et al. [14] asserted that about 50 % of the time and cost of software development is related to the testing of the software. To hasten the software release, the practice of *continuous integration* was proposed [2]. According to this practice, every software developer needs to submit locally tested code to a mainstream repository, and each developer should submit their code at least several times daily. The mainstream repository is an independent server which re-builds, integrates and re-runs test cases after each submission from the developer. The process of re-running test cases after each iteration of software development is referred to as *regression testing*. It is crucial that regression testing is executed in the minimal possible time to obtain feedback for the software developer to fix the bugs before the submission of their code to the main repository. However, re-running the test cases is time-consuming and may sometimes take a day or occasionally more than a week. This might be even more complicated when each developer needs to submit their code multiple times in a day.

© Springer International Publishing Switzerland 2016
M. Bertogna et al. (Eds.): Ada-Europe 2016, LNCS 9695, pp. 78–93, 2016.
DOI: 10.1007/978-3-319-39083-3_6

To make the regression testing more effective, several techniques have been proposed in the past including *test suite minimization* (TSM), *test case selection* (TCS) and *test case prioritization* (TCP). For the first two techniques, a subset of test cases from a test pool is selected to be run against the software. In TCS, test cases are selected based on the modifications created between two *different* versions of the software, and they are then extracted from the test pool temporarily for a specific version the software [16]. In TSM, on the other hand, test cases are selected based on an execution path in the *same* version of the software [21], and they are then permanently excluded test cases from the test pool. In contrast, TCP does not exclude test cases from the test pool but orders them based on the likelihood of capturing faults. The goal of the TCP technique is to reveal possible existing faults at an early stage of the execution of the test case. Early detection of the faults during test case executions enables software developers to be notified of a fault in the software in a shorter time in comparison to not prioritizing the test cases. Therefore software developers can fix the software faults faster and ultimately reduce the processing time of developing software.

A classic approach for TCP techniques is based on *offline information* (e.g., a study by Zhou [26]), i.e., the *static* knowledge about the test case and the program to prioritize the test cases before their main execution. In our approach, we recommend using the *online information* for these purposes, i.e., the *dynamic* knowledge about the test case and the program execution. This idea follows the *continuous integration* practice and enables speeding up the testing process.

Many approaches rely on the assumption that faults are distributed evenly through out the program and are based on the number of program statements. However, the research on Microsoft Windows and Office programs showed that 80 % of faults occur in 20 % of the program code [17,25], which is referred to as *80-20 rule* also known as the *Pareto principle* [15]. Moreover, in the same study by Microsoft researchers, it was found out that 50 % of the crashes come from only 1 % of the program code. These findings indicate that the previous assumptions of the even distribution of faults are not always valid, and further highlight the importance of historical information on the previously identified faults to be used for the detection of new faults. Therefore, using *online* information about previous execution of test cases could enhance the effectiveness of detecting new faults in the software. Particularly, online information about the previous *location* of detected fault in the software could help to identify new faults close to the previous fault location. In this study, the locations of previously identified faults from executed test cases are captured to prioritize unordered test cases based on their coverage close to the captured locations.

Contributions: In this paper, we present a new online test case prioritization approach, which utilizes the location of previously identified faults to prioritize the test cases. This approach is evaluated by a number of empirical techniques, which significantly out-perform previous approaches.

Outline: The rest of the paper is organized as follows: in Sect. 2, we discuss the related work on TCP techniques. In Sect. 3, we introduce the TCP baselines and how they can be adapted using our approach, which is presented in Sect. 4. We further describe the experimental design of this study in Sect. 5, followed by the evaluation of the approach in Sect. 6. Section 7 presents future work directions and concludes the paper.

2   Related Work

A number of different offline prioritization techniques have been proposed [19]. In previous studies, two greedy approaches, namely 'Total' and 'Additional' TCP are the most studied techniques [24]. For example, the 'Total-Statement' (TS) TCP orders test cases based on the number of statements in the program that each test case could cover. On the other hand, the 'Additional-Statement' (AS) TCP uses the same metric to order test cases; however, it excludes the statements covered by the test cases that have already been selected. Zhang et al. [24] recommended a new TCP technique which delivers performance results between the classic approaches. This technique relies on the offline information about test cases and programs. The researchers applied static parameters that were manually set based on experimental studies. By contrast, our study utilizes dynamic parameters that are systematically adjusted throughout testing process.

Kim and Porter [11] argued that historical information about previous executions of tests was ignored by researchers but it could be potentially useful. They employed historical information about the previous execution of test cases to improve the effectiveness of TCP for a system with a resource constraint. The approach introduced by Kim et al. also relies on offline information. Our work can be seen as an extension of this approach, as we rely on the testing history, but use the dynamic version of it and base the test case prioritisation on the online information.

The risk of faults occurring in a particular section of the code could potentially help to improve TCP techniques by focusing on the error prone part of the software, which is referred to as the risky part of the software. Thus, the test cases covering the risky parts of code are assigned a higher rank in prioritization results. Rothermel et al. [19] introduced a metric to measure faults exposed by the potential of test cases. They used this measurement to built new TCP techniques which have better overall effectiveness in comparison to traditional coverage based techniques. Yoon and Choi [22] also measured the risks in code by asking human experts during the risk assessment stage to propose a new TCP technique. In our approach, we measure the risk in code by analysis of the previously selected and executed test cases that detect a fault.

There are a number of approaches aiming at estimating the probable location of a fault in the program, e.g., [9,23], as this could potentially save the time of the developer to find the faults. Jiang et al. [8] recommended integrating TCP with statistical fault localization to facilitate the identification of fault locations for developers. They claimed that existing prioritization techniques did not consider the fact that identifying the location of the fault is as important as detecting the faults; whereas, existing techniques aimed at detecting a higher number of faults even at the expense of interrupting the execution of test cases. To address this gap, researchers have discovered that statistical fault localization techniques cannot be degraded even by executing fewer test cases using prioritization techniques. In contrast, our approach looks at the effect of location of faults on the effectiveness of TCP techniques.

3   Preliminary-Baseline Techniques for TCP

As introduced in Sect. 1, a TCP function is mainly based on an iterative selection process. We model this main selection process in an equation which chooses a test case for prioritization in each iteration. This iteration ends after selecting all test cases for prioritization. The selection equation can be implemented in different ways depending on which TCP technique is used. The differences between the techniques are explained in the specification of the selection equations in the rest of this paper. A set of notions is used to explain the specification of equations. P and t represent a program and a test case. NST is a set of Not Selected Test cases, where from this set, a test case would be selected and added to the Selected Test cases (ST) in each iteration of the TCP function. Test cases are run against partial parts of the corresponding program P. These parts are usually referred to as the *coverage* of the test cases. To measure test case coverage, two main metrics, known as *statement coverage* and *branch coverage*, have been proposed previously. The statement coverage counts all executed statements of the program; whereas, the branch coverage criterion indicates what fraction of control branch statements have been executed while running a test case against the program. If there is complete coverage, the metrics are referred to as *full branch coverage*, and *full statement coverage*.

***Random* (R) TCP:** R TCP is the simplest approach to perform prioritization over test cases. This technique employs test cases which are randomly ordered, i.e., the *selection equation* in this case is a simple random selection. Compared to other TCP techniques, this method represents the lower bound of least effectiveness.

***Optimal* (O) TCP:** This method represents an optimal solution for the TCP problem. It orders test cases based on decreasing numbers of detected faults. For this purpose, this technique runs each test case against the program to identify the number of captured faults. However, executing test cases before prioritization defeats the purpose of TCP. The goal of using the TCP technique is to order test cases by the maximum number of faults so that the test case can be identified without having to execute the test case itself. This technique represents the upper bound of the TCP effectiveness. In the optimal TCP, the *selection equation* can be specified as follows, where FD denotes a Fault Detector that identifies a set of faults that can be captured by each test case.

$$t \in NST \text{ and } |FD(t, P)| \text{ is maximum} \Rightarrow \text{return } t \qquad (1)$$

Total-Statement **(TS)/*Total-Branch*** **(TB) TCP:** The TS TCP technique prioritises the test case which examines the larger portion of the program. To measure the portion of the program under test, the coverage of test cases over the program is used. In TS TCP and TB TCP, test cases are ordered based on the number of covered statements or branches respective to the TCP technique. Test cases with equal statement coverage are randomly ordered. In the TS TCP, we specify the *selection equation* as follows, where *SC* denotes a Statement Coverage function which calculates a set of statement covered by a test case. Another variant (TB TCP) can implemented by replacing SC with *BC* which returns a set of branch coverage statements.

$$t \in NST \text{ and } |SC(t, P)| \text{ is maximum} \Rightarrow return \ t \qquad (2)$$

Additional-Statement **(AS)/*Additional-Branch*** **(AB) TCP:** The aim of the 'Additional' techniques are to obtain a full test coverage of the program by executing test cases in the shortest amount of time. These types of TCP techniques select a test case which covers the highest number of program parts that have not been covered by other already selected test cases. This is contrary to 'Total' techniques, where the covered part of program through executing previous selected test cases can also be counted for selecting new test cases. Based on the statement or branch coverage criteria uses in 'Additional' TCP, two techniques of AS and AB TCP techniques were proposed. In the AS TCP, we specify the *selection equation* by Eq. 3, where already covered statements set (*CS*) is defined in Eq. 4.

$$t \in NST \text{ and } |SC(t, P) - CS(ST, P)| \text{ is maximum} \Rightarrow return \ t \qquad (3)$$

$$CS(ST, P) = \cup_{t \in ST} \cup_{S \in SC(t,P)} S \qquad (4)$$

4   The Proposed Approach-Online TCP

'Additional' and 'Total' coverage methods are limited in terms of capturing faults. 'Total' coverage techniques select a test case that covers the largest portion of the program in each iteration of prioritization. This type of technique assumes that every covered unit of the program has an equal chance of capturing faults. Therefore, test cases with higher coverage are more qualified to capture faults. However, the qualified test cases might miss faults located in rarely covered parts of the program by a few test cases, which might not have the coverage for a large portion of the program. On the other hand, the 'Additional' techniques aim to reach full coverage of the program in the fastest possible time. With this aim, the 'Additional' techniques place a higher priority on a test case which covers part of the program that has not yet been covered by other test cases. This could potentially address the limitation of the 'Total' techniques that only focus on a test case with a higher coverage, regardless of achieving the full coverage of the program. However, test cases with full coverage of the program might not necessarily reveal all faults in the program [13]. In other words, it is

Algorithm 1. Line of Code Weight

```
1: function W(s,ST, NST,P)
2:       CoveredStatements = CS(ST,P)
3:       if s ∈ CoveredStatements then
4:             return CoveredW(s,ST,P)
5:       else
6:             return UCW
7:       end if
8: end function
```

s: statement, UCW: UnCovered unit Weight, W: weight for statement

Algorithm 2. Covered Statements Weight

```
1: function CoveredW(s,ST,P)
2:       AF = ⋃_{t∈NST} DF(t)
3:       CW = ∑_{(t∈NST)&(s∈SC(t,P))} |DF(t, P)|/AF
4:       return CW
5: end function
```

AF: a set of All detected Faults, CW: Covered unit Weight

possible that only a specific test case could find existing faults in a particular line of the program, even though that line might be covered several times by other test cases. This limitation of the 'Additional' techniques could be addressed by the strategy in 'Total' techniques, which would give another chance to statements already covered to be covered again.

It appears that both 'Total' and 'Additional' types of techniques have their own limitations, which could each be addressed by the strengths of the other technique. This suggests that a solution to these limitations should take advantage of both techniques. Our proposed approach addresses the mentioned limitations, and is inspired by the 80-20 rule [15]. This principal is interpreted by the software engineering community as 80 % of faults exist in only 20 % of the program. Our approach, *online TCP*, initially works in a similar way to the 'Additional' techniques which try to rapidly reach full code coverage of the program. This could potentially help reach a faulty part of the program (20 % faulty portion of the code). By revealing more faults, our online techniques gradually become similar to the 'Total' coverage strategy especially in the area of the already revealed faults. This enables new faults to be found clustered near the previously clustered detected faults.

Online techniques prioritize test cases based on a weight assigned to their own *covered units*. Here, we abstract two coverage metrics (statement and branch) introduced in Sect. 3 as a generic *coverage unit*. Our technique assigns a weight to the covered unit of the program, and the test case that obtains the higher total weight is given a higher priority to be selected, which is represented in the selection Eq. 5. The weight of uncovered and covered statements in the previous selected test case is calculated using the W() function in Algorithm 1. The way of calculating the weight of covered units would differ depending on whether that unit has already been covered or not (i.e., *uncovered*) by selected test cases. UnCovered Weight (UCW) in Algorithm 1 is a constant value, either 0 or 1 based on variant of online TCP for uncovered statements. The covered unit weight (CW) is the ratio of revealing the fault detected by test cases that previously covered the same unit, over all faults that have been found, which is explained in Algorithm 2. This ratio is always between zero and one. In Algorithm 2, AF (All Covered Faults) holds all these faults that are retrieved by already selected the test cases. For explaining these online TCP techniques, the same notions in Sect. 3 were used.

$$t \in NST \text{ and } \sum_{s \in SC(t,P)} W(s, ST, NST, P) \text{ is maximum} \Rightarrow \text{return } t \qquad (5)$$

As more faults are discovered in a particular area of code, the weight of covered unit in the same area approaches one, which makes the online prioritization techniques behave similarly to the TS technique. However, the weight of covered units in an area with no or a few faults would be zero or near to zero respectively. Around this area of the program, our online TCP techniques work similarly to the 'Additional' types of techniques. The uncovered unit receives a constant weight (UCW). UCW with a zero value makes online TCP to act similarly to 'Total' TCP, while online TCP with UCW equal to one is similar to 'Additional' techniques. The above explanation is based on statement coverage for their calculation and form two variants OS0 and OS1 based on UCW zero and one respectively. Branch based online TCP (i.e., OB0 and OB1) use the same algorithm but with branch based covered units and using UCW zero and one constant for each of them. Let us discuss our online TCP technique using the example of a sample program presented in Fig. 1. We denote the program statements (si) by nodes of a tree, where the path of executing statements is represented by the corresponding edges. Those edges that are labeled as bi are representative of branch statements. In total, there are 11 statements and 8 branches. The execution of the program begins from the root node (s1) to the leaf nodes (s5, s6, s8, s9, s10). Assume that there are also five test cases to test this program (t1, t2, ..., t5), which are to be executed from the start to the end of the program. For simplicity we also assume that running test cases against the program will not break in the middle of execution. Given the notions described in Fig. 1, the statement and branch coverage of the test cases are shown in Table 1. For example, t2 covers statements s1, s2, s5 and branches b1 and b4. This Table also presents the faults captured by each test case. We assume that our provided program has 10 faults which are shown in the fault column fi. For example, t1 captures faults f1, f6 and f10.

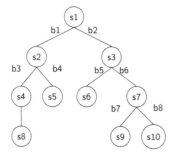

Fig. 1. A sample program, represented as a tree structure (si: statement, bi: branch)

Table 1. Fault (fi), statement coverage (si) and branch coverage (bi) from executing test case (ti) against the sample program in Fig. 1.

si	t1	t2	t3	t4	t5	bi	t1	t2	t3	t4	t5	fi	t1	t2	t3	t4	t5
s1	✓	✓	✓	✓	✓	b1	✓	✓				f1	✓	✓			
s2	✓	✓				b2			✓	✓	✓	f2			✓	✓	
s3			✓	✓	✓	b3	✓					f3					✓
s4	✓					b4		✓				f4			✓		
s5		✓				b5					✓	f5			✓		
s6					✓	b6			✓	✓		f6	✓	✓			
s7			✓	✓		b7			✓			f7			✓	✓	
s8	✓					b8				✓		f8				✓	
s9			✓									f9			✓	✓	✓
s10				✓								f10	✓				

Our approach is illustrated using the sample test cases in Table 1. For the sake of simplicity, we only illustrate the statement based online technique with uncovered statement weight equal to one (OS1). The initial selected test case would be the one with the highest coverage which could be any of t1, t4 or t5 from the test cases shown in Table 1. Since the initial weight for test cases t1, t4 and t5 is equal, a random test case is selected. Assuming that the test case t1 is randomly selected, the execution of test case t1 would reveal three faults (f1, f6 and f10). The statements that are covered by t1 are s1, s2, s4, and s8, which would result in the covered weight of 3/3, as the ratio of discovered faults over the total number of detected faults at the current stage of the algorithm execution. In the next iteration, the weights of t4 and t5 are equal again. Assuming that t5 is randomly selected and executed, faults f3 and f9 would be detected. The covered statement weight for t4 (s3, s7 and s10 except s1) would be 2/5. Finding new faults would also impact on the weight of covered statements of t1, and therefore the weight of statement would be changed from 1 to 3/5. Both t1 and t5 cover s1, and therefore, the weight of s1 would be the sum of both weights, equal to 1 (2/5 + 3/5). The weight for remaining test cases t2, t3, and t4 would be 2.6 (1 + 0.6 + 1), 2.4 (1 + 0.4 + 1), and 2.8 (1 + 0.4 + 0.4 + 1) respectively. Therefore, in the next step, test case t4 would be selected. Continuation of this algorithm selects test cases t3 and t2 respectively. Using our algorithm, the final order of test cases is t1, t5, t4, t3, and t2, which is different from orders obtained by other existing techniques, which were explained in Sect. 3.

5 Empirical Study

This experimental study first investigates the effectiveness of online techniques in comparison to baseline techniques for TCP, and next the impact of factors, such as different test cases coverage, are examined. The research questions of this study are given as follows:

- RQ1: Can a test case prioritization technique be improved using the location of previously detected faults?
- RQ2: How can different coverage criteria affect the effectiveness of test case prioritization based on the location of previously detected faults?

Independent Variables: In the design of this experimental study, first we explain a set of independent variables. Two coverage criteria, statement and branch coverage, are used in this study. Statement coverage is mainly used in our test prioritization techniques; however branch coverage is used not only for the TCP, but also to form the test pool for this research. Moreover, ten different TCP techniques are used in this research. Six of them form baseline methods to compare against the four methods proposed in this paper. The baseline methods include 'Additional' and 'Total' TCP with each of the two different coverage criteria (4 in total), in addition to the optimal and the lower bound effectiveness techniques (the further two methods). These techniques were discussed in Sect. 3.

The proposed techniques in this study (Sect. 4) are based on two main methods, which are further extended using the introduced coverage criteria, leading to a total of 4 techniques.

Dependent Variables: There is one dependent variable in this study, which is referred to as *APFD* (Average Precision Fault Detection). APFD is the main metric for comparing TCP techniques. In a study by Elbaum et al. [5], the effectiveness of a TCP technique is defined using the following formula:

$$APFD = 1 - \frac{\sum_{i=1}^{m} TF_i}{nm} + \frac{1}{2n}$$

In the above formula, n is the number of test cases in a test suite, and m is the number of faults that are revealed by the execution of the test suite. Given different orders of test cases in the test suite, TF_i returns the index of first test case with which the Fault i has been detected for the first time [5].

Experimental Object Programs, Test Cases, Faults and Test Suites: Seven C programs are used in our experimental study, which were initially used by Siemens engineering researchers [6]. The researchers explored how effective dataflow and controlflow-based techniques can be selecting the number of test cases that are adequate for detecting faults. These programs have been extensively used by the software testing research community, particularly in the TCP (e.g., the study by Rothermel et al. [18], Li et al. [12] and Jiang et al. [7]). Each of these seven programs has an oracle version and multiple faulty versions, in addition to the test cases and an input file. As described in Sect. 3, running all test cases is not practical or feasible in real-world applications; therefore, we select a subset of test cases from the test pool to form a test suite. In this study, the test suite must have full branch coverage of the oracle version, in addition to having the coverage of detecting all faulty versions. The branch coverage is selected because it is more complete compared to statement coverage, in terms of the number of possible different coverage criteria produced by the test cases, as used in the literature.

The experiments in this study are repeated 1000 times to make the results independent from a specific generation of test pools. The average size of the test suite, the number of test cases in the test pool, and the number of Lines of Code (LoC) in our experimental object programs are presented in Table 2. The explanation of experimental object could be found in the study by Hutchins et al. [6].

Threats to Validity: A set of risks has been previously identified in validating research projects and consists of internal, external, construct and conclusion threats.

The internal threats are related to errors that could occur within the development of the research project. In our study, the implementation of the prioritization technique, and also the APFD metric can be at the risk of internal threats. In order to reduce these risks, the implementation of this study has been reviewed multiple times.

Table 2. Experimental object program specification in a study by Do et al. [3].

Program	LoC	Number of faulty versions	Number of test cases	Test suite avg. size[†]
print-tokens	726	7	4130	21.061
print-tokens2	570	10	4115	17.066
replace	564	32	5542	38.223
schedule	412	9	2650	15.341
schedule2	374	10	2710	16.049
tcas	173	41	1608	30.8
tot-info	565	23	1052	14.523

[†]Avg. size is constructed from our experimental study.

External threats come from the errors of other research projects that have been used for the current study. The external threat for our study is related to the experimental object of the program, the Siemens program [6], and their faulty versions. The Siemens program is implemented in C language and cannot be generalized to all other programming languages. This limitation has also been highlighted in past research [4], which requires further investigations on the TCP for different programming languages, which are beyond the scope of this study and we plan to explore in future work. Another external threat to this study might come from the faulty versions of the object program, as they might not be representative of the real-world faults. The use of the Siemens program reduces this type of risk, as Software-artifact Infrastructure Repository (SIR) [1] has stated that Siemens engineers seed faults manually to the faulty versions in such a way as to simulate faults in real-world applications. Moreover, the Siemens object program has been broadly used in software testing research. Just et al. [10] reported that about 1,400 papers in Google Scholar have used the Siemens program in their research, and over 677 papers have been published by using the SIR repository for their empirical study [1].

The construct threats are related to the evaluation measures of the research. In this study, we use APFD as an evaluation metric, and therefore, this can be considered as the construct risk. Although some limitations of using APFD have been mentioned in past research (e.g., a study by Elbaum et al. [5] found that APFD does not differentiate between the cost for detecting faults and test cases), it is still the main metric for comparing TCP techniques.

The conclusion threat refers to errors in the interpretation of the experimental results. In this study, this risk was controlled by running experiments multiple times, and further using statistical tests for significant interpretations of the results.

6   Experimental Results

There are multiple runs and techniques involved in this experiment. To better illustrate the results for each object program, the statistical analyses are explained in this Section. A detailed illustration of results is also provided for a sample object program (tcas) in Fig. 2 using boxplots. In this figure, the x-axis represents different prioritization techniques, and the y-axis demonstrates the APFD score for each of the techniques. The test prioritization techniques are shown by abbreviations explained in Sects. 3 and 4. Every technique has a box plot which shows the mean ($\star$), median ($-$), 90th and 10th percentile and also any outlier ($+$). The actual APFD average of each technique is reported on top of each whisker. This way of presentation has been previously used by other studies [24]. The rest of detailed results are available online[1].

Statistical tests were run for techniques in the same experimental object program to indicate the significant differences between the techniques using ANOVA test followed by a post-hoc analysis. The results of the ANOVA test indicate significant differences (p-value < 0.0001) for all groups of techniques in each experimental object program. Following ANOVA in order to identify which pairs of techniques are significantly different, a post-hoc test, LSD, was employed which has been previously used in a similar study by Zhang et al. [24]. The results of the LSD test for each object programs in Table 2 are shown in the top part of Table 3, where statistically different techniques are assigned different grouping labels and are ordered from left to right with their *mean* values. For example, technique O achieved the highest mean value, whereas technique R is in the lowest rank for object print-tokens.

The labels could have two different signals based on the commonalities in the letters of the labels: (1) The labels are different, which means that they are statistically different from each other: for example in print-tokens, techniques O and OS1 have different labels 'a' and 'b' respectively. (2) On the other hand, the labels are the same or share common parts of the label, which means that the techniques are not statistically significant and are independent: for example, OB1 and OB0 have taken the same label of 'cd', likewise OS1 and OS0 share the letter 'b' in their labels ('b' and 'bc' respectively), which shows that they are not statistically different.

Comparisons Between Statement-Based Techniques: As mentioned before in Sects. 3 and 4, statement-based techniques consist of OS0, OS1, AS and TS. APFD scores for the statement-based techniques indicate that at least one of our proposed techniques (OS0 and OS1) could significantly improve both statement-based baselines (AS and TS). However, note that statistical results of APFD score for two programs of *replace* and *print-tokens2* indicate that there are no significant differences between proposed or baseline techniques.

Our observation indicates that the APFD score for OS0 is always significantly better than for the AS technique in all experimental object programs. The APFD score of OS0 is also always better than or at least similar to that for TS with the exception of *print-tokens2*, where the APFD score of AS significantly outperforms OS0. Similar to OS0, the APFD score of OS1 is always significantly better than for AS. In comparing the APFD scores for OS1 against TS, it appears that OS1 is significantly better than TS in most of the cases, and there is no case where TS outperforms OS1 significantly. Our proposed techniques in most

---

[1] http://tinyurl.com/detailed-graphs

of the programs did not outperform each other significantly except in *schedule2* and *print-tokens2*, where OS1 is significantly better than OS0 in terms of the APFD score.

Comparisons Among Branch-Based Techniques: Recall from Sects. 3 and 4, branch-based methods consist of OB0, OB1, AB and TB. Similar to the statement-based techniques, our proposed branch-based techniques (OB1 and OB0) either out-perform baselines (AS and TS) significantly, or there is no significant difference in effectiveness. However in contrast to the proposed statement-based techniques, which out-perform baselines significantly in most cases, our branch-based techniques are among the best performing group of techniques, which are not significantly different. The only exception is for *tcas*, where both of our branch-based techniques performed significantly better than the baselines. In terms of APFD score, OB0 performs significantly better than AB in all cases, except for one case of *print-tokens2*, where both techniques are not significantly different. On the other hand, comparing OB0 with TB shows that these techniques are not significantly different except in two cases where TB performs significantly better than OB0 (*print-tokens2* and *totinfo*), and there is one case where OB0 out-performs TB(*tcas*).

Summary and Implications: The statistical analysis of techniques is summarized in the bottom part of Table 3. In this part of the table, the rows are filled with proposed techniques while the columns are dedicated to the baseline techniques. The statement-based and branch-based techniques are illustrated on the left and right hand sides of the bottom table respectively. The numbers in the summary table represent how many times our proposed techniques are significantly different from corresponding baselines. In addition to the numbers, there are two notions of > and < which denote whether the mean score of our technique is either greater than or smaller than the corresponding baselines.

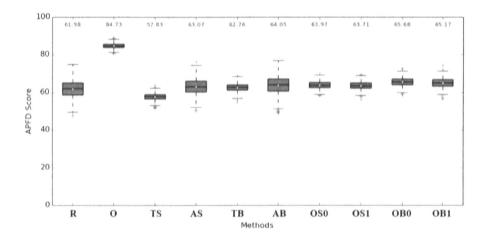

Fig. 2. Techniques comparisons based on 1000 test runs on program tcas

Table 3. Statistical comparison between techniques (top: details and bottom: summary).

Method	O	OS1	OS0	TS	OB1	OB0	TB	AS	AB	R	print-tokens
Grouping	a	b	bc	cd	cd	cd	d	e	f	g	
Method	O	TS	OS1	TB	OB1	OS0	AB	AS	OB0	R	print-tokens2
Grouping	a	b	b	c	c	c	d	d	d	e	
Method	O	TB	OB1	OB0	OS0	OS1	TS	AB	AS	R	totInfo
Grouping	a	b	bc	c	d	d	e	f	g	h	
Method	O	OB1	OB0	TB	OS1	OS0	TS	AS	AB	R	schedule
Grouping	a	b	bc	bc	c	c	d	d	e	e	
Method	O	OB1	TB	OB0	OS1	TS	OS0	AS	R	AB	schedule2
Grouping	a	b	b	bc	c	d	d	e	f	g	
Method	O	OB1	TB	OS1	TS	OB0	OS0	AB	R	AS	replace
Grouping	a	b	b	b	b	b	b	c	d	e	
Method	O	OB0	OB1	OS0	AB	OS1	AS	TB	R	TS	tcas
Grouping	a	b	b	c	cd	cd	de	e	f	g	

Statement	AS		TS		Branch	AB		TB	
OS1	6 (>)	0 (<)	5 (>)	0 (<)	OB1	7 (>)	0 (<)	1 (>)	0 (<)
OS0	7 (>)	0 (<)	3 (>)	1 (<)	OB0	6 (>)	0 (<)	1 (>)	2 (<)

For example, from the left side of the summary Table 3, OS0 has a mean score significantly greater than TS in three object programs, whereas TS is significantly greater in one object program. It can be seen that in this table, the two baselines of random and optimal were not considered, since they are representative of the upper and lower bounds of the prioritization techniques respectively. Given the above summarized results on differences between our proposed techniques and the baselines, we draw the following conclusions for the research questions of this study. The first research question in Sect. 5 is regarding the effect of using online information about the location of faults, and how it could affect the TCP techniques. The results summarized in bottom Table 3 indicate that using the fault location can outperform the baseline techniques. As can be seen in this table, the average APFD score of the proposed new techniques are always among the leading group, and mostly they outperform the baselines significantly (53 out of 56 cases, i.e., 4 'pairs of comparison' × 2 'coverage criteria' × 7 'programs' = 56), while there are only a few cases where baselines statistically outperform the proposed techniques.

The second research question (RQ2) relates to the effect of different coverage criteria on the performance of proposed techniques compared to the base line. The summarized results indicate that the proposed branch-based techniques have overall better performance over the statement-based techniques. Statistically speaking, proposed statement-based techniques, most of the time, outperform the statement baselines; however, the number of significant differences for proposed branch-based techniques that outperform the branch baselines are not as large as that for the statement based techniques, particularly for TB techniques. Our proposed branch-based techniques outperform the branch baselines in most of the cases as can be seen in the summary part of Table 3. An underlying reason for the lower performance of our statement-based techniques in comparison to branch-based techniques could be due to the more fine-grained coverage of branch-based techniques, which makes the effectiveness of the techniques less distinctive. Another observation from the results is that the order of TB and AB coverage is similar to the order of the proposed techniques with uncovered unit weights of 0 and 1 respectively for each coverage criterion. For example, in the *replace* object program, Table 3, TB works better than the AB, and similarly OB1 is better than OB0. On the other hand, for *tcas*, AB is better than TB, and likewise OB0 works better than OB1. This is in line with what we assumed in Sect. 4 that the uncovered unit with 0 and 1 values make our proposed techniques work similarly to the 'Total' and 'Additional' baselines respectively.

Overall, this paper has provided several contributions towards improving the effectiveness of current TCP techniques: (a) online branch-based techniques outperform branch-based baselines (b) online statement-based techniques outperform statement-based baselines; and (c) online branch-based techniques outperform both branch and statement-based baselines.

7   Conclusions and Future Work

In this paper we proposed a family of TCP techniques based on online information about the previously executed test cases, to further improve the prioritization of the remaining test cases. The approach relies on covering the location and area around previously identified faults, which is motivated by the 80-20 rule, where 80 % of faults in a program are related to only 20 % of its code. However, most of traditional TCP techniques only used greedy information in the coverage of test cases. To measure the effectiveness of the proposed approach, we performed an empirical study. The results of the study showed that in most cases, the suggested techniques significantly outperform baselines. These techniques were categorized in two subcategories based on the coverage of statements or branches of the program. The statement-based techniques mostly improve existing baselines, which utilize the statement coverage. However, in comparing branch-based techniques with the corresponding baselines, it appeared that this type of technique was not as effective as the statement-based results. This may suggest that branch-based techniques have a broader coverage in comparison to the statement-based techniques, and it is more likely that faults can be captured after a few times of covering code branches.

Our current approach is based on the assumption that each statement or branch near the location of previously identified faults has even probability of encountering a new fault. However, it is also likely that some particular types of statements or branches have higher chance of having faults. It is also likely that some types of statements or branches have higher chance of having faults. Another possible future work direction is to integrate the presented approach with the analysis of human factors in software reliability engineering [20]. We plan to study the behaviours of developers to further distinguish the likelihood of faults occurring in different statements and branches.

References

1. Software-artifact Infrastructure Repository. http://sir.unl.edu. Accessed 24 Mar 2015
2. Booch, G.: Object Oriented Design with Applications. Benjamin-Cummings Publishing Co., Inc., Redwood City (1991)
3. Do, H., Elbaum, S., Rothermel, G.: Supporting controlled experimentation with testing techniques: an infrastructure and its potential impact. Empir. Softw. Eng. **10**(4), 405–435 (2005)
4. Do, H., Rothermel, G., Kinneer, A.: Empirical studies of test case prioritization in a junit testing environment. In: ISSRE 2004, pp. 113–124. IEEE (2004)
5. Elbaum, S., Malishevsky, A.G., Rothermel, G.: Test case prioritization: a family of empirical studies. IEEE Trans. Softw. Eng. **28**(2), 159–182 (2002)
6. Hutchins, M., Foster, H., Goradia, T., Ostrand, T.: Experiments of the effectiveness of dataflow-and controlflow-based test adequacy criteria. In: ICSE, pp. 191–200. IEEE Computer Society Press (1994)
7. Jiang, B., Zhang, Z., Chan, W.K., Tse, T.: Adaptive random test case prioritization. In: ASE 2009, pp. 233–244. IEEE (2009)
8. Jiang, B., Zhang, Z., Chan, W.K., Tse, T., Chen, T.Y.: How well does test case prioritization integrate with statistical fault localization? Inf. Softw. Technol. **54**(7), 739–758 (2012)
9. Jones, J.A., Harrold, M.J.: Empirical evaluation of the tarantula automatic fault-localization technique. In: ASE 2005, pp. 273–282. ACM (2005)
10. Just, R., Jalali, D., Inozemtseva, L., Ernst, M.D., Holmes, R., Fraser, G.: Are mutants a valid substitute for real faults in software testing. In: FSE 2014 (2014)
11. Kim, J.-M., Porter, A.: A history-based test prioritization technique for regression testing in resource constrained environments. In: ICSE 2002, pp. 119–129. IEEE (2002)
12. Li, Z., Harman, M., Hierons, R.M.: Search algorithms for regression test case prioritization. IEEE Trans. Softw. Eng. **33**(4), 225–237 (2007)
13. Malaiya, Y.K., Li, M.N., Bieman, J.M., Karcich, R.: Software reliability growth with test coverage. IEEE Trans. Reliab. **51**(4), 420–426 (2002)
14. Myers, G.J., Sandler, C., Badgett, T.: The Art of Software Testing. Wiley, New York (2011)
15. Newman, M.E.: Power laws, Pareto distributions and Zipf's law. Contemp. Phys. **46**(5), 323–351 (2005)
16. Orso, A., Rothermel, G.: Software testing: a research travelogue (2000–2014). In: FoSER, pp. 117–132. ACM (2014)
17. Rooney, P.: Microsofts CEO: 80–20 rule applies to bugs, not just features. ChannelWeb, October 2002
18. Rothermel, G., Untch, R.H., Chu, C., Harrold, M.J.: Test case prioritization: an empirical study. In: ICSM 1999, pp. 179–188. IEEE (1999)
19. Rothermel, G., Untch, R.H., Chu, C., Harrold, M.J.: Prioritizing test cases for regression testing. IEEE Trans. Softw. Eng. **27**(10), 929–948 (2001)
20. Spichkova, M., Liu, H., Laali, M., Schmidt, H.: Human factors in software reliability engineering. In: WAHESE 2015 (2015, to appear)
21. Yoo, S., Harman, M.: Regression testing minimization, selection and prioritization: a survey. JSTVR **22**(2), 67–120 (2012)
22. Yoon, H., Choi, B.: A test case prioritization based on degree of risk exposure and its empirical study. Int. J. Softw. Eng. Knowl. Eng. **21**(02), 191–209 (2011)

23. Yu, Y., Jones, J.A., Harrold, M.J.: An empirical study of the effects of test-suite reduction on fault localization. In: ICSE 2008, pp. 201–210. ACM (2008)
24. Zhang, L., Hao, D., Zhang, L., Rothermel, G., Mei, H.: Bridging the gap between the total and additional test-case prioritization strategies. In: ICSE 2013, pp. 192–201 (2013)
25. Zheng, Z., Zhou, T.C., Lyu, M.R., King, I.: FTCloud: a component ranking framework for fault-tolerant cloud applications. In: ISSRE 2010, pp. 398–407. IEEE (2010)
26. Zhou, Z.Q.: Using coverage information to guide test case selection in adaptive random testing. In: COMPSACW 2010, pp. 208–213. IEEE (2010)

An Experience in Ada Multicore Programming: Parallelisation of a Model Checking Engine

Franco Mazzanti$^{(\boxtimes)}$

ISTI - Istituto di Scienza e Tecnologie dell'Informazione "A. Faedo",
Consiglio Nazionale Delle Ricerche, Pisa, Italy
franco.mazzanti@isti.cnr.it

Abstract. Even if multicore architectures are nowadays extremely wide-spread, the exploitation of this easily available degree of parallelism is not always straightforward. In this paper we describe the experience gained in our ongoing effort to parallelise the model checking engine of a family of model checkers (KandISTI) developed at ISTI. The main focus of our experimentation is the evaluation of the minimal efforts needed to take advantage of our everyday multicore hardware for model checking purposes. Our early results relative to an initial fragment of the logic show a speedup factor of about 2.5 when 4 physical cores are available. This result, however, can only be achieved by complementing the initial high level Ada design with a second round of code fine-tuning which exploits nonstandard low level features in the implementation of the needed thread-safe data structures.

Keywords: Model checking · Parallel programming · Multicore processor architectures · Ada programming language

1 Introduction

KandISTI [4], is a family of model checkers being developed at ISTI in the last ten years aimed to the experimentation of innovative formal verification techniques. The family is constituted by four model checkers each of which is oriented to a particular system design approach, but all of which share the same underlying abstract model and verification engine. The basic underlying idea behind KandISTI is that the evolution in time of the system behaviour can be seen as a graph where both edges and states are associated with sets of (composite) labels [9]. Labels on the states represent basic state properties, and labels on the edges represent properties of system transitions. The different flavours of the various tools have to do with the choice of one of the supported specifications languages, which range from process algebras to sets of UML-like statecharts.

The properties that can be verified on such a graph are expressed in a branching time, state and action based, temporal logic [8] which includes both the basic fix point operators and the more friendly (A)CTL-like [7] operators. The verification of a formula and the generation of the relevant part of the system evolutions

© Springer International Publishing Switzerland 2016
M. Bertogna et al. (Eds.): Ada-Europe 2016, LNCS 9695, pp. 94–109, 2016.
DOI: 10.1007/978-3-319-39083-3_7

graph occur *on the fly*. Given an initial system state and a top-level formula, only the actually needed subformulas of the initial formula are analysed, and only the actually needed next states of the current state are generated. The graph generation is driven *on demand* from the ongoing formula verification. All the various tools of the KandISTI framework are programmed in Ada, and are freely usable online through a public web interface.[1] These tools are being used mainly for didactic and academic research purposes, and have not yet reached the engineering level actually needed for full-scale industrial use.

All these tools are usually executed upon consumer level hardware that normally supports at least 4 cores. The current version of KandISTI is however not able to exploit this easily available degree of parallelism. We are therefore interested to observe which degree of redesign is needed and to measure the amount of benefits that could be gained by the exploitation of the multicore structure of our systems. The parallelisation effort is still ongoing, but the early results already show a reasonable picture of the situation and of the novel design.

In Sect. 2 we describe the overall structure of the original sequential version of the tools, while in Sect. 3 we describe two possible approaches for introducing some parallelism during the verification. In Sect. 4 we describe a recent case study to which our KandISTI framework has been applied and we show the results of the parallelisation efforts. In Sect. 5 we draw some final conclusions.

2   The Basic Sequential Approach

In the following we will consider just a few operators of the logic supported by KandISTI, which are however sufficient to illustrate the overall structure of the verification mechanism. One of these is the *EX* (Exists neXt) operator.

The formula: *EX{action} subform* holds on a state *s* if and only if there exists an outgoing transition from *s* whose edge labels satisfy the transition predicate *action* and which leads to a target state *s'* in which the formula *subform* holds. A second operator we consider is the *AG* (Always Globally) operator.

The formula: *AG subform* holds on a state *s* if and only if for all the states reachable (in any number of steps) from *s*, the formula *subform* holds. We also make use of the *True* formula which holds in any state, and the *true* action predicate which holds for any transition.

The skeleton of the sequential verification algorithm is quite simple: we have an EvalFormula function which, depending on the kind of formula passed to it, dispatches to the appropriate specific version returning a TT or FF value according to the validity of the formula on the given state. When the formula to be evaluated is of the *EX* kind, the evaluation has the following structure:

```
1: function EvalEX(Formula, State) return Computation_Status is
2:    Result: Computation_Status;
3: begin
```

---

[1] http://fmt.isti.cnr.it/kandisti.

```
4:    Result = Computations_DB.CheckComputation (Formula, State)
5:    if  Result = NOT_YET_STARTED then
6:      Result := FF;
7:      for E of GetEvolutions(State) loop
8:        if E.Labels satisfy Formula.Action then
9:          Result := EvalFormula(Formula.Subformula,E.TargetState);
10:         if Result = TT then
11:             exit;
12:           end if;
13:         end if;
14:      end loop;
15:      Computations_DB.Set_Status(Formula,State,Result);
16:   end if;
17:   return Result; -- either TT or FF
18: end EvalEX;
```

We assume the existence of a Computations_DB, i.e. a global container keeping track of all partial or completed subcomputations being performed. By calling CheckComputation (Line 4), each time a new subcomputation (i.e. a pair [formula, state]) is needed we check whether that computation has already been performed. In the positive case we can return the already known result, otherwise we return a NOT_YET_STARTED value. This global container is essentially a large global hashed set. The Computations_DB is not the unique global structure: also the graph representing the possible system evolutions, which is dynamically generated as the evaluation proceeds, needs to be saved and recorded as some kind of hashed map from nodes to edges (Configurations_DB). Both these global data structures are in our case programmed using custom hash tables, which allow easier monitoring and ad hoc optimisations of the code (e.g. deletions are never needed). In the previous example of EvalEX code, the call of GetEvolutions (Line 7) interacts with the underlying Configurations_DB potentially triggering the analysis of a new node and the expansion of the system evolutions graph. The case of recursive operations like the *AG* formula is a little more complex especially in the case of cyclic models. In this case the evaluation has the following structure:

```
1: function EvalAG(Formula, State) return Computation_Status is
2:    Result: Computation_Status;
3: begin
4:    Result = Computations_DB.CheckComputation (Formula, State)
5:    if Result  = NOT_YET_STARTED  then
6:      Result := EvalFormula(Formula.Subformula, State);
7:      if Result = TT then
8:        Computations_DB.Set_Status(Formula,State, TT);
9:        for E in GetEvolutions(State)  loop
10:         Result := EvalAG(Formula, E.TargetState);
11:         if Result = FF then
12:           Computations_DB._DB.Set_Status(Formula, State,FF);
13:           exit;
```

```
14:            end if;
15:          end loop;
16:        else
17:          Computations_DB._DB.Set_Status(Formula, State,FF);
18:        end if;
19:   end if;
20:   return Result;
21: end EvalAG
```

As in the previous case we first check whether a result is already known (Line 4). If the result is not known we first evaluate whether the AG subformula actually holds in the current state (Line 6). If it does not, the evaluation is completed and the FF value is saved and returned (Lines 17, 20). If the subformula holds in the current state we save this initial partial result (Line 8) and proceed with the recursive evaluation on all the successor states. If for the some successor the AG formula does not hold we save the FF status, and exit the loop. If the AG formula holds for all successors we finally return the already saved TT result. If during the evaluation of AG we meet a nested recursive evaluation of AG (because of loops in the graph) we take its already saved TT value and continue the analysis, according to the maximum fix point semantics of AG.

The above verification structure is actually a simplification of the real sequential algorithm used in the KandISTI framework. In particular we have not shown the overhead needed to save the information required to generate a counter-example (or the proof) for the formula together with the final result. Moreover, we have not shown the possibility to truncate the recursive evaluations at increasing levels of depth (bounded model checking) in order to search for counter-examples or proofs smaller than those otherwise generated by a purely depth first evaluation approach.

3   Towards a Parallel Approach

The introduction of parallelism in the verification process has to successfully overcome three difficulties.

- **Memory model**: A sequential program may usually rely on a flat view of the available memory; it is a compiler/hardware task to optimise the performance by keeping data inside registers, local caches or physical RAM in a way is completely transparent to the programmer. In the case of parallel programs the programmer has to apply Volatile/Atomic aspects to the shared objects and types, and apply the appropriate synchronisations mechanisms to serialise the accesses to the shared objects, in order to preserve a coherent inter task view of the memory. This also implies hardware/compiler efforts that may greatly reduce the overall performance of the program.
- **Synchronisations**: The executions of operations over shared data (hash tables/queues) need to be properly synchronised, and this requires additional overhead in the execution of otherwise simple operations.

– **Parallel design**: Finally, the parallelisation of the evaluation algorithm may introduce additional complexities and overhead with respect to the plain sequential depth-first approach.

These problems do not have a known unique solution, as the most effective choice may actually depend on the details of the hardware, on the structure of the state-space, on the structure of the formula, on the desired degree of parallelism, and on the overall structure of the parallel design. Some experimentation is therefore needed. In the following we describe two possible approaches that differ in the amount of redesign they require, and in the reasonable benefits that we can expect from them.

3.1   Parallel Graph Generation

In many cases the complexity of generating the needed fragment of state-space can be higher than the complexity of evaluating a formula over it. A first experiment that could be done is therefore letting the sequential verification program to proceed in parallel with one or more other tasks that simply speedup the evolutions graph traversal and state-space generation. Since the evaluation task and the additional model-generating tasks both work upon the shared hash tables used to elaborate the nodes and to store the representation of the graph, we still need to use a thread safe implementation for these tables. Clearly it is not possible to model the whole hash table as a single protected object, but we need to synchronise the accesses to the data in a more fine-grained way. We can do that, for example, by partitioning the table and associating locks to the various regions so that accesses to different parts need not to get synchronised. In Ada, the classical abstract, portable way to implement a semaphore requires the use of a protected object; however if we choose this implementation we see that the choice has pernicious effects on the program performance (specific data is shown in Sect. 4). The problem lies on the high overhead introduced by protected objects for synchronising very small operations. Indeed, these may require expensive context switching each time a task not allowed to immediately proceed with its operations. An alternative solution is that of using custom, system dependent, implementations of spinlocks, exploiting the compiler built-in lock-free primitives,[2] based on atomic compare-and-swap and memory fence processor operations. Using these lightweight non context switching (busy waiting) primitives our parallel version of the program actually shows some significant speedups, especially in the case of verification of simple properties requiring the full state space analysis. The advantage of this approach is that, since we do not touch the evaluation algorithm, only rather small modifications have to be done to the model checker code. However, since the model generation is now separated and independent from the evaluation algorithm we completely lose the advantages of the on-the-fly model generation.

---

[2] In our case we use the GNAT run-time component System.Atomic_Primitives.

3.2 Parallel Formula Evaluation

The above considerations suggested to further investigating how to introduce the parallelism directly inside the evaluation algorithm. Our scenario is that we have only a limited number of cores on a single processor, therefore it might not be necessary to push the parallelism of the evaluation to its limits. As a first approach we plan to introduce the parallelism only into the recursive AG operators. The worst-case complexity of the verification (which for the CTL-like fragment of the logic is linear w.r.t. the number of states, number of edges and size of the subformula) is only obtained when recursive operators (like AG) need to explore the whole state-space before producing a result. Therefore our approach directly targets this worst case of evaluation.

Handling of Non-recursive Operators. In the sequential case the evaluation proceeded by constructing (in a depth first mode) a graph of subcomputations. Our goal is now to build that same structure in a concurrent way. We start by associating to each logical subcomputation, corresponding to a pair [formula, state], an evaluation fragment. All evaluation fragments are stored inside a global shared container implemented as a thread-safe hashed set. Each evaluation fragment has references to the set of fragments on which it depends, and references to the set of fragments that depend on it. In this way we have a graph structure modelling the ongoing evaluation process.

From the point of view of this data type, the main difference with respect to the sequential case is that now evaluation fragments must synchronise the operations working upon them, and that also the shared global hashed set of all fragments must synchronise all operations of insertion and retrieval. We suppose to have a pool of worker tasks, where each task performs a cycle in which the task takes one item from a shared container of needed fragments and elaborates the fragment, until the whole verification is completed. The parallel evaluation process begins with the insertion in the shared container of the initial fragment corresponding to the top-level formula and the initial system state.

The precise effect of the elaboration of a fragment associated to a pair [formula, state] depends on the kind of the formula, on the possible evolutions of the state, and on several design choices to be performed (like the amount of parallelism we want to introduce or the order of analysis of subfragments). The overall structure of the evaluation process for a fragment comprises the following steps:

- The fragment internal structure is initialised. In particular, the current system state is analysed and its next successors states (and edge labels) are computed (if not yet known). This is the point that may trigger the evaluation-driven model generation step. The eventually needed subfragments are identified, and if not already existing they are created and added to the global shared container.
- We start the check of the status of the needed subfragments. The status of a fragment can be one of: JUST_CREATED, NEEDED, TT, FF.

- If the status of a subfragment is JUST_CREATED, then a reference to the current fragment is recorded inside the subfragment parents' list. Moreover the subfragment is introduced into the global shared container of *needed fragments* (to be eventually elaborated by some worker task). The status of the subfragment is also changed to NEEDED.
- If the status of the subfragment is already NEEDED, then just the recording of a reference to the current fragment inside the parents' list of the subfragment is sufficient.
- If the status of a subfragment is TT, or FF, we take care of this information deciding if is it sufficient or not in order to complete the evaluation of the current fragment. For example, in the case of an *or* formula, an early TT result is sufficient to establish the TT status of the current fragment without any further evaluation.

If during the elaboration of a fragment we can establish its definitive TT or FF status, this information is recorded (if not already present) inside the fragment data and the same information is notified back to all the registered parents so that they can handle it.

If a fragment is intended to be elaborated in a sequential way (e.g. as in the case of fragments associated to *EX*, operators) the evaluation of subfragments proceeds as long as the previous subfragments have an already computed TT or FF value. As soon as a subfragment is found with no definitive value (i.e. a JUST_CREATED or NEEDED value), the elaboration of the current fragment is temporarily abandoned after the recording of the current fragment in the parents' list of the subfragment. When a notification from the subfragment arrives, depending on the delivered TT or FF value, either a final result is established (and notified back to the parents), or the elaboration of the remaining list of subfragments is resumed.

The operations working over fragments must behave in an atomic way, guaranteeing that the semantics of a set of parallel invocations is the same as if they were executed in some sequential order. This can be achieved by implementing fragments as Ada protected objects, or by implementing them as plain records and manually encoding the needed synchronisations of the calls using spinlocks or semaphores. We have experimented with both approaches and the results are illustrated in the Sect. 4.

Handling of Recursive Operators. The above description describes well the behaviour of the evaluation for all the fragments referring to non-recursive logical operators (e.g. *and, or, not, EX, AX, <>,* [] operators). In the case of recursive parallel operators (like *AG,*) the situation is more complex.

Handling cycles in the state space: Let us consider a system having just three states, as shown in Fig. 1.

The evaluation of the initial fragment F1 leads to the creation of the two other fragments F2 and F3, which are evaluated in parallel. The evaluation of F2 finds the fragment F3 in the NEEDED state, and just registers itself as a parent fragment depending on F3. The same happens during the evaluation of

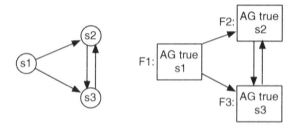

Fig. 1. Mutually dependent fragments in the evaluation of *AG true*

F3: fragment F2 is found as already NEEDED and therefore F3 just registers itself in the F2 parents list. Now all the possible elaborations are completed (there are no more fragments to elaborate) but no result has been produced. If the evaluation of an *AG* operator completes (in the sense that there is nothing more to compute) without producing any result, then the TT result is the correct result to be returned. The situation is partly similar to the sequential case when the discovery of a still in progress subcomputation was treated as if a TT result was found. The difference is that we can discover these cases only when the full exploration of the *AG* formula is ended.

Handling Early Completions: The evaluation of an *AG* fragment spreads the parallel elaboration of its subfragments. If formula *subform* is eventually found to be FF in some state, then the corresponding parent *AG subform*, and all its ancestor fragments up to the root *AG* formula, must be set to the state FF. This is already done by the backward notification procedures. However we must also stop all the still ongoing parallel spreading of *AG* fragments. The specific evaluation procedure for *AG* fragments aborts its elaboration when the status of the root *AG* formula is found to be FF (another global shared variable AGSTATUS is used for this purpose), therefore stopping the further spreading of subfragments. When an *AG* fragment is aborted, its status is reset to JUST_CREATED, and the same happens recursively to all its not yet resolved ancestors. Done that, the remaining still unresolved *AG* fragments can instead be set to the TT status, as they are related to isolated loops in the graph, not affected by the nodes for which the formula is false.

Dealing with Parallel Root Evaluations: Another limitation of the evaluation of *AG* formulas is that we cannot start two parallel evaluations from two different root states. If that happened the two evaluations could interfere. For example, it would become particularly difficult to understand which fragments to abort when an FF result if found in some state (we should not abort fragments being used also by other root *AG* evaluations). Therefore, we decide to concentrate all parallel efforts to the recursive evaluation of one *AG* formula at a time. Considering our relatively limited degree of expected hardware parallelism, this is in practice not a big limitation. While the evaluation of some *AG* formula is in progress, we enqueue all the concurrently arising evaluation requests for the same root AG formula, and when one evaluation completes we just resume another root evaluation from that queue. Notice that we do not prevent different AG formulas to be evaluated in parallel. For example, let us consider the formula:

$$AG \; ((not \; EX\{b\} \; True) \; or \; AG \; EX\{a\} \; True)^3$$

In this case we would have a parallel evaluation of the outer AG (searching for nodes which have outgoing $\{b\}$ transitions), and a set of root AG evaluations looking for $\{a\}$ transitions that would happen to be serialised and executed one at the time. The full implementation of the parallel version of our model checkers is still in progress. We have to support further recursive and not recursive CTL-like operators, the parameterisation of formulas, and to understand how to deal with fix points. Nevertheless we can already experiment with the current framework to evaluate the current design strategies and to optimise the implementation of the shared data types. In the next section we will show a case study that we have adopted as an initial benchmark to evaluate our progress.

4   Case Study

In order to have an early feedback about the performed design choices, we have tested our parallel approach with a case study recently analysed within our KandISTI framework. The case study is taken from the railway domain, and is related to the verification of a deadlock avoidance technique implemented inside the software which controls the movements of (driverless) trains inside a given yard [12,13]. In that case study we had a formal model of the system based on the railway layout shown in Fig. 2, including a certain number of trains moving inside the yard according with their predefined set of missions. The purpose of the verification of the formal model is to verify that the deadlock avoidance kernel of the control system is actually able to dispatch the trains on the layout without ever causing situations of deadlock, even in presence of arbitrary delays with respect to the planned timetable. Several models of different complexity can be built, depending on layout region in which the trains are moving, on the number of trains considered and on the length of their missions.

The whole model has been described by a UML statechart and the verification is carried out with the UMC model checker [5]. We have considered three models of growing complexity as illustrated in Table 1.

Table 2[4] shows the evaluation time for an exhaustive deadlock analysis performed by verifying the formula $AG \; EX \; \{true\} \; True$ (which simply states that all

---

[3] For all reachable nodes it is true that either the node has no outgoing $\{b\}$ transitions, or the node and all its successors have at least one outgoing $\{a\}$ transition.

[4] The data in the following tables are taken on a MacBook Pro early 2013, with a quad-core Intel Core i7-3740QM @ 2.70 GHz CPU, 16 GB RAM, running OS X El Capitan Version 10.11.3. The code has been compiled with GNAT GPL 2015 (20150428-49). Execution times computed by performing calls to Calendar.Time at the beginning/end of each evaluation. Sources, executables, models and test data are available from http://fmt.isti.cnr.it/WEBPAPER/AE2016-data.zip.

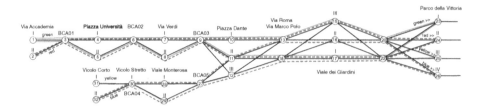

Fig. 2. The yard layout and the missions for the trains of the green, red, yellow and blue lines (Color figure online)

Table 1. The three reference models

M1:	7 trains moving with short missions (one way traversal of the yard)	(323,195 states)
M2:	8 trains moving with short missions (one way traversal of the yard)	(1,636,538 states)
M3:	8 trains moving with long missions (one way traversal of the yard)	(8,878,643 states)

reachable states do have at least one successor), using the original purely sequential version of the tool UMC (with and without all compile time optimisations turned on).

Table 2. Sequential evaluation times for $AG\ EX\{true\}\ True$

Model	Evaluation time	-O3 (optimized version)
M1:	21 s	11 s
M2:	110 s	57 s
M3:	660 s	371 s

In Tables 3 and 4, instead, we show the evaluation times resulting from the first approach in which the sequential evaluation of the formula is helped by the parallel model generation by 1, 2 or 3 worker tasks. We show two data sets, one for the case in which data synchronisation is achieved using semaphores implemented by protected objects (Table 3), and one in which semaphores are implemented by custom (busy waiting) spinlocks (Table 4).

The data in Table 3 shows clearly that, when protected types are used for implementing semaphores, the presence of worker tasks instead of improving the overall performance of the model checker, drastically reduces it. In particular, the introduction of a second worker has the immediate effect of more than doubling the execution time. Moreover we can see that the execution times of the parallel version with zero worker tasks (i.e. still using thread-safe global containers, but running only the sequential evaluator task), suffers only a small

Table 3. Parallel graph generation (using protected objects)

Model		+1 task	+ 2 tasks	+3 tasks
M1:	22 s	49 s	72 s	84 s
M1(-O3)	14 s	42 s	65 s	73 s
M2:	121 s	259 s	382 s	446 s
M2 (-O3)	75 s	220 s	349 s	394 s

reduction of performance w.r.t. the original purely sequential version when no optimisation is performed on the compiled code. This small reduction is caused by the presence of atomic/volatile aspects in the shared data types and by the overhead introduced by the calling of the semaphore primitives (which however never happen to block the executing task). The negative effect of the presence of atomic/volatile data is more evident when optimisations are turned on, since this aspect directly prevents many memory based optimisations.

Table 4. Parallel graph generation (using spinlocks) - times and speedups

Model		+1 task	+ 2 tasks	+3 tasks
M1:	22 s	15 s *(1.46)*	13 s *(1.69)*	15 s *(1.46)*
M1 (-O3)	14 s	9.8 s *(1.42)*	9 s *(1.55)*	8 s *(1.75)*
M2:	116 s	79 s *(1.46)*	69 s *(1.68)*	82 s *(1.43)*
M2 (-O3)	72 s	48 s *(1.50)*	45 s *(1.60)*	50 s *(1.44)*
M3:	701 s	480 s *(1.46)*	408 s *(1.71)*	485 s *(1.43)*
M3 (-O3)	452 s	294 s *(1.53)*	265 s *(1.70)*	296 s *(1.52)*

With the use of spinlocks instead of protected objects we see some gains in the exploitation of the multicore architecture. As shown in Table 4, the evaluation time in this case decreases of a percentage varying from 35 % to 42 % when +2 worker tasks are activated. However the big gain is obtained by the activation of the first worker, the second and other workers have a much smaller effect. This effect can be explained by the fact that the more worker tasks we create, the sooner the generation of the full model completes (while the inter-tasks interferences grow): once the model is fully generated no more gains are given by the parallelism. We can see that these gain are mostly preserved also in the case of compilations with full optimisations turned on.

Finally, let us see what happens with our parallel evaluation approach, when both the model generation and the fragment evaluation are being carried out in parallel by several evaluator tasks. Also in this case we take into consideration the possibility of achieving mutual exclusion in the fragment data manipulation either using a protected type or by using custom spinlocks (Table 5). In both

Table 5. Parallel formula evaluation

Model	Using protected objects				Using spinlocks			
	1 task	2 tasks	3 tasks	4 tasks	1 task	2 tasks	3 tasks	4 tasks
M1　(-O3)	12.7 s	7.4 s	5.9 s	5.4 s	12.5 s	7.2 s	5.4 s	4.5 s
speedup		*1.71*	*2.13*	*2.32*		*1.73*	*2.31*	*2.77*
M2　(-O3)	66 s	37 s	29 s	28 s	65 s	36 s	27 s	24 s
speedup		*1.78*	*2.27*	*2.35*		*1.8*	*2.4*	*2.7*
M3　(-O3)	437 s	265 s	207 s	189 s	414 s	251 s	192 s	164 s
speedup		*1.64*	*2.15*	*2.31*		*1.64*	*2.15*	*2.5*

Table 6. Parallel formula evaluation, using spinlocks, on eight-core workstation

Model	1 task	2 tasks	3 tasks	4 tasks	5 task	6 tasks	7 tasks	8 tasks
M1　(-O3)	10.9 s	6.61 s	5.10 s	4.42 s	3.94 s	3.67 s	3.51 s	3.45 s
speedup		*1.64*	*2.13*	*2.46*	*2.76*	*2.97*	*3.10*	*3.15*
M2　(-O3)	55.1 s	34.2 s	25.9 s	21.9 s	19.7 s	19.1 s	18.4 s	17.9 s
speedup		*1.61*	*2.12*	*2.51*	*2.79*	*2.88*	*3.01*	*3.07*
M3　(-O3)	346 s	207 s	153 s	146 s	131 s	124 s	120 s	124 s
speedup		*1.67*	*2.26*	*2.36*	*2.64*	*2.79*	*2.88*	*2.79*

cases we use custom spinlocks for the synchronisation of the accesses to the shared global containers.

In this case the differences between the two implementations of thread-safe fragments are smaller, but there is still an advantage is using a handmade locking mechanism rather than a protected type implementation of these objects. This is especially true if we consider that the current locking mechanism is very trivial (we just model full mutual exclusion between state-changing operations) and could be much improved by a more careful design. On the other side, the protected type based implementation is more abstract and less error prone, and we are happy with the choice of having selected it as our first implementation, leaving to a possible second round of optimisations the task of replacing it with something more fine-tuned with the actual optimisation needs.

The version that makes use of spinlocks for synchronising the accesses to fragment data and shared containers has been tested also on an 8-core Linux workstation. We want to observe the program behaviour when the number of available physical cores is increased. The results are shown in Table 6,[5] and a graphical comparison with the speedups reported in the right side of Table 5 is shown in Fig. 3.

Overall, when the number of parallel tasks passes from 1 to 4, but even more when it passes from 4 to 8, the speedup factor grows much less than in the

---

[5] Test executed on a eight-core workstation with a Intel(R) Xeon(R) E5-2630 v3 @ 2.40 GHz CPU, 64G RAM, running Ubuntu 14.04.4 LTS (GNULinux 3.13.0-83-generic x86_64), GNAT GPL 2015 Compiler.

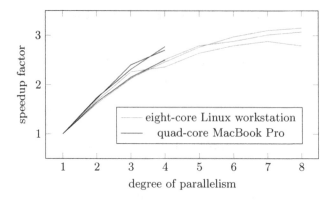

Fig. 3. Best speedups on a 4-core and 8-core processors

optimal linear scale. Surely much work can, and has to be done, in reducing the conflicts on the shared data, e.g. with more careful designs of the shared containers and of the overall parallelisation strategy.

5   Related Work

The definition of highly efficient thread-safe containers is surely one of the key factors for an efficient multicore programming. Many suggestions in this sense are available in the literature. Indeed the use of distributed/lock-free hash tables, both in the case of single processors multicore and in the case of multiprocessors with local and shared memory, has been widely studied (e.g. for parallel state space generation) and several solutions have been illustrated which allow a linear speedup w.r.t the degree of available parallelism [2,3,10,14].

Also the parallelisation of model checking algorithms is a widely investigated field. Most of the studies, however, are related to the parallelisation of linear time logics (LTL), or to global model checking approaches, where the whole state space is generated and available before the beginning of the evaluation process, or to symbolic (e.g. BDD based) approaches to model checking were the state space is finite and all states have the same size. A survey of the currently adopted LTL approaches can be found in [1,11].

In our case, instead, we want to deal with potentially infinite state spaces, where the states may have an unbounded size (e.g. because of the presence of unbounded data structures like queues). Moreover we want to deal with a CTL-like branching time logic (as initial fragment of the logic supported by our KandISTI framework). Finally, we want to preserve our explicit, local (i.e. on-the-fly), approach on which the sequential versions of our model checkers are based.

From this point of view we have several points in common with the approaches in [6,15]. The main difference w.r.t them is that we are more focused on multicore single processor architectures while these other works are more oriented towards highly parallel/distributed architectures. It is interesting to observe that the speedup factor of about 2.5 that we obtain for our worst evaluation case when all our 4 cores are used, is obtained in [6] only on parallel architectures with at least 10 processors. Cleary the difference is that, in their case, they can reach speedup factors of 14 with 50 processors, while we are constrained to our small number of cores. However, since single processors with 16 cores are already on the market it would be interesting to see how our approach behaves on such more powerful systems. Another major difference with respect to the approach in [15] is that the logic taken into consideration by those authors is constrained to a fragment of the CTL logic where state subformulas are restricted to atomic propositions. That simplification rules out all the complexities related to existence of multiple concurrent root evaluations of recursive operators.

6   Conclusions

We have presented some early experiences gained from an ongoing process of code rewriting relative to the multicore parallelisation of a sequential model checking Ada program. In our case we have initially constrained the parallelism inside the *AG* operator (to be followed by all the other recursive operators), as this directly allows to target our worst-case execution times for finite systems. It is however reasonable (and will be the target of future studies) to introduce the parallelism in a much more widespread way. In that case the target would not much be the reduction of the worst case execution time, rather than to open the path towards a fully parallel breadth-first evaluation strategy which would allow to capture the shortest counter-examples and would allow to better deal also with potentially infinite-state systems (in presence of a finite proof or counter-example).

Computationally intensive programs making heavy use of shared data must employ highly optimised thread-safe data structures. Unfortunately this kind of abstractions are not currently available in the standard Ada container libraries, therefore we must resort to some manual implementation of them. In doing that we cannot make use of the Ada standard synchronisation mechanisms like protected types, but we need to make use of compiler-dependent, system dependent libraries providing access to low-level lock free atomic primitives. It is indeed a pity that these basic building blocks for multicore programming are not made immediately available by the language definition.

It is well known that debugging a parallel program is much harder than debugging a sequential program. However, when dealing with a shared memory architecture, just missing the volatile/atomic aspect over an object would give raise to spurious errors extremely difficult to find. The situation is worsened when the programmer is forced to use handcrafted versions of thread-safe data types and containers, and handcrafted synchronisation primitives. The result is that debugging a parallel program might easily become a nightmare. Definitely, the aid of a tool from this point of view would be extremely desirable (especially for the analysis of the volatile/atomic variables).

One of the confirmed strong points of Ada, however, is that it allows a nice, abstract design of the parallel algorithms using the language-defined, concurrency-oriented constructs. The optimisations needed for the best exploitation of the underlying hardware can be added at second round of code fine-tuning, with a relatively little effort.

In the design of a parallel system it is also quite easy to introduce logical design errors caused by unexpected thread interactions. From this point of view the construction of a formal model of the system and the exhaustive verification of the robustness the design might become an almost necessary help. Indeed this is another direction in which our project intends to move, with the goal of having a fully validated parallel evaluation engine. In spite of all difficulties and of the incompleteness of the experiment, the introduction of just a limited form of parallelism (e.g., 4 cores) allows us to obtain a performance speedup factor around 2.5, and this is surely a satisfactory initial result.

References

1. Barnat, J., Brim, L., Leucker, M.: Parallel model checking and the FMICS-jETI platform. In: 12th International Conference on Engineering of Complex Computer Systems, ICECCS 2007, pp. 330–338. IEEE Computer Society (2007)
2. Barnat, J., Rockai, P.: Shared hash tables in parallel model checking. Electron. Notes Theor. Comput. Sci. **198**(1), 79–91 (2008). Elseiver
3. Barnat, J., Ročkai, P., Štill, V., Weiser, J.: Fast, dynamically-sized concurrent hash table. In: Fischer, B., Geldenhuys, J. (eds.) SPIN 2015. LNCS, vol. 9232, pp. 49–65. Springer, Heidelberg (2015)
4. ter Beek, M.H., Gnesi, S., Mazzanti, F.: From EU projects to a family of model checkers. In: De Nicola, R., Hennicker, R. (eds.) Wirsing Festschrift. LNCS, vol. 8950, pp. 312–328. Springer, Heidelberg (2015)
5. ter Beek, M.H., Fantechi, A., Gnesi, S., Mazzanti, F.: A state/event-based model-checking approach for the analysis of abstract system properties. Sci. Comput. Program. **76**(2), 119–135 (2011). Elseiver
6. Bollig, B., Leucker, M., Weber, M.: Local parallel model checking for the alternation-free μ-calculus. In: Bošnački, D., Leue, S. (eds.) SPIN 2002. LNCS, vol. 2318, p. 128. Springer, Heidelberg (2002)
7. De Nicola, R., Vaandrager, F.: Action versus state based logics for transition systems. In: Guessarian, I. (ed.) Semantics of Systems of Concurrent Processes. LNCS, vol. 469, pp. 407–419. Springer, Heidelberg (1990)
8. Fantechi, A., Gnesi, S., Lapadula, A., Mazzanti, F., Pugliese, R., Tiezzi, F.: A logical verification methodology for service-oriented computing. ACM Trans. Softw. Eng. Methodol. **21**(3), 16:1–16:45 (2012)
9. Gnesi, S., Mazzanti, F.: An abstract, on the fly framework for the verification of service-oriented systems. In: Wirsing, M., Hölzl, M. (eds.) SENSORIA. LNCS, vol. 6582, pp. 390–407. Springer, Heidelberg (2011)
10. Laarman, A, van de Pol, J, Weber, M.: Boosting multi-core reachability performance with shared hash tables. In: Formal Methods in Computer-Aided Design, Lugano, Switzerland. IEEE Computer Society (2010)
11. Laarman, A.: Scalable multi-core model checking. CTIT Ph.D. thesis, Formal Methods and Tools, University of Twente (2014). http://dx.doi.org/10.3990/1.9789036536561

12. Mazzanti, F., Spagnolo, G.O., Della Longa, S., Ferrari, A.: Deadlock avoidance in train scheduling: a model checking approach. In: Lang, F., Flammini, F. (eds.) FMICS 2014. LNCS, vol. 8718, pp. 109–123. Springer, Heidelberg (2014)
13. Mazzanti, F., Spagnolo, G.O., Ferrari, A.: Designing a deadlock-free train scheduler: a model checking approach. In: Badger, J.M., Rozier, K.Y. (eds.) NFM 2014. LNCS, vol. 8430, pp. 264–269. Springer, Heidelberg (2014)
14. Saad, R.T., Zilio, S.D., Berthomieu, B.: A general lock-free algorithm for parallel state space construction. In: 9th International Workshop on Parallel and Distributed Methods in Verification (PDMC 2010). IEEE (2010)
15. Saad, R.T., Dal Zilio, S., Berthomieu, B.: An experiment on parallel model checking of a CTL fragment. In: Chakraborty, S., Mukund, M. (eds.) ATVA 2012. LNCS, vol. 7561, pp. 284–299. Springer, Heidelberg (2012)

Program Correctness and Robustness

Lessons Learned in a Journey Toward Correct-by-Construction Model-Based Development

Laura Baracchi[1], Silvia Mazzini[1(✉)], Stefano Puri[1], and Tullio Vardanega[2]

[1] Intecs SpA, Pisa, Italy
{laura.baracchi,silvia.mazzini,stefano.puri}@intecs.it
[2] Università di Padova, Padua, Italy
tullio.vardanega@math.unipd.it

Abstract. This paper discusses lessons learned in the attempt to apply the long-known principles of correct-by-construction (CbyC) first promoted by Dijkstra, to modern model-based development practices. We recall the intent and scrutinize the outcomes of a string of research projects that focused explicitly on the pursuit of CbyC by means of model-driven methods and technologies. The lessons learned show that when CbyC extends from the algorithmic and functional dimension to extra-functional concerns, some of the strength of original CbyC concept and its pull dilute. One of the possible causes of that phenomenon, is that – in some situation – the assertive style of algorithm refinement gives way to more tentative exploration of an unknown solution space where the known truths are insufficient to steer the development.

Keywords: Model-based development · Model transformation · Correctness by construction · Formal methods · Contract refinement

1 Background

1.1 On the Origin of the Quest for Correct by Construction

In formulating some of his early ideas about programming as a discipline [12], Dijkstra pointed out that software productivity is closely related to rigor in design, which is a sound and predictable method to eliminate software bugs at an early stage, before they creep in actual software products. The approach to be pursued is not, as common practice had it (and, sadly, still continues to) to first write a program and then test it, but rather to provide a mathematical proof of correctness before committing the corresponding algorithm to code.

Dijkstra promoted a program derivation method, which can be summarized in the engagement to "develop proof and program hand in hand". One starts with a mathematical specification of what a program is supposed to do and applies successive mathematical transformations to the specification until it equates to a program that can be executed (passed to a compiler, that is). The program that results from that process can then be claimed *correct by construction*. Testing is still performed on it, but only to validate the correct-by-construction process rather than to find bugs in the program.

© Springer International Publishing Switzerland 2016
M. Bertogna et al. (Eds.): Ada-Europe 2016, LNCS 9695, pp. 113–128, 2016.
DOI: 10.1007/978-3-319-39083-3_8

The work of Dijkstra has been furthered by other authors, for example Kurie and Watson in [2], essentially with the goal of detecting and removing as early as possible any errors that may occur in the development of the program, as close as possible to the point at which they were introduced. The approaches by the followers of Dijkstra essentially concentrated on nailing down a formal specification of the problem at hand, leaving the solution open for successive refinements. The central tenet of those methods was to capture, formulate and valuate specification constraints expressed in terms of pre- and post-conditions and invariants, to associate them to subprograms, and to prove them locally on them. Not surprisingly, therefore, the ambit where the concept of Correct by Construction development (shortened by CbyC in the sequel) subsequently flourished was in *Formal Methods*, as in [15, 29]. In those initiatives, the main carrier of specification information was the formal language of choice, with program artefacts seen as a derivative product, though not necessarily via automated transformation.

However, while mainstream software production methods and practices embraced model-based development techniques, and started using UML and its derivatives, they never went the full way toward formal methods, which caused CbyC to retreat to the periphery of their vision, not quite what its originator had hoped.

Researchers who attempted to cast CbyC to the model-based development practice (which in this work we refer by extension as MDE, for model-driven engineering [11]), assumed the program specifications to correspond to models, and consequently sought to devise appropriate transformation techniques to apply to them. The authors of [16], for example, reported: "[…] in some simple cases, we may be able to specify a transformation using a sequence of declarative specified steps, and provide an argument for its correctness by construction. However, we do not yet have a model transformation tool that can take a purely declarative specification and produce an automated transformation". In the quoted passage, an MDE transposal of CbyC would take more abstract program specifications than classic CbyC did. In fact, in the view of the cited authors, this would be the essential power of being model-driven, thus closer to conceptual thought than to algorithm formulation. Yet, the ultimate operation and product of the CbyC process would be entirely the same, that is, an implementation artefact that could be deemed correct by construction, by virtue of the sequence of transformative steps that eventually produced it.

Pursuing the CbyC principles to the furthest extent, and adhering with the MDE paradigm, leads to an ideal process of automated software production where CbyC is achieved through a sequence of model transformations – whose correctness is proven by some algebra – that start from the initial input of a formal specification of the solution and finally produce a correct implementation. The final product of this implementation process is guaranteed to be correct by construction, owing to the provable correctness of the applied transformations.

This kind of approach is elegant and "clean" conceptually, but it requires highly sophisticated formal language for the problem specification and complex software development for the transformations. It therefore entails considerable effort from theoretical computer scientists for both developing the transformations and expressing the program specification in the chosen formal language(s). The resulting investment may not pay sufficient dividends in the development of specific software products, especially when much of it is highly specialized, thoroughly dedicated, scarcely factorized and ill fit for re-use. Indeed, this one factor arguably hampered the effort reported in [16].

The quest of CbyC was revived by the late Peter Amey, when at Praxis High-Integrity Systems, who argued that the ambitious goals of CbyC can be attained by the combined application of the following six principles [9]:

1. (Specialization) use of formal and precise tools and notations for any product of the development cycle, it being a design document or a piece of source code.
2. (Automated step-wise validation) use of tool support to validate the product of each step: since formal tools have been used to develop every artefact (cf. point 1), it is possible to constructively reason on their correctness.
3. (Divide-and-conquer) break the development down in smaller steps to defeat error persistence: products of every step must be verified against their formal specification as soon as possible.
4. (Dryness) say things only once, to avoid any contradictions and repetitions.
5. (Beware of complexity) design software that is easy to validate, for example using safer language subset or explicit coding and design patterns
6. (Rigor and discipline) do the hard things first: this includes thorough requirement analysis and the development of early prototypes.

Amey's concept approached the nature of a CbyC process, which extended the programmer's scenery to mightier software engineering concerns, to include user requirements, as the semi-formal starting point that leads to the high-level design and test specifications, and the need to break software down to master complexity. Yet, Amey's approach was still "code-centric", in that it concentrates on the programming perspective, thereby on the production of program artefacts.

We are not satisfied with this interpretation of CbyC, which we deem too narrow for satisfactory exploitation in MDE. Fortunately, a significant boost to the "engineering" of CbyC and its promotion into the embedded real-time systems domain, arrived from the work of Sifakis in [3], with the promotion of the concept of (software) components and the associated qualifying properties of composability and compositionality. The former ensure the stability of component properties across integration, which is a vital principle to software integration. The latter facilitate inferring system properties from individual properties of constituent components, which is vital to ascertaining the feasibility, the viability, the quality, the performance of the overall system.

Since we consider pursuing this line of reflection wholly beneficial to good software engineering, we have devoted considerable effort in the last few years, to arrive at the definition and experimentation of "an MDE way to CbyC". In this work, we report and discuss the principal lessons we have learned in the attempt.

1.2   A Modeling Approach to Correct by Construction

In our view, an effective CbyC approach, ultimately geared to making it increasingly difficult to introduce errors in the software development process, would have two main ingredients: one, the adoption of MDE to manipulate more malleable and yet powerful abstractions than program artefacts; the other, rigor at each development step, to enable (possibly automated) formal reasoning or analysis of the correctness of the step, and (possibly automated) derivation, whenever possible, of correct base input for the subsequent step.

We advocate that using models in most of the development steps, supported by adequate MDE techniques and tooling (far more productive today than in the early age of CbyC), makes it easier to define correct requirements, to design a system that meets the requirements, and to develop an implementation that preserves the desired correctness properties.

The concept of "stepwise refinement" is naturally related to a CbyC process. In formal methods, program refinement is the verifiable, possibly multi-staged, transformation of a high-level, hence more abstract, formal specification into a low-level, hence more concrete, artefact of implementation. Following a stepwise refinement process, one may progress from a high level of abstraction, with the solution's specification, gradually across lower levels of abstraction, in a systematic (and provably correct) manner, while preserving (and possibly enriching) the properties that characterize the specified solution.

Components are a fitting abstraction of software construction: associating formalized contracts – broadly speaking, pairs of assume/guarantee statements – to model components (primarily to their interfaces, in the quest for encapsulation and information hiding) across the development phases provides solid background to enable the selective use of formal methods for the verification of the stepwise refinement process.

Contract based-design [8] allows focusing on the specification of entities in isolation, so it naturally fits component-based development well, where components are designed in isolation and only their provided and required interfaces are published to the outside, for binding and assembly.

Contracts also allow deriving system-level properties by composing the properties sustained by individual components, thereby earning the guarantee that the properties derived from them at system level, hold as long as the contracts stipulated by the individual components hold after composition.

As Amey noted in [1], "CbyC combines the best parts of two superficially unlikely bedfellows: formal methods and agile development. For example, we take from the former precise notations, and from the latter incremental development". The adoption of contracts is a further important enabler for CbyC: with it, the system and its components are characterized by formally defined contracts, and the designer iteratively envisages suitable system/contract decompositions and refinements, converging towards the identification of qualified lower-level components. The system development is thus incremental in nature, and each refinement step in it can in principle be formally verified, provided that the system and component contracts are formally described.

The remainder of this paper is organized as follows: Sect. 2 describes the initial steps of this work; Sects. 3 and 4 discuss the immediate extensions of it, which were consistent for intent and equally successful in outcome; Sect. 5 examines the hurdles in the latest and more recent effort to extend the reach and coverage of the approach. Section 6, finally, presents the principal lessons learned in the whole endeavour.

2   Pursuing CbyC in Model-Driven Engineering: The ASSERT Experience

The ASSERT project [4, 5], led by the European Space Agency under funding from the 6th Framework Program of the European Commission, was a first attempt to realize a model-driven methodology for embedded software system development with dedicated component model, explicitly focused on CbyC.

The primary goal that the ASSERT project set itself was to assure the prevention of errors in the model space, in particular in the specification of real-time attributes and in the derivation of claims of real-time properties for individual software components and of their assembly.

ASSERT pursued that goal by defining a specialized metamodel, enriched with extra-functional attributes crafted for the specification of component interfaces. Using the ASSERT metamodel for modeling, the user would be able to attach sound properties to the concurrent structure of the system, require and verify the safeness of the interaction protocols involved in the system operation, and ascertain the timing feasibility of the system overall.

Interestingly, in the traditional development style of real-time embedded systems, the above concerns were verified "a posteriori", predominantly by testing, and usually without guarantees on exact correspondence between the intended design (on which certain properties were claimed) and the actual implementation (which may have considerably deflected from the designer's intent).

With ASSERT's MDE methodology instead, correctness can be ensured either by construction (as the user is enabled to stipulate binding assertions on individual model components and on their assembly, which can be attached to sound proofs) or by static verification of properties anticipated in the implementation artefacts yielded by the model, and by automated generation of implementation artefacts that provably produce the (concurrency and real-time) semantics captured in the verified model.

Ultimately, the essence of the ASSERT approach relied on the adoption of a methodology that:

1. Allows the user to express functional and timing properties for component interfaces using a restricted, sound and coherent set of annotations and constraints (for all respects and purposes, precursor of contracts), to facilitate the specification of functional and timing requirements of components in a manner amenable to rigorous verification.
2. Allows the user to model components at a level of abstraction higher than actual, target-specific, implementation, hence easier to verify as correct and reuse for intent, as well as to attach to clear and distinct obligations on the part of the subsequent implementation. The concrete form of this model was called Platform Independent Model (PIM) in the MDE literature of the time.
3. Provides a suite of automated model transformations capable of converting the user PIM into a refined model, closer to implementation concerns (and called Platform Specific Model, PSM, in MDE jargon) that:

(a) Assures conformance to the concurrent model of computation sanctioned in the Ravenscar Profile [13], which causes the system to exhibit well-formed semantics for its concurrent and real-time behaviour;

(b) Makes its resulting run-time behaviour amenable to sound, advanced, composable and tight feasibility analysis, by construction;

(c) Ensures that a semantic-preserving implementation of it can be produced with state-of-the-art industrial-quality technology, and be bound to a property-preserving run-time environment, i.e., one that can be proven to correctly, efficiently and accurately implement the corresponding concurrency semantics.

The results from the ASSERT project have enabled important progress in narrowing the earlier divide between CbyC and MDE, and have since become terms of reference for the subsequent industrial research work. One particularly important contribution of ASSERT was in providing initial evidence that the incorporation of CbyC in MDE needs a dedicated component model to enable architectural (i.e., rule-based) composition, as an essential enabler to the compositional assembly of locally asserted attributes into system-level properties.

3   CHESS: Bringing ASSERT to the Next Level

The CHESS project [18] started off from the foundations of the ASSERT research, with the goal to promote a disciplined approach to mastering complexity by enforcing *separation of concerns* [10] between the functional and the extra-functional dimensions, the latter regarded as the value-adding pillars for the next software generation and the basis for a mature model-based development.

Indeed, the motivation behind CHESS was that, for a given component, the functional and the extra-functional properties can and should be specified separately, through distinct views of one and the same the development problem. Functional attributes and properties can be provided first (largely in a reusable and platform-independent way), before timing and failure-propagation attributes (specified) and properties (verified) can be attached on top of them, facilitating the reuse of the same functionality in different extra-functional scenarios.

Consider for example a component C that exposes an operation Op1 in its provided interface. Component C can be instantiated multiple times in the same system or even in different systems. For each individual instance of it, the user should be able to decide whether the implementation of Op1 should be attached to a dedicated thread, so that Op1 would be executed solely and exclusively by that thread, or else to a procedure, so that any flow-of-control on the caller side with a required interface that matched Op1, would be able to execute it. In the former case, Op1 would be labelled "active"; in the latter, "passive". Obviously, the latter is free of data races only when Op1 should not persist local state across calls; otherwise the correct attribute would be "protected", which would require the implementation to provide appropriate synchronization protocols to warrant absence of data races and boundedness of priority inversion.

CHESS sought and promoted separation of concerns first by the adoption of a *multi-view* approach, where the system is designed as a single model via the use of dedicated views, each representing a specialized projection of the system with respect to a particular and cohesive set of development concerns (e.g., Requirements, System, Software, Deployment, and Analysis).

CHESS enforced its most manifest form of separation of concerns by promoting separation between the functional aspects of the system (which address the local, internal behavior of individual components, assuming that external needs are satisfied) from the extra-functional aspects (such as, for example, real-time constraints). To this end, CHESS built around a component model [6] that resolves all of a component's functional properties in the component internals (so that they can be implemented only considering local concerns), and delegates the implementation of all extra-functional properties to the component's infrastructure, outside of the component itself (that is, the run-time environment that sustains the existence, interaction, persistence, and resilience semantics stipulated in extra-functional attributes). The component internals are bound to the component infrastructure by means of platform-specific containers: such containers are responsible for the realization of all the extra-functional properties that are specified for the components that they embed. Components are bound to one another (via matching required and provided interfaces) by connectors: such connectors are also artefacts of the component infrastructure and realize the interaction between components as a mediated communication between containers.

Consistent with the principles of component-based software engineering [25], the adopted component model is characterized by the definition of "strong interfaces" that are the basis for structural composability, and precursors of contracts.

In CHESS, the user model is a PIM artefact that can be *automatically* transformed into a PSM artefact. The transformations that map the attributes of component interfaces to containers and those of component-to-component bindings to connectors, can be claimed correct by construction as the run-time entities that implement containers and connectors provably conform to the semantics assumed in the interface specifications. Thanks to that important quality, the PSM that corresponds, by transformation, to the user PIM is amenable to mathematical evaluation in the dimensions of interest. For example, the real-time feasibility of the user model expressed with CHESS, can be ascertained by transforming its PSM into a model artefact fit for input to MAST [21], an open-source tool to perform schedulability analysis in accord with state-of-the-art scheduling theory. That very same PSM is also used to generate code that provably conforms to the run-time semantics assumed in schedulability analysis, which is another important obligation required to claim correctness by construction in the eventual implementation product.

The CHESS method is enacted by a tool-chain that implements the sought extent of CbyC by supporting:

- Automated analysis of extra-functional properties (e.g., predictability and dependability) claimed for assemblies of components;
- Direct propagation of the analysis results back to the user model (by backward traversal of the transformation chain from the analysed artefact to the originating PIM artefacts) so that the user would have all elements to iterate the model to satisfaction, before committing it [5];

- Automated generation of implementation code and deployment on the target platform provably consistent to the PSM submitted to analysis, and transitively, to the user model in the PIM space.

3.1   Modelling Extra-Functional Properties

Real-time Concerns. The component model and model annotation concept needed to pursue CbyC in a component-based approach, first sketched in the ASSERT project, was refined, extended and consolidated in CHESS. The intent was to support the definition of software building blocks (i.e., components) owning pure functional and reusable behaviour, using UML, and the annotation of model elements with extra-functional (especially, real-time) attributes, using MARTE [14].

Every individual operation that appears in the provided interface of a component instance (hence, candidate to become part of a deployable system) must be decorated with real-time attributes that specify the guarantees that other components using that provided operation may assume for its real-time behaviour. For a real-time embedded system, those attributes are determined assuming a particular allocation of the component instance to a given executing platform, inclusive the component infrastructure, the real-time operating system, the communication drivers, and the board support package for the target processor.

Interestingly, using UML and MARTE for the specification of those interface attributes undermined our quest for CbyC in subtle yet important ways. For one thing, UML and MARTE offer different constructs to convey the same meaning: this freedom is a source of confusion for the user and may cause inconsistency to creep in the model if not prevented by dedicated tool support (in the model editor, in the model representation, in the model repository). The solution to this kind of problem is to define specific UML and MARTE profiles, which set appropriate constraints to avoid unwanted specification overlaps. In fact, profiles are also essential to fix the semantic variation points intrinsically available in the original specifications for UML and MARTE.

The CHESS profile chose to augment the UML component model with MARTE, so as to provide the user model with the ability to express rich component interfaces and ports, decorated with real-time attributes. The alternative would have been to use low-level extra-functional resources like schedulable or protected resources directly in the user model, but that would have caused mixing multiple levels of abstraction in a single modelling space, which is obviously undesirable.

CHESS followed the OMG model-driven architecture approach, using elements of MARTE in the high-level, more abstract, platform-independent model, solely MARTE in the low-level, implementation-oriented, platform-specific model, and automated transformations capable of deriving the MARTE representation of the PSM starting from the information contents present in the PIM.

Dependability Concerns. Dependability was a further dimension of interest to CHESS, in the exploration of extending CbyC to extra-functional concerns. A technique called Failure Logic Analysis (FLA) was developed to this end, to enable the specification of *safety contracts*, in the form of failure-propagation rules (i.e., stipulated mechanisms) between input and output ports of specific components. The assumption/ guarantee relations determined for safety contracts by binding required interfaces to provides interfaces was expressed in CHESS with the Fault Propagation and Transformation Calculus (FPTC) formalism [22]. FPTC analysis analyses system-level behaviour, reasoning compositionally on the behaviour of individual components considered in isolation (in fact, on the safety contracts expressed on their provided interfaces). With that provision, CHESS enables the reuse of safety artefacts within safety-critical systems [23], an interesting ramification of CbyC in the realm of reuse.

4 SafeCer: Adding Contract-Based Refinements

To allow experimenting with contract-based development processes, which was the focus of the SafeCer project [19], we augmented the CHESS toolset with OCRA (Othello Contracts Refinement Analysis) [20]. OCRA supports checking the refinement of contracts specified in a linear-time temporal logic. The OCRA specification language allows expressing discrete as well as metric real-time constraints. The underlying reasoning engine allows checking whether the contract refinement (on the guarantee side of the assume/guarantee pair) is correct.

Contract-based refinement enables compositional reasoning that strengthens the verification of components. When used in conjunction with hierarchical decomposition of architectural components, the contracts set on the parent component are refined with contracts set on the child components: if the refinement steps are proven correct, any implementation of the leaf components that satisfies the leaf component contracts can be used to implement the system. The verification is therefore compositional and conducive to early verification of incomplete (partial) architecture specifications.

The integration of OCRA in the CHESS toolset [7] provides a framework that assists the user throughout the entire development process: starting from the description of the system and its hierarchical decomposition, the definition of requirements associated to components and the formalization of requirements as contracts, through a stepwise refinement process with explicit verification of contract refinements and of component implementations.

However, no automation or wizard tool or method currently exists, which is capable of devising a feasible system decomposition and contract refinement, where feasibility is one (arguably essential) dimension of correctness when extra-functional concerns enter the picture: at the present state of the art, this depends entirely on human engineering experience. All that technology aids can offer in this regard for now is to measure the goodness (i.e., fitness for purpose) of a proposed solution against given criteria, and consequently rank alternative decompositions and refinements. The deficient part is an efficient method for proposing solutions, which one might perhaps conjecture as the analogous of genetic algorithms [28] applied to this problem domain.

A system development process normally crosses multiple levels of abstraction (e.g., between system and software), each expressed with its own conceptual model(s). Classic examples of this progression include the functional architecture at the high level, and the physical architecture at the low level, with software specification and deployment configuration to unite the two.

Formally-verified stepwise refinement may in principle be performed at each level of abstraction. On the transition from one level of abstraction to the next (e.g. from system to software architecture), however, entirely new models may have to be created, using the formalisms, the concepts and the notations proper of that level. When that happens, the trace relation in place between corresponding entities at different conceptual levels become the sole link that contract refinement can traverse. Unfortunately, establishing the link that relates corresponding model entities of different conceptual levels is the responsibility of the user: no automated formal verification can be applied (at the present state of the art) to ascertain correctness without semantic knowledge of the respective conceptual models. This is a tremendously complex problem, which reveals a break in desired continuity of the CbyC connotation of the development process.

Interestingly, when applied in the face of the re-use of existing qualified components, the formally-verified stepwise refinement process just evoked may take on a *correctness-by-correction* connotation (less pure and attractive than Dijkstra's CbyC), as a result of verification failures. This is generally the case when the development process is not a mere top-down progression, but involves iterations and re-work prompted by bottom-up feedback. The important aspect, however, is that, with the CbyC-geared provisions discussed so far, the re-work is limited to the models and the relevant contracts, without involving costly *human* retries of the implementation.

5   Further Challenges

The CONCERTO project [17], funded by the ARTEMIS JU, extended the CHESS model-based methodology and language to:

- Allow the user to include multi-core processors among the possible target platforms, with the same level of CbyC guarantees as had for traditional single-core processor targets;
- Widen the coverage of industrial application domain needs.

In the following, we briefly review some of the challenges that those goals presented, and the main results that were achieved in the regard of the CbyC focus of this work.

5.1   Addressing Multi-Core Processor Platforms

One distinctive character that CONCERTO inherited from CHESS is strong emphasis on supporting model-based feasibility analysis and back propagation of the analysis results to the user model [26]. The intent of the former is to allow consolidation of the user model by advancing feasibility analysis (as part of the real-time concerns) so that the implementation product to be deployed on the target platform is assuredly satisfactory. The intent of the latter was to mend the divide between the way analysis results are conveyed by specialized analysis tools (which use their own concepts) and their meaning on the individual constituents of the user model. Back propagation walks backward the transformation relations between the implementation model (PSM) and the user model (PIM), and attaches analysis findings (such as the response time for the operations and the utilization percentage of the HW component instances) obtained for PSM artefacts to the PIM artefacts from which they originate. In that manner, the user has a more direct perception of what needs to be fixed in the model to achieve feasibility and the costs of the correctness-by-correction distortion of CbyC are lowered.

CONCERTO extends CHESS in these two respects by supporting a wider range of advanced feasibility analysis (including of course for multi-core processor targets) and by enriching back-propagation with observation data obtained from the run-time environment. The latter feature aims to aid the user in the timing characterisation of applications run on novel multi-core processors, for which the real-time systems community acknowledges as necessary to refine the (otherwise poor) accuracy of state-of-the-art timing analysis techniques [27].

Worst-case execution time (WCET) analysis for multi-core processors is an open research problem, with numerous research actions investigating it. CONCERTO does not perform WCET research, but rather approaches the timing verification problem from the angle of feasibility analysis, which is the next level up in the verification process. Schedulability analysis for multi-core processors is challenged in several respects:

1. The need to get WCET bounds for individual application programs, capable of accounting, soundly and tightly, for the contention overhead resulting from parallel execution on multiple cores, which is a research topic of unprecedented difficulty. The obvious (but highly penalizing) countermeasure to this problem is to schedule the system so that only one core is active at any one time, losing $m - 1$ of the m available cores.

2. The need to determine a sound and tight bound on the run-time overhead incurred from the extent of task migration caused by non-strictly-partitioned scheduling algorithms, and by the repercussion that migration has on the WCET bounds of the migrating task, e.g., by losing warm caches across the memory hierarchy. The obvious (but highly penalizing) countermeasure to this problem is to use strictly partitioned scheduling for the system, losing much (> 50%) in schedulable utilization.

The ideal CbyC progression of system development breaks in front of challenges of this hardness, whereby correctness-by-correction becomes the only way forward. Acknowledging this predicament in the multi-core processor domain, CONCERTO adopts a "round-trip analysis methodology". It uses run-time data (drawn from observation of the actual application execution in its run-time environment and the comparison with the initial model assumptions and analysis results) to increase the confidence in the prediction of model-based analysis; and run-time monitoring to ensure that possible violations are detected and – where possible – mitigated. Design failures (specifically, solutions that do not meet their extra-functional requirements) continue to be possible, but they are detected early enough, and managed accordingly.

Figure 1 captures the main steps of the CONCERTO methodology, which we also itemize below in narrative.

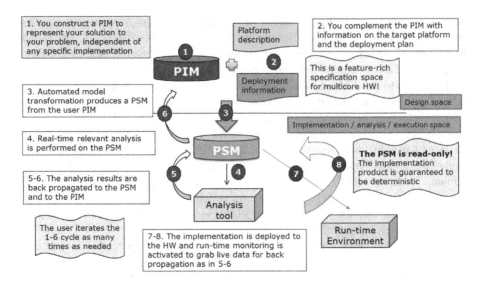

Fig. 1. The CONCERTO process

1. Define the PIM to represent the solution, independent of any specific platform implementation;
2. Complement the PIM with information on the target platform and on the deployment plan: this is a feature-rich specification space for multi-core HW;
3. Apply automated model transformation to produce a PSM from the PIM. The PSM is read-only and the implementation product is guaranteed to be deterministic;
4. Perform relevant real-time analysis on the PSM;
5. Back propagate analysis results to the PSM and to the PIM;
6. Iterate steps 1 to 5 as many times as needed, until a satisfactory solution is achieved;
7. Deploy the implementation on the target hardware;
8. Activate run-time monitoring to grab live data that is back propagated to the PSM and to the PIM (as in 5).

By accompanying the developer through every step of the way, from presenting clean, uncluttered, single-concern design spaces to providing constant, informative verification feedback to the modelling actions, CONCERTO promotes a disciplined, productive development experience, which yields concrete, platform-specific implementations with high-integrity runtime guarantees.

5.2 Cross-Domain Extensions: Automotive

While CHESS set the foundation of a cross-domain model-driven development method and language centred on CbyC, the experience made in CONCERTO revealed how difficult it is to keep a controlled balance between core (hence, transversal) elements, and domain-specific extensions in the quest for larger domain coverage. The problem one soon faces in that endeavour is that each domain is likely to have its own baggage of "preferred" ingredient (languages, methods, practices, conventions) whose presence is seen as a mandatory element in any solutions candidate for industrial adoption.

A clear manifestation of this problem occurred to us while investigating the viability of fitting CONCERTO to the automotive domain practices. In that effort, we attempted to parallel the AUTOSAR [24] and the CONCERTO development approaches, for methodology and component model, with focus on functional and real-time concerns.

We first mapped the entities defined in the CONCERTO component model to semantically equivalent entities available in AUTOSAR. Out of that, we were able to devise sound model transformations from CONCERTO to AUTOSAR. The opposite direction was a problem, however, as the AUTOSAR component model is considerably richer in constructs and in "modelling freedom" than CONCERTO. The net consequence is that not all AUTOSAR models find correspondence in a legal CONCERTO models, for syntax and for semantics. This taught us that AUTOSAR has less attention than CONCERTO in fostering CbyC by means of constraints placed on what to model, how to model it, and when in the development flow. One particular exemplar of this difference in intent is worth recalling here. CONCERTO sets restrictions on the component model (directly in the modelling language and modelling actions availed to the user) to ensure that the chosen forms of feasibility analysis can always be performed *soundly* on the user model that is decorated with sufficient information attributes. This is necessary to ensure that the model transformation that uses the user model to feed the analysis can be proven correct by construction, i.e., such that the semantic meaning of each analysis artefact and analysis operation corresponds to the semantic meaning of the modelling artefact and decoration attribute in the user model. For instance, in CONCERTO, a provided operation that is attached to a thread at run time, can only receive release events from a single source (a clock, an external interrupt, another thread, etc.). This restriction causes the run-time semantics of that operation to conform to the abstraction of thread in feasibility analysis. AUTOSAR lifts that restriction, so that the run-time semantics of operations specified in the user model is *not* guaranteed, by construction, to be statically analysable for feasibility.

The bottom line of the experiment is that a complete (for process coverage and for automation) bi-directional integration between CONCERTO and AUTOSAR is presently not possible without unsatisfactory compromises. This is product of the confrontation between the rigidity of seeking adhesion to the CbyC principles (manifest in CONCERTO), and the permissiveness of wanting to assist without imposing too much perceived burden on the user (manifest in AUTOSAR).

6 Lessons Learned and Conclusions

The ASSERT and the CHESS development processes and modelling steps had a strong connotation of CbyC ingrained in them. This trait manifested in a number of constraints being applied to remove (i.e., statically resolve) semantic variation points originally present in the language substrate used to express model artefacts (i.e., UML and MARTE), and to propagate those constraints upward into the model editor, so that the user is actively guided into "doing the right thing".

SafeCer augmented the CHESS heritage with a rigorous stepwise contract refinement approach for system and software design. This effort however showed that decompositions and refinements may occasionally have a more *tentative* nature than assertive (as presumed in CbyC, where the refinement is guided by the need for conformance), which may therefore fail and require backtracks, as in correctness-by-correction.

In CONCERTO, we observed two phenomena of interest. First, the wider the sought coverage of non-contiguous industrial domains, the more difficult the application of CbyC, in accord with its original intent and course. Second, when what determines correctness in a particular dimension of concern (e.g., feasibility on a multi-core processor platform) is not solid enough in the state of the art, the verification of correctness can only be done retrospectively: not enough prescriptions (design and implementation recipes, if you will) are known to causally warrant correctness, to guide development in a top-down fashion.

In CONCERTO the satisfaction of some (modelling and semantic) constraints had to be deferred to later stages, enabled by ad-hoc transformations toward specialized analyses (e.g., for dependability, conformance to given restrictions, feasibility in the time domain), with consequent deflection of CbyC into correctness-by-correction. When a model transformation needs to take place to enable verification, then the modelling infrastructure defers to the user for explicit action and for discipline of method. The act of requesting a verification is up to the user. Hence, the method no longer is a tool-assisted (in fact, enforced) traversal of design steps that follow a rigid ordering with CbyC guarantees.

Acknowledgements. This work has been partially supported by ARTEMIS-JU grants for the CONCERTO [17], CHESS [18] and SafeCer [19] projects. The considerations represented in this work are the authors' only and do not engage the opinions of the other project members, whose contributions however we acknowledge.

References

1. Amey, P.: Correctness by Construction, Praxis High Integrity Systems Ltd., 05 December 2006. https://buildsecurityin.us-cert.gov/articles/knowledge/sdlc-process/correctness-by-construction. Accessed 22 Jan 2016
2. Kourie, D.G., Watson, B.W.: The Correctness-by-Construction Approach to Programming. Springer, Heidelberg (2012)
3. Sifakis, J.: Embedded systems - challenges and work directions. In: Higashino, T. (ed.) OPODIS 2004. LNCS, vol. 3544, pp. 184–185. Springer, Heidelberg (2005)
4. Bordin, M., Vardanega, T.: Correctness by construction for high-integrity real-time systems: a metamodel-driven approach. In: Abdennadher, N., Kordon, F. (eds.) Ada-Europe 2007. LNCS, vol. 4498, pp. 114–127. Springer, Heidelberg (2007)
5. Cancila, D., Passerone, R., Vardanega, T.: Composability for high-integrity real-time embedded systems. In. Proceedings of the First Workshop on Compositional Theory and Technology for Real-Time Embedded Systems (CRTS 2008), Barcelona, Spain. ACM/IEEE, 30 November 2008

6. Mazzini S., Puri S., Veran G., Vardanega T., Panunzio M., Santamaria C., Zovi A.: Model-driven and component-based engineering with the CHESS methodology. In: Proceedings of DASIA Conference, Malta, May 2011

7. Baracchi, L., Cimatti, A., Garcia, G., Mazzini, S., Puri, S., Tonetta, S.: Requirements refinement and component reuse: the FoReVer contract-based approach. In: Bagnato, A., Quadri, I.R., Rossi, M., Indrusiak, L.S. (eds.) Industry and Research Perspectives on Embedded System Design. IGI Global, Hershey (2014)

8. Benveniste, A., Caillaud, B., Nickovic, D., Passerone, R., Raclet, J.B., Reinkemeier, P., Sangiovanni-Vincentelli, A., Damm, W., Henzinger, T., Larsen, K.: Contracts for Systems Design

9. Chapman, R.: Correctness by construction: a manifesto for high integrity software. In: Proceedings of the 10th Australian Workshop on Safety Critical Systems and Software, vol. 55, Sydney, Australia

10. Panunzio, M., Vardanega, T.: A component-based process with separation of concerns for the development of embedded real-time software systems. J. Syst. Softw. **96**, 105–121 (2014)

11. Schmidt, D.: Guest editor's introduction: model-driven engineering. Computer **39**(2), 25–31 (2006)

12. Dijkstra, E.: On the role of scientific thought. In: Dijkstra, E. (ed.) Selected Writings on Computing: A personal Perspective. Texts and Monographs in Computer Science, pp. 60–66. Springer, New York (1982)

13. Panunzio, M., Vardanega, T.: Ada ravenscar code archetypes for component-based development. In: Brorsson, M., Pinho, L.M. (eds.) Ada-Europe 2012. LNCS, vol. 7308, pp. 1–17. Springer, Heidelberg (2012)

14. The Object Management Group: UML Profile for MARTE: Modeling and analysis of real-time embedded systems (2011). http://www.omg.org/spec/MARTE/1.1/. Accessed 22 Jan 2016

15. Estivill-Castro, V., Hexel R.: Correctness by construction with logic-labeled finite-state machines – comparison with event-B. In: 2014 23rd Australian Software Engineering Conference (ASWEC), pp. 38–47, 7–10 April 2014

16. Anand, M., Fischmeister, S., Kim, J., Lee, I.: Generating sound and resource-aware code from hybrid systems models. In: Broy, M., Krüger, I.H., Meisinger, M. (eds.) ASWSD 2006. LNCS, vol. 4922, pp. 48–66. Springer, Heidelberg (2008)

17. CONCERTO Project: Guaranteed component assembly with round trip analysis for energy efficient high-integrity multi-core systems. Artemis Call 2012 333053. http://www.concerto-project.org/. Accessed 22 Jan 2016

18. CHESS Project: Composition with guarantees for high-integrity embedded software components assembly. http://www.chess-project.org/. Accessed 5 May 2015

19. SafeCer Project: Safety certification of software-intensive systems with reusable components. http://safecer.eu/. Accessed 22 Jan 2016

20. OCRA: A command-line tool for the verification of logic-based contract refinement for embedded systems. https://es-static.fbk.eu/tools/ocra/. 22 Jan 2016

21. MAST: Modeling and analysis suite for real-time applications. http://mast.unican.es/. Accessed 22 Jan 2016

22. Wallace, M.: Modular architectural representation and analysis of fault propagation and transformation. Electron. Notes Theoret. Comput. Sci. (ENTCS) **141**(3), 53–71 (2005)

23. Sljivo, I., Gallina, B., Carlson, J., Hansson, H., Puri, S.: A method to generate reusable safety case fragments from compositional safety analysis. In: Schaefer, I., Stamelos, I. (eds.) ICSR 2015. LNCS, vol. 8919, pp. 253–268. Springer, Heidelberg (2014)

24. AUTOSAR: Software architecture specification. http://www.autosar.org. Accessed 22 Jan 2016
25. Crnkovic, I.: Component-based software engineering for embedded systems. In: ICSE 2005, pp. 712–713 (2005)
26. Cicchetti, A., Ciccozzi, F., Mazzini, S., Puri, S., Panunzio, M., Zovi, A., Vardanega, T.: CHESS: a model-driven engineering tool environment for aiding the development of complex industrial systems. In: ASE 2012, pp. 362–365 (2012)
27. Baker, T.P.: What to make of multicore processors for reliable real-time systems? In: Real, J., Vardanega, T. (eds.) Ada-Europe 2010. LNCS, vol. 6106, pp. 1–18. Springer, Heidelberg (2010)
28. Srinivas, M., Patnaik, L.M.: Genetic algorithms: a survey. Computer **27**(6), 17–26 (1994). doi:10.1109/2.294849
29. Romanovsky, A., Thomas, M.: Industrial Deployment of System Engineering Methods. Springer, Heidelberg (2013). doi:10.1007/978-3-642-33170-1

Extension of the Ocarina Tool Suite to Support Reliable Replication-Based Fault-Tolerance

Wafa Gabsi[1(✉)], Bechir Zalila[1], and Mohamed Jmaiel[1,2]

[1] ReDCAD, University of Sfax, B.P. 1173, 3038 Sfax, Tunisia
wafa.gabsi@redcad.org, bechir.zalila@enis.tn,
mohamed.jmaiel@enis.rnu.tn
[2] Digital Research Center of Sfax Technopark of Sfax,
B.P. 275, Sakiet Ezzit, 3021 Sfax, Tunisia

Abstract. Replication is a reliability technique that involves redundancy of software or hardware components to guarantee availability for fault tolerance purposes. Several studies focused on modelling fault tolerance of real-time embedded systems using replication of AADL (*Architecture Analysis & Design Language*) components. Manual replication with AADL is a tedious task, error-prone and increases design time.

To support the automatic replication of AADL components, we propose in this paper an extension of the AADL Ocarina tool suite. For that, based on a set of transformation rules, we assist the designer to automatically generate standard AADL models enriched with variants and adjudicators. This is based on a three-step model driven approach. First, we enable the designer to model his or her core application using AADL. Second, the designer enriches the model with a property set that we defined to describe replication concepts. Finally, applying a set of transformation rules, we generate an intermediate AADL model enriched with different replicas using Ocarina. This generated model can be analysed, formally verified, used for application code generation or even replication of other components. To illustrate our approach, we apply an active replication to a robot system chosen as a case study.

Keywords: Fault-tolerance · Replication · AADL modelling · Ocarina · Active replication · Passive replication

1 Introduction

With the evolution of distributed real-time embedded systems, new requirements for high dependability and fault tolerance are emerging. These requirements have to be satisfied at design time since that systems can address critical domains like avionics, space and medicine. Such systems must be highly dependable in order to increase their performance, effectiveness and reliability. In this context, some work [13,14] provide design supports of fault tolerance techniques dedicated to such systems such as model weaving or passive replication applied to AADL models. But such techniques do not offer neither automatic code generation of

© Springer International Publishing Switzerland 2016
M. Bertogna et al. (Eds.): Ada-Europe 2016, LNCS 9695, pp. 129–144, 2016.
DOI: 10.1007/978-3-319-39083-3_9

fault tolerance elements nor reuse of such techniques which may help to avoid significant number of failures for dependability purposes.

We proposed in previous work [4], a development process for the design and the implementation of fault tolerant reconfigurable real-time systems. In our work, we ensured separation of concerns at the model level as well as generated code level. We used AADLv2 (`Architecture Analysis & Design Language, version 2`) to model the core system and its Error Model Annex [17] to model fault tolerance requirements. This annex not only allows designers to model different kinds of faults, but also fault propagation affecting related components, fault behaviour, fault detection as well as fault recovery mechanisms. This annex provides strong support for fault tolerance elements and more general dependability requirements. However, it does not support automatic redundancy, a well-known technique used to achieve fault tolerance in distributed real-time embedded systems. It relies on manually-specified redundancy of AADL components, connections, and behaviours. However, the more the replicas or the replicated components we have, the more complex and error prone the model is. Thus, supporting automatic replication of AADL components would be an important contribution and very considerable to assist the designer modelling the fault tolerant system by integrating replication techniques from the design phase.

In this paper, we present an approach relying on automatic replication of AADL components since the design level. We propose a model driven approach based on an AADL model extension and automatic code generation of both active and passive replication. Therefore, the workload of the designer is minimized to only indicating the original component subject to replication, specifying the replication style (active or passive) and setting the number of variants. In addition, the designer has to define the consensus algorithm for each replicated component. These concepts have to be set by the designer through a set of properties. After specifying all properties, the designer validates them before automatically generating an intermediate AADL model enriched with different variants and adjudicators. To ensure the model generation process, we define a set of transformation rules, in order to map between the basic AADL model and its extended version with replication concepts. The mapping process concerns the generation of either new components (like variants and adjudicators) or connections between original and generated ones. It treats also the behaviours of the variants and adjudicators relying on user defined properties. These rules are first manually established and then translated into algorithms that we implemented to ensure model transformation. We implemented these rules as an extension of the Ocarina tool suite [10] as it is dedicated to perform analysis and verification on AADL models. Therefore, we ensure the separation of concerns at design level as well as at application level. We provide better code quality and modularity. This separation also enables the validation of either model or code application without affecting each other. Using Ocarina, we ensure model analysis, verification of the resulting AADL model, and generation of its corresponding application code (into Ada, C or RTSJ). Thus, we benefit from the reusable aspects of our extension.

The remainder of this paper is structured as follows: Sect. 2 discusses the related work. Section 3 provides then background concepts related to AADL language, Ocarina tool suite and finally replication. In Sect. 4, we introduce our replication-based fault tolerance approach and we give details about the defined property set, the transformation rules and the extension of the Ocarina tool suite. Then, we validate our approach by a case study in Sect. 5. Finally, conclusions and a road-map for future work are given in Sect. 6.

2 Related Work

A survey of software techniques to handle software faults developed in the fault tolerance and the autonomic computing domains was given in [2]. As these techniques are all practically exploiting some form of redundancy, they considered the impact of replication on the software architecture.

In particular, authors in [7], extended the framework FT-CORBA (Fault-Tolerant CORBA) with support of fault-tolerance mechanisms such as fault detection and redundancy. They also proposed a modelling process, based on UML with CCM (CORBA Component Model) as well as the QoS & FT (Quality of Service and Fault Tolerance) profile, in order to be able to design fault tolerance components and generate their corresponding code. After that, this model is deployed and executed by means of CCM descriptor files. Yet, this approach is not well adapted to dynamically reconfigurable systems. Also, the authors restricted their tests to a unique replication style that is the active replication with voting.

Authors in [3] applied redundancy patterns in the architecture design level using Aspect Oriented Paradigm. They focused on weaving an original architecture model with redundancy related design patterns. This approach aims at separating functional and non-functional design. The base model is designed using UML. Then, an aspect model is integrated within the base one using a model weaver. Thus, reusable fault tolerance and redundancy management mechanisms together with their specific analysis sub-models were available in the form of a design pattern library. Based also on UML designs, authors in [1] propose MARTE-DAM (MARTE-Dependability Analysis and Modelling): a profile which extends the MARTE (UML Modeling and Analysis of Real-Time and Embedded systems profile) to support the dependability modelling and quantitative analysis. Unlike several works aiming at extending UML models with dependability annotations, this profile covers different dependability aspects through rich domain models. The defined domain concepts are then mapped to elements of the UML profile. In particular, a redundancy model introduces fault tolerant components which can provide a redundant structure such as variants, adjudicators, and FT strategies. For performance and dependability analysis and assessment purposes, authors translated the annotated MARTE-DAM into DSPN (Deterministic and Stochastic Petri Nets) models. They highlighted model refinement and dependability assessment but they did not support code generation for MARTE-DAM.

While UML, without using the MARTE profile, is not well adapted to design real-time embedded systems and AADL has sufficiently proved its power in this domain, a significant number of works have been proposed as solutions for designing replication with AADL. In [13], authors proposed an approach to model and to formally verify replication patterns in the AADL language and then analyse potentially unintended behaviours. This approach is based on designing two AADL models. The first defines the intended behaviour in synchronous call sequences and the second describes the replication architecture. This approach supports only the primary-backup replication using AADL based on modes and mode transitions. It limits also the number of variants. It proposes only two replicas: one primary and one backup unlike our approach which does not fix the number of replicas. The designer can vary this number when needed. In [9], authors gave an example of a manual primary-backup replication strategy designed with AADL and its Behavioural Annex (AADL-BA). They modelled the core system using AADL components and their connections through features. Threads in this case are synchronized using dispatched events. Then, based on AADL-BA, they modelled the automaton showing different states where the application can be blocked to describe the executed call sequences of different threads. They proved also that AADL-BA provides an interesting additional strategy to define critical regions.

The difference between this approach and ours is that it focuses only on passive replication while we support both replication styles. In addition, this work challenges resides in the modelling of complex synchronization mechanisms commonly used in distributed system design such as mutual exclusion. Besides, designers who applied this approach must manually specify both their core system and the replication pattern. There are no automatic tasks to help them generate a consistent model contrary to our approach that facilitates the replication design through automatic generation of variants and adjudicators.

Most of the stated work deal with manual replication addressing only one style (active or passive replication). However, manually modelling replication not only can increase the risk of errors on the design time but also needs considerable efforts especially when it introduces a significant number of variants and/or replicated components. Using our extension of the Ocarina tool suite based on properties, designers can significantly reduce design time and risk of errors especially in case of large number of replicas or replicated components. Besides, the designer benefits from the variable number of variants and the two supported replication styles.

3   Background

3.1   Overview of AADL

AADL [16] is a standard consisting of both textual and graphical representations with precise execution semantics for embedded software systems. AADL is a typed language providing formal modeling concepts to design the runtime architectures of complex embedded real-time systems and the map of software components onto hardware ones. All hardware (`device`, `processor`, `memory` and `bus`), software (`process`, `thread`, `subprogram` and `data`) or hybrid (`system`) AADL components correspond to concrete entities, which is why AADL is a concrete language. Each of these components can be connected to others through features. These features contain event and data ports, subprogram access, data access and bus access, among others. Moreover, AADL can be extended with properties to specify characteristics of a component within its architectural context. AADL annex libraries enable a designer to extend and customize the AADL core specification with other concepts specified in a language other than AADL. For example, we enrich an AADL model with clauses from Error Model Annex [17] to describe dependability requirements or from Behavioral Annex [15] to express components behavior. Besides, AADL provides a support to describe operational modes of a system and then manages dynamic reconfiguration. Modes and mode transitions describe the reconfiguration processes of existing components. A mode represents an operational state, which manifests itself as a configuration of contained components, connections, and mode-specific property value associations. However, a configuration is statically defined and consists of a set of components linked with connections.

3.2 Ocarina

Ocarina [10] is an open source tool suite of the AADL language written in Ada. In addition to the lexical, syntactic and semantic analysis of AADL models, Ocarina allows the code generation into different languages such as Ada and C. Besides, this tool supports scheduling analysis of AADL models with Cheddar [18] based on both real-time scheduling theory and queuing system theory. Ocarina offers also the transformation of AADL models into LNT language [12]. The Ocarina compiler can be easily extended thanks to its well organized architecture as shown in Fig. 1. It is composed of three main parts:

- A central library used to build and manipulate syntactic trees. It consists of a set of builder and finder routines. This part allows the frontends and backends to manipulate and analyse syntactic trees of any supported language.
- A set of frontends that analyse the syntax and semantics of AADL models extended with annexes. Each of these annexes is related to a frontend part. The output of frontends is an abstract syntactic tree generated using routines defined in the central library.
- A set of backends dedicated to automatically produce code. Their inputs are AADL trees obtained from the frontends. This part enriches received trees and produces more structured and richer trees to generate appropriate code.

3.3 Replication

Replication is a well-known technique to achieve fault tolerance [6]. It is defined as the redundancy of software, hardware or both parts. This technique involves repetition and multiplicity of different or identical components or behaviors in order to mitigate the effects of component failures and then create a system

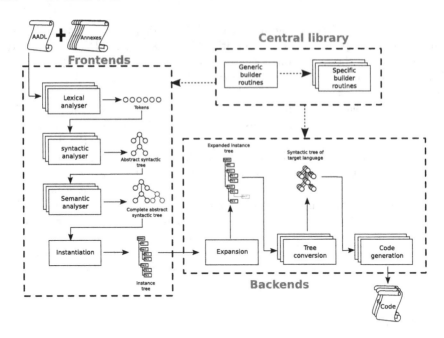

Fig. 1. Architecture of OCARINA [10]

more reliable than a single component. Thus, critical hardware or software components, or even entire systems, can be replicated. Three main replication techniques are distinguished in the literature [14]:

1. *Active replication*: all replicas have the same input, keeping their internal state synchronized and voting all on the same output. In this case, we must have a voting algorithm to choose one between all outputs.
2. *Passive or primary-backup replication*: Only one replica, called primary copy, can handle the input. When the primary copy fails, one of the others, called backup copies, is elected to take its place to provide the same functionality.
3. *Semi-Active replication*: It consists of a replica group containing a leader replica (primary copy) and one or more follower replicas (backup copies). Similar to the active one, all replicas receive the same input and can treat them. However, similar to the passive replication, only the leader is responsible for processing a request and taking decisions. The leader processes a request as soon as it receives it, whereas backup copies must wait for notification from the leader to handle a request.

There is a trade-off between active and passive replication techniques [11]. Each of them has its own advantages and drawbacks. In active replication, all the copies should process the request, so it costs more system resource than passive replication. But a crash of the primary copy in passive replication, may significantly increase the latency of an invocation. Moreover, passive replication

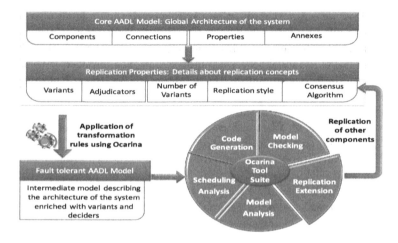

Fig. 2. Replication design process

requires additional support for the primary copy to update the state of the other copies. Furthermore, passive replication provides a less predictable and generally slower response time than the active one. Finally, the passive replication is more flexible as it does not require the synchronisation between the replicas.

4   Overview of the Approach

We propose in this section a model driven approach based on model transformation to ensure replication-based fault tolerance for distributed real-time embedded systems. Our idea is to assist the designer modelling his or her system by automation of the replication design. This is by encapsulating the needed replication parameters into a property set and then integrating it in the base model through a model transformation. Doing so, the designer has to model the core system with AADL and then set the parameters needed to automatically generate the replication such as the replication style, the replica number and the agreement algorithm using a property set. Then, a model transformation is performed in order to generate a new model enriched with variants and adjudicators. As shown in Fig. 2, we propose a design process to produce an extension of an existing tool to support replication of AADL components based on our defined property set baptised `Replication_Properties`. The steps of the proposed process are described in the following.

We start from a core AADL specification model describing an embedded system. The designer models the core application using AADL and enriches her/his model with properties and annexes. For example, the designer can extend his model with clauses from the Error Model Annex [17] to describe fault tolerance requirements. This annex lets us design all kinds of faults, fault behaviour, fault propagation, fault detection and also fault recovery mechanisms. Nevertheless, this annex does not support replication. At this level, the designer also enriches his model with our property set defined to integrate replication concepts.

After specifying the set of replication properties, we apply a model transformation on the core model to get an intermediate one enriched with replicas. It consists in a direct-manipulation M2M (Model To Model) transformation to integrate replication policies to the core model in order to save efforts and reduce errors. Based on an automatic build and modification of models when possible, we aim at applying a set of transformation rules to get a new enriched model that has to be itself consistent and coherent.

The model transformation is ensured by a set of transformation rules defined and implemented within an existing tool. We propose, in this paper, the extension of the Ocarina tool suite to support the analysis and the generation of the replication properties. As we have already mentioned in Sect. 3.2, Ocarina is a powerful tool supporting analysis and verification of AADL models. In addition, the Ocarina tool is designed and implemented around a modular architecture that can be easily extended to support analysis of the replication properties as well as replication code generation. For that, we extended Ocarina in order to automatically generate replicas. We enriched the existing compiler with a backend part to expand the original model with variants, adjudicators and establish necessary connections. Finally, once the intermediate model is automatically generated by Ocarina, the designer can then apply different analyses. On one hand, the designer can use Ocarina again either to formally verify or analyse the generated model using its Petri nets backend or to produce the application code into Ada or C. On the other hand, the designer can in turn use Replication_Properties to specify the replication of another hardware, software or hybrid component of the system. Thus, we enable the designer to have the benefit of all analysis and verification tools offered by Ocarina to manipulate AADL models especially the fault tolerant ones.

In the following, we detail the description of the replication property set and the extension of the Ocarina tool suite to support it.

4.1   Description of the Property Set

To set replication requirements, we defined an AADL property set baptised Replication_Properties [5]. We help the user to simply express the replication expect using a set of properties in order to specify the desired replicated architecture as explained above:

- **Description.** The designer gives details about the purpose of replication, its manner or its requirements. This property provides information about the context of replication without any impact on the replication policies.
- Our approach allows supporting several replicated components even in a single model through the defined property **Replica_Number** applied to a given replicated component. This property represents the number of replicas that we intend to model.

- We defined a property named **Replica_Identifiers** in order to identify each of the generated replicas.
- We are interested in our context in both active and passive replication of hardware, software and even hybrid components. For that, we have defined a property called **Replica_Type** to describe the adopted style of replication. Such a property specifies the associated replication type to a given replicated component. The value of this property may be either PASSIVE or ACTIVE.
- **Consensus (agreement) algorithm**: It is required in two cases related to the replication style. The first is to elect from one or more secondary copies a new primary copy in case of failure of the current one. This is in the context of passive replication unlike the active one. The latter consists in voting between the different replicas. In both cases, this algorithm can be described via an AADL subprogram component. This subprogram can describe an existing algorithm within the base model or define a new one through a source code file. We can support predefined consensus algorithms like majority voters as well as personalized ones.

All of these properties are required to establish replication mechanisms. They have no default values and have to be explicitly set.

4.2   Model Transformation

As mentioned previously, we propose in this paper a replication-based fault tolerance approach for distributed real-time systems relying on replication at design level. Our idea is to help the designer modelling its system by automation of the replication design using a selective approach. It means that the designer has to encapsulate the needed replication parameters (replication style, replica number, agreement algorithm...) into a property set and then integrate it in the core model. Then, through an automatic model transformation we generate a new AADL model enriched with variants and adjudicators. Then, this model can be subject to model checking, model analysis, code generation or replication of other components.

Regarding the model transformation, it consists in a direct-manipulation M2M transformation to integrate replication policies into the core model. Based on automatic generation, we apply a set of transformation rules to get a new enriched model that has to be itself consistent and coherent. The transformation rules, to map the replication concepts into the enriched AADL model, depend on various constraints listed hereafter.

Supported AADL Components: The objective of our research work is to meet dependability requirements and to cope with faults since the design level. Numerous research work are carried out to model fault tolerance techniques using AADL. AADL components correspond to concrete software and hardware entities. FT communities (for example in [8]) assert that software and hardware fault tolerance architectures and even implementations are not similarly applicable. In particular, replication of software components is quite different from hardware components. This difference is due to the specific characteristics of each AADL component including their possible features and then the prospective connections that can be established, the containment hierarchy of these components, the modes clauses that can be or cannot be declared and finally the coordination with the adjudicator regarding the AADL hierarchy.

For that, we conducted an in-depth study to explore all possible situations even the complex cases. Then, we have applied the property declarations defined in the `Replication_Properties` property set into only a subset of the AADL components that we find necessary and consistent. For software components, we support the replication of `threads` and `processes` unlike `data` and `subprogram` components as we require in this case to apply diversity concepts and not replication ones [2]. In fact, the **diversity**, specifically developed to tolerate design faults in software arising out of wrong specifications and incorrect coding, aims at providing the same service through a distinct model and/or implementation. The most popular techniques which are based on the design diversity are the Recovery Blocks (RB), the Distributed Recovery Blocks (DRB) and the N-Version Programming (NVP). The second strategy is the distributed nature of the first one which is based on rollback recovery. While the third strategy is based on masking errors and the majority voting to select the correct response. In this case, replication of identical subprograms does not guarantee better reliability from the treatment viewpoint. For that, we do not support replication of `subprogram` nor `data` components. As for hardware components, we support the replication of `processors` and `devices`. We also ensure replication of the hybrid component (`system`). Moreover, the type of features of the replicated component (`ports`, `data access` or `subprogram access`) affects the assumed replication policies. For each feature of replicated component of type `in` out, `out port` or `data access`, we specify its corresponding voter subprogram. That means that the consensus algorithm property is applied to each feature of the replicated component and not to the component itself in the case of active replication contrary to the passive one.

Replication Style: The generated intermediate AADL model enriched by variants and adjudicators strongly depends on the type of replication defined by the property `Replication_Properties::Replica_Type`. The adopted replication policies are not the same in the case of primary-backup or active replication.

- **Active Replication**: The generated model contains `Replica_Number` replicas generated inside the same containment hierarchy of the replicated component. Each of them is then connected directly or remotely to a generated or called adjudicator (voter in this case) depending on the property used to specify the consensus algorithm and the type of the replicated component. Active replication type treats differently all types of components (hardware, software and system).
- **Passive Replication**: Unlike active replication, primary-backup approach does not differentiate between types of component subject to replication. This type of replication, based on the migration between two or more configurations, imposes the generation of `Replica_Number` identical components

supporting the dynamic reconfiguration to obey the adaptation needs. To describe the dynamic behaviour of the runtime architecture, we used the modes and mode transitions concepts provided by the AADL standard.

Consensus Algorithm: we defined a set of properties describing the consensus algorithm which has in turn a significant impact on the generated model. Among a number of variants, the consensus problem (adjudicator) requires agreement for a single data value. Some of the variants may fail or be unreliable in other ways. One approach to generate consensus for all variants, is majority voting. In our case, the consensus algorithm property specifies the way that connects variants to adjudicators even by remote connection in the case of hardware components. For that, we discussed all possible cases of AADL components replication to tolerate both software and hardware faults. The description of the consensus algorithm is set through one of the three properties that we have already defined. This property, applied to the replicated component or to each of its features, is then transformed to an AADL subprogram. To be executed, this subprogram must be called by an already existing or a generated thread. Deployment and timing properties of the generated software components (like `Dispatch_Protocol`, `Period` and `Deadline`) are also considered when applying the transformation rules. Due to space limitation, the issue of the replication overhead that may have on timeliness is not addressed in this paper.

The different transformation algorithms are implemented as an extension of the Ocarina tool suite to support replication mechanisms.

4.3   Extension of the Ocarina Tool Suite

Our approach is developed as an extension of the Ocarina tool suite. Not only, Ocarina can analyze and verify the use of the replication properties but also generate the intermediate AADL model enriched with different variants and adjudicators. This generation process includes:

1. The validation of the properties use. In this part, we check the validity of the use of our property set items using Ocarina. The designer must specify the replica number, which must be bounded between the minimal and the maximal number of replicas. The designer must also specify the type of the replication which is either active or passive.Then, we check the consensus algorithm that must be specified to decide about replicas. All these properties have to be coherent and not redundant.
2. The extraction of the list of properties for each replicated component if all properties are validated. This is ensured by collecting all replication properties specified to one replicated component as a record and then invoking the suitable transformation.
3. The expansion of the base AADL model with replicas. We are able in this case to expand the AADL model with replicas based on transformation rules. This is done by manipulating AADL tree retrieved from the base model. Depending on the type of replicated component and on the selected replication strategy,

a replication algorithm is applied to extend the model by the replication mechanisms. For that we have defined and implemented the transformation rules for each supported component in the replication.

4. The generation of the enriched AADL model (.aadl file) from the expanded AADL tree.

We have implemented the different transformation algorithms as an extension of the Ocarina tool suite to support replication mechanisms. We have validated the developed parts by a set of examples. We verified manually if (1) all requirements are satisfied for each generated component and (2) the performed extensions do not violate the structure and behaviour of the core AADL model. If either a requirement was not met or an extension was not mapped to Ocarina, we went back to the previous step in order to refine it. This activity enabled both the completeness and the consistency checking of the replication extensions mapped into the Ocarina tool suite.

5 Case Study

Several case studies have been performed to validate our development process and to verify the correctness and consistency of our tool suite extension[1].

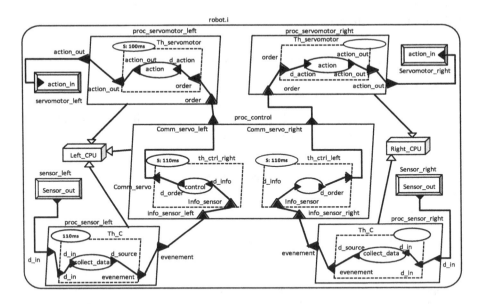

Fig. 3. AADL core model of the robot system

---

[1] More details about this case study, the textual description of its core AADL model as well as generated intermediate models are available at http://goo.gl/QeXJMr. The description of the property set Replication_Properties, the transformation algorithms and other case studies are also given at the same link.

Listing 1.1. Replication of process components in the robot system

```
system implementation robot.i
...
properties
  Replication_Properties :: Description => "Replication_of_the_process_
    component_proc_sensor_right" applies to proc_sensor_right;
  Replication_Properties :: Replica_Number => 2 applies to
    proc_sensor_right;
  Replication_Properties :: Replica_Type => ACTIVE applies to
    proc_sensor_right;
  Replication_Properties :: Replica_Identifiers => ("proc_sensor_right_1",
    "proc_sensor_right_2") applies to proc_sensor_right;
  Replication_Properties :: Consensus_Algorithm_Source_Text => "robot.
    Do_Vote" applies to proc_sensor_right.evenement;
  Replication_Properties :: Description => "Replication_of_the_process_
    component_proc_sensor_left" applies to proc_sensor_left;
  Replication_Properties :: Replica_Number => 2 applies to
    proc_sensor_left;
  Replication_Properties :: Replica_Type => ACTIVE applies to
    proc_sensor_left;
  Replication_Properties :: Replica_Identifiers => ("proc_sensor_left_1","
    proc_sensor_left_2") applies to proc_sensor_left;
  Replication_Properties :: Consensus_Algorithm_Source_Text => "robot.
    Do_Vote" applies to proc_sensor_left.evenement;
end robot.i;
```

To illustrate the effectiveness of our approach, we choose as a case study a robot system. This system has a symmetrical architecture for both right and left sides. It is composed of a set of processes responsible for collecting data (position) from sensors, treating them by a control unit and finally reacting with movements applied by the servomotor. This system is composed of five processes. proc_sensor_left and proc_sensor_right are two processes responsible for collecting data from sensors respectively for the left and right sides of the robot. They send the position of the robot to the proc_control process which is in turn responsible for treating received data. After analysing the possible movements of the robot, the proc_control sends orders to the proc_servomotor_left and proc_servomotor_right to move respectively left and right servomotors of the system. Figure 3 illustrates the core AADL model of the robot system in a graphical representation.

To avoid the false detection of the position of the robot and then its movement in an undesired direction, we apply an active replication to both proc_sensor_left and proc_sensor_right components to be sure about the motor action. Each of these processes is dually replicated to vote on the collected data (positon) of the robot. Besides, we replicate three times sensor_left and sensor_right device components. (We consider in the Fig. 4 only the replication of processes due to the lack of space).

Listing 1.1 shows the replication properties clauses that we added to the core AADL model of the robot system to replicate processes and devices respectively.

When applying the automatic generation of the intermediate model through our developed backend, Ocarina generates an AADL model enriched with replicas like depicted in Fig. 4. It consists of two similar processes generated inside

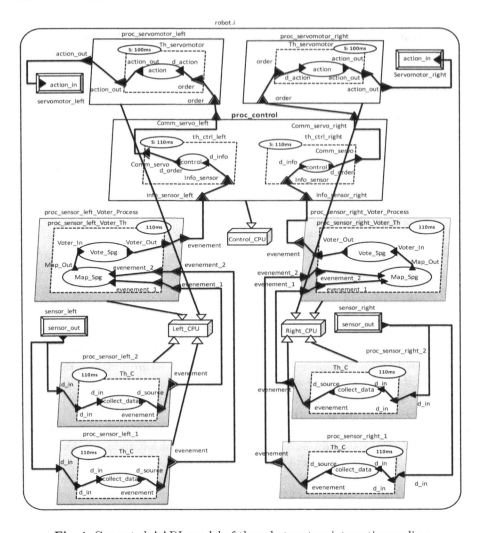

Fig. 4. Generated AADL model of the robot system integrating replicas

the system component connected to a voter process generated also inside the system component. The voter thread calls two subprograms Map_Spg and Vote_Spg. The first is to construct an array of collected data that will be the input of the second which calculates the average of all detected positions. This is to have both algorithms independent from the replica number.

We deduce from this case study how much the generated model is complicated with respect to the initial one even that we have applied dual replication only to two components. Thus, we help the designer to generate it while reducing the risk of errors and decreasing the number of lines of code in a meaningful way (up to 50 %). In case of replication of several components with various number of replicas, this generated model will be certainly more complicated. Our approach helps the designers save efforts, reduce the design time and the risk of errors that may appear due to the significant number of components and connections. This is through an automatic generation of replicas and adjudicators by ensuring automatic model transformation using our extension of the Ocarina tool suite.

Finally, to validate the consistency of the generated intermediate model, we used Ocarina again to parse it and to generate Ada code using the PolyORB-HI middleware. The automatic code generation using Ocarina, its compilation with GNATforLEON, its simulation using TSIM were performed successfully.

6   Conclusion and Future Work

As replication is a well-known technique used to ensure fault tolerance, a wide range of studies aims at designing and implementing fault tolerance for distributed real-time systems based on replication. Most of these work deal with only one replication style and limited number of variants. In addition, they perform manual redundancy. In case of a large number of variants and/or replicated components, the replication design can cause significant increase of the design time and the risk of errors. For that, to assist the designer when modelling his or her fault tolerant application, we proposed a new approach based on automation of the replication of AADL components. Our approach supports also active and passive replication. Besides, it enables the designer to choose different number of variants even in a single model to overcome limits of existing approaches.

Accordingly, we defined a replication property set consisting on a group of properties encapsulating the replication parameters set by the designer to reach desired replicated architecture. We described, in this paper, how AADL and our defined property set are used for automated generation of a replication-based fault tolerant AADL model. An extension of an existing tool suite to create AADL system architecture has been implemented to transform the base model enriched with replication properties into an intermediate model rich with variants and adjudicators. An application to a robot system was finally provided as a case study.

After accomplishing the extension of this tool by passive replication, we plan in the future to extend the POLYORB-HI middleware with fault tolerant concepts. To benefit from its support, we aim at enriching it with various consensus algorithms that are well used to ensure software fault tolerance including all agreement, weak validity, strong validity and termination [19].

References

1. Bernardi, S., Merseguer, J., Petriu, D.: A dependability profile within MARTE. Softw. Syst. Model. **10**(3), 313–336 (2011)
2. Carzaniga, A., Gorla, A., Pezzè, M.: Handling software faults with redundancy. In: de Lemos, R., Fabre, J.-C., Gacek, C., Gadducci, F., ter Beek, M. (eds.) Architecting Dependable Systems VI. LNCS, vol. 5835, pp. 148–171. Springer, Heidelberg (2009)

3. Domokos, P., Majzik, I.: Automated construction of dependability models by aspect-oriented modeling and model transformation. In: ARCS Workshops, pp. 66–75 (2006)

4. Gabsi, W., Zalila, B.: Fault tolerance for distributed real time dynamically reconfigurable systems from modeling to implementation. In: WETICE - AROSA, Hammamet, Tunisia, pp. 98–103. IEEE Computer Society (2013)

5. Gabsi, W., Zalila, B.: Towards a model level replication technique for fault tolerant systems using AADL. In: Lee, R. (ed.) Software Engineering, Artificial Intelligence, Networking and Parallel/Distributed Computing 2015. SCI, vol. 612, pp. 159–175. Springer, Heidelberg (2015)

6. Guerraoui, R., Schiper, A.: Software-based replication for fault tolerance. Computer **30**(4), 68–74 (1997)

7. Hamid, B., Radermacher, A., Vanuxeem, P., Lanusse, A., Gerard, S.: A fault-tolerance framework for distributed component systems. In: EUROMICRO-SEAA (2008)

8. Laprie, J.-C., Arlat, J., Béounes, C., Kanoun, K.: Definition and analysis of hardware- and software-fault-tolerant architectures. Computer **23**(7), 39–51 (1990)

9. Lasnier, G., Robert, T., Pautet, L., Kordon, F.: Behavioral modular description of fault tolerant distributed systems with AADL behavioral annex. In: NOTERE, pp. 17–24 (2010)

10. Lasnier, G., Zalila, B., Pautet, L., Hugues, J.: Ocarina: an environment for AADL models analysis and automatic code generation for high integrity applications. In: Kordon, F., Kermarrec, Y. (eds.) Ada-Europe 2009. LNCS, vol. 5570, pp. 237–250. Springer, Heidelberg (2009)

11. Liu, L., Wu, Z., Ma, Z., Cai, Y.: A dynamic fault tolerant algorithm based on active replication. In: Seventh International Conference on Grid and Cooperative Computing, 2008, GCC 2008, pp. 557–562 October 2008

12. Mkaouar, H., Zalila, B., Hugues, J., Jmaiel, M.: From AADL model to LNT specification. In: de la Puente, J.A., Vardanega, T. (eds.) Ada-Europe 2015. LNCS, vol. 9111, pp. 146–161. Springer, Heidelberg (2015)

13. Niz, D.D., Feiler, P.H.: Verification of replication architectures in AADL. In: ICECCS, pp. 365–370 (2009)

14. Pinho, L., Vasques, F., Wellings, A.: Replication management in reliable real-time systems. Real-Time Syst. **26**(3), 261–296 (2004)

15. SAE: Architecture Analysis and Design Language Annex: Behavioral Annex (2006)

16. SAE: Architecture Analysis and Design Language, April 2011

17. SAE: Architecture Analysis and Design Language Annex E: Error Model Annex, June 2014

18. Singhoff, F., Legrand, J., Nana, L., Marcé, L.: Cheddar: a flexible real time scheduling framework. In: International ACM SIGADA Conference, Atlanta, pp. 1–8 (2004)

19. Warns, T.: Structural Failure Models for Fault-Tolerant Distributed Computing. Vieweg + Teubner Research : Software Engineering Research. Vieweg + Teubner, Wiesbaden (2010)

Kronecker Algebra for Static Analysis of Barriers in Ada

Robert Mittermayr$^{(\boxtimes)}$ and Johann Blieberger

Institute of Computer Aided Automation,
Vienna University of Technology, Vienna, Austria
{robert,blieb}@auto.tuwien.ac.at

Abstract. Kronecker algebra until now has been applied to concurrent programs that use semaphores and protected objects for synchronization. Like many other programming languages, Ada uses barriers, too. In this paper, we present a new synchronization construct for barriers. By applying this, we are able to statically analyze Ada multi-tasking programs that employ barriers for synchronization issues. It turns out that we can use our existing Kronecker algebra implementation completely unmodified for concurrent program graphs using such barrier synchronization primitives.

Keywords: Static program analysis · Ada tasking · Synchronization primitives · Thread synchronization · Barriers · Kronecker algebra

1 Introduction

Since multi-core processors even for safety-critical applications increasingly become a state-of-the-art technology, scientific and industrial research focuses on analysis and verification of multi-threaded programs. It is widely agreed that such concurrent systems are hard to understand and that it is difficult to prove properties.

At this point Kronecker algebra comes into play. It has proven to be an elegant and adequate vehicle in that field and was already used to model stochastic automata [20] and calculate reachable sets [4]. In order to model shared memory concurrent systems the ordinary Kronecker algebra was extended by additional operations in [17]. An adapted version of the Kronecker product is introduced and important properties of the generated models are proved. The operations of that *extended Kronecker algebra* are used to generate *concurrent program graphs* (CPGs) out of the *control flow graphs* (CFGs) of the threads and *synchronization primitives*. Until now this approach was applied to multi-threaded concurrent programs synchronized via *semaphores* [17,18] and higher level synchronization primitives like Ada's *protected objects* (POs) [5]. Applying Kronecker algebra to Ada's *barriers* is novel in this area. The contributions of this paper are as follows.

© Springer International Publishing Switzerland 2016
M. Bertogna et al. (Eds.): Ada-Europe 2016, LNCS 9695, pp. 145–159, 2016.
DOI: 10.1007/978-3-319-39083-3_10

1. We show how to model Ada's barriers such that Kronecker algebra can be employed for static analysis. This is done by introducing a novel synchronization primitive modeling the semantics of barriers.
2. We compare our barrier synchronization primitive with a barrier implementation based on semaphores. As a byproduct, we show how our CPG-based approach can be used as a basis for proving such implementations correct. It turns out that our barrier construct is better suited for program analysis because it fully can be analyzed by static analysis[1], while the implementations using semaphores, in order to omit dead paths, require advanced techniques (e.g. symbolic analysis [6]).

The outline of the paper is as follows: In Sect. 2, after presenting basic definitions and extending Kronecker algebra such that it can be used for modeling and analysis of concurrent systems, we show how semaphores can be incorporated into our approach. In Sect. 3, we introduce novel synchronization primitives for modeling the semantics of barriers. We compare our barrier construct with barriers modeled by semaphores. Related work is discussed in Sect. 4 before we draw our conclusion in Sect. 5.

2   Preliminaries

The preliminaries described in this section can be found in more detail in [5,18]. In contrast to these papers, we give just a brief overview and introduce initially locked and unlocked semaphores.

We represent Ada tasks and synchronization primitives (e.g. semaphores [8]) by slightly adapted control flow graphs (CFGs). Each of the CFGs is stored in form of an adjacency matrix. We assume that the CFG edges are labeled by elements of a semiring. Definitions and properties of the semiring can be found in [14,18]. Our semiring consists of a set of labels $\mathcal{L}$ which is defined by $\mathcal{L} = \mathcal{L}_V \cup \mathcal{L}_S$, where $\mathcal{L}_V$ is the set of non-synchronization labels and $\mathcal{L}_S$ is the set of labels representing calls to synchronization primitives ($\mathcal{L}_V$ and $\mathcal{L}_S$ are disjoint). From now on, we use matrices out of $\mathcal{M} = \{M = (m_{i,j}) \mid m_{i,j} \in \mathcal{L}\}$ only.

Sometimes we find it convenient to refer to CFGs as automata, both of which are represented by matrices. To keep things simple, we refer to edges, their labels and the corresponding entries of the adjacency matrices synonymously. Since our matrix calculus processes on the matrix entries (which correspond to edges on CFG-level), we require that the basic blocks are situated on the (incoming) edges. The matrices have entries which are referred to as labels $l \in \mathcal{L}$ as defined in [5,18]. The labels refer to a certain basic block. A basic block consists of multiple consecutive statements without jumps. For our purpose, we need a finer granularity which we achieve by edge splitting. Especially for synchronization

---

[1] Programs using our barrier synchronization primitive from within loops or conditional statements will still require advanced techniques.

primitive calls (e.g. p- and v-calls to semaphores [8]) edge splitting is required. Such calls have to be the only statement on the corresponding (split) edge.

Formally, the system model (see, e.g., [18]) consists of the tuple $\langle \mathcal{T}, \mathcal{S}, \mathcal{L} \rangle$, where $\mathcal{T}$ is the finite set of CFG adjacency matrices describing tasks, $\mathcal{S}$ refers to the finite set of CFG adjacency matrices describing synchronization primitives (e.g. semaphores), and the labels in $T \in \mathcal{T}$ and $S \in \mathcal{S}$ are elements of $\mathcal{L}$ and $\mathcal{L}_S$, respectively.

A *Concurrent Program Graph* (CPG) is a graph $C = \langle V, E, n_e \rangle$ with a set of nodes V, a set of directed edges $E \subseteq V \times V$, and a so-called *entry node* $n_e \in V$. The sets V and E are constructed out of the elements of $\langle \mathcal{T}, \mathcal{S}, \mathcal{L} \rangle$. Details on how we generate the sets V and E follow below. Similar to CFGs, the edges of CPGs are labeled by $l \in \mathcal{L}$.

Kronecker product ($\otimes$) and Kronecker sum ($\oplus$) form Kronecker algebra [18]. Proofs, properties, and examples can be found in e.g. [2,7,11,17]. In the following, we equip the ordinary Kronecker algebra with additional operations. With this what we call *extended Kronecker algebra*, we will be able to state a formula calculating the adjacency matrix of a CPG representing the corresponding multi-threaded program.

Let $T^{(i)} \in \mathcal{T}$ and $S^{(j)} \in \mathcal{S}$ refer to the matrices representing thread i and synchronization primitive j, respectively. We obtain matrix T representing k interleaved tasks and matrix S representing r interleaved synchronization primitives by

$$T = \bigoplus_{i=1}^{k} T^{(i)}, \text{ where } T^{(i)} \in \mathcal{T} \text{ and } S = \bigoplus_{j=1}^{r} S^{(j)}, \text{ where } S^{(j)} \in \mathcal{S}.$$

Because the operations $\otimes$ and $\oplus$ are associative (cf. [17]), the corresponding n-fold versions are well defined. In the following, we define the selective Kronecker product which we denote by $\oslash_L$. This operator limits synchronization of the operands to labels $l \in L \subseteq \mathcal{L}$.

Definition 1 (Selective Kronecker Product). *Given an m-by-n matrix A and a p-by-q matrix B, we call $A \oslash_L B$ their selective Kronecker product. For all $l \in L \subseteq \mathcal{L}$ let $A \oslash_L B = (a_{i,j}) \oslash_L (b_{r,s}) = (c_{t,u})$, where*

$$c_{(i-1)\cdot p+r,(j-1)\cdot q+s} = \begin{cases} l & \text{if } a_{i,j} = b_{r,s} = l, \ l \in L, \\ 0 & \text{otherwise}. \end{cases}$$

The selective Kronecker product ensures that, e.g., a semaphore p-call in the left operand is paired with the p-operation in the right operand and not with any other operation in the right operand. In practice, we usually constrain $L \subseteq \mathcal{L}_S$.

In the remainder of this section, we refer to the identity matrix of order n as I_n. Furthermore we write $o(M)$ to denote the order of matrix M.

Definition 2 (Filtered Matrix). *We call M_L a filtered matrix and define it as a matrix of order $o(M)$ containing entries of $L \subseteq \mathcal{L}$ of $M = (m_{i,j})$ and zeros elsewhere:*

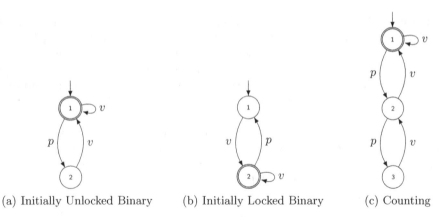

(a) Initially Unlocked Binary   (b) Initially Locked Binary   (c) Counting

Fig. 1. Semaphores (synchronization primitives)

$$M_L = (m_{L;i,j}), \ where \ m_{L;i,j} = \begin{cases} m_{i,j} & if \ m_{i,j} \in L, \\ 0 & otherwise. \end{cases}$$

We refer to the ordinary Kronecker algebra equipped with the operations defined above as *extended Kronecker algebra*.

The adjacency matrix representing program $\mathcal{P}$ is referred to as P. In [17] it is shown that P can be efficiently computed by

$$P = T \oslash_{\mathcal{L}_S} S + T_{\mathcal{L}_V} \otimes I_{o(S)}. \tag{1}$$

Intuitively, the selective Kronecker product term on the left allows for synchronization between the tasks represented by T and the synchronization primitives S. Both T and S are Kronecker sums of the involved tasks and synchronization primitives, respectively, in order to represent all possible interleavings of the concurrently executing tasks. The right term allows the tasks to perform steps that are not involved in synchronization. Summarizing, the tasks (represented by T) may perform their steps concurrently, where all interleavings are allowed, except when they call synchronization primitives. In the latter case the synchronization primitives (represented by S) together with Kronecker product ensure that these calls are executed in the order prescribed by the (incomplete) deterministic finite automata (DFA) of the synchronization primitives.

So, for example, a task cannot do semaphore calls in the order v followed by p when the semaphore DFA only allows a p-call before a v-call (this would be the case when we remove the self-loop at node 1 in Fig. 1a). The CPG of such an erroneous program will contain a node from which the final node of the CPG cannot be reached. This node is the one preceding the v-call. Such nodes can easily be found by traversing CPGs. Thus deadlocks of concurrent systems can be detected with little effort.

In Fig. 1 an initially unlocked (a) and locked (b), respectively, binary and a counting semaphore (c) are depicted. The latter allows two threads to enter at the same time. In a similar way it is possible to construct semaphores allowing n non-blocking p-calls ($n \in \mathbb{N}, n \geq 1$).

Figure 2 shows a small example. The program in Fig. 2a has two branches. The left one employs calls p and v to an initially unlocked semaphore (Fig. 1a) in the correct order, the second one contains two p-calls. Applying Kronecker algebra (cf. (1) and Fig. 2b) we obtain the CPG in Fig. 2c. Node 6 shows that there is a self-deadlock in the underlying program.

In general, a thread's CPG may have several final nodes. We refer to a node without outgoing edges as a sink node. A sink node appears as zero line in the corresponding adjacency matrix. A CPG's final node may also be a sink node (if the program terminates). However, CPG sink nodes and final nodes can be distinguished as follows. We use a vector determining the final nodes of thread i, namely $F^{(i)}$. In addition, vector $G^{(j)}$ determines the final node of synchronization primitive j. Both have ones at places q, when node q is a final node, zeros elsewhere. Then the vector $\bigotimes_{i=1}^{k} F^{(i)} \otimes \bigotimes_{j=1}^{r} G^{(j)}$ determines the final nodes of the CPG. Again, a one in the resulting vector states that the corresponding node is a final node. In the remainder of this paper, we assume that all threads do have only one single final node. Our results, however, can be generalized easily to an arbitrary number of final nodes.

In [17] it is shown that CPGs have at most n^k nodes and at most $2k\,n^k$ edges, if k is the number of threads and each thread has n nodes in its CFG. CPGs have sparse adjacency matrices ($|E| = O(|V|)$). Hence, memory saving data structures and efficient algorithms suggest themselves. However, in the worst-case (i.e. no synchronization used), the number of CPG nodes increases exponentially in k.

3   Barriers

Kronecker algebra until now has only been applied to concurrent programs that use semaphores and Ada's protected objects (POs) for synchronization. In this section, we propose a new synchronization primitive modeling the behavior of barriers.

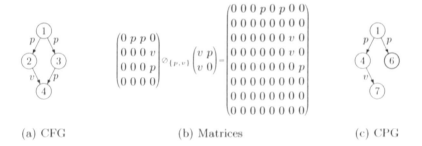

(a) CFG   (b) Matrices   (c) CPG

Fig. 2. (a) An example program with a correct (left path) and incorrect (right path) use of a binary semaphore that is initially unlocked; (b) Kronecker matrix operation; (c) CPG after Kronecker analysis with the self-deadlock in CPG-node 6

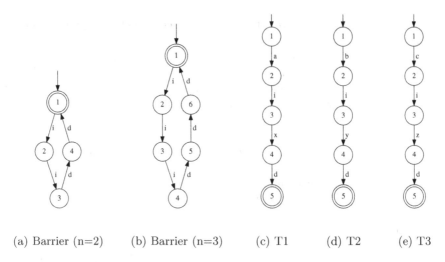

(a) Barrier (n=2)   (b) Barrier (n=3)   (c) T1   (d) T2   (e) T3

Fig. 3. CFGs of tasks T1, T2, and T3 using a barrier

We will give examples and we will compare our solution with the barrier implementation found in [8]. Several other implementations of barriers can be found in [12].

A barrier is a synchronization construct available in most modern programming languages (e.g. Ada and Java). It is used when threads have to wait for each other. Thus a barrier is used to synchronize a set of n threads. The first thread(s) reaching the barrier will be blocked. When the nth thread reaches the barrier all the threads are released and continue their work. A barrier is called reusable, when it can be re-used after the threads are released. In general, dynamic and static barriers are distinguished. Static barriers have a statically fixed number of participating tasks/threads, while the number of threads can vary at runtime for dynamic barriers.

In Ada, barriers are available in form of synchronous barriers [3, D.10.1] available in the package **Ada.Synchronous_Barriers**. Tasks calling its procedure **Wait_For_Release** will be blocked until the **Release_Threshold** is reached. Java supports barriers in form of the class **CyclicBarrier** [10]. The method **await** is called when the barrier is reached. Also a dynamic barrier (i.e. **Phaser** [10]) is supported in Java. Both, Ada's synchronous barrier and Java's **CyclicBarrier** are reusable. With the class **CountDownLatch**, Java has also some sort of a non-reusable barrier, where one or more threads can wait until a set of operations being performed in other threads completes. The approach presented in this paper works for both, Ada's and Java's static barriers. Anyway, in the remainder of this paper we elaborate on Ada's barrier in more detail.

We model a call of the barrier operation **Wait_For_Release** with label i. This indicates that the counter within the barrier implementation is incremented by one during such a call. In order to set the current counter to zero all the tasks call d (decrements counter). Both labels i and $d \in \mathcal{L}_S$. We require that the

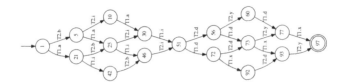

Fig. 4. CPG for the program consisting of T1 and T2

barrier labels have to be unique, i.e., the labels of two different barriers have to be different (the same applies for all synchronization primitives e.g. semaphores) thus the jth barrier uses the labels i_j and d_j. Because the examples in this paper use at most one barrier, we do not have to pay much attention to this fact.

Similar to the semaphore synchronization primitives, we now model our barrier synchronization primitive. A barrier construct includes n subsequent edges labeled by i followed by n subsequent edges labeled by d. Examples for such barrier constructs are depicted in Fig. 3a,b. These barriers synchronize two and three threads, respectively. In a similar way it is possible to model barriers synchronizing any number of threads. After releasing the tasks, each of them, before allowed to continue, calls the barrier's d-operation. This sets the counter back to zero and ensures that the barrier is reusable.

During CFG construction each call of the procedure `Wait_For_Release` is being replaced such that i and d of the corresponding barrier synchronization primitive are called. This replacement implies that the actually used barrier implementation has to be provably correct. Otherwise, a proof could state correctness while abstracting away from a faulty implementation. This proof can be done independently from proving a barrier usage scenario correct. From a certain point of view, our barrier construct is based on the semantics of barriers. A different approach is to use any implementation of a barrier based on semaphores to verify a barrier usage scenario together with the barrier's implementation. As we will see in the following examples, the verification of programs using our barrier synchronization primitive will be easier compared to barriers implemented using semaphores.

3.1   Examples

As an example consider the CFGs of the tasks T1, T2, and T3 shown in Fig. 3. The CPG of a program consisting of the two tasks T1 and T2 is depicted in Fig. 4 whereas the CPG of the program consisting of the three tasks T1, T2, and T3 is shown in Fig. 5. The first program uses the barrier construct presented in Fig. 3a whereas the second program uses the barrier depicted in Fig. 3b. Note that these graphs are generated with our standard CPG generating software. The input programs just use our new barrier synchronization primitive. It can easily be seen that the barrier synchronizes the tasks correctly.

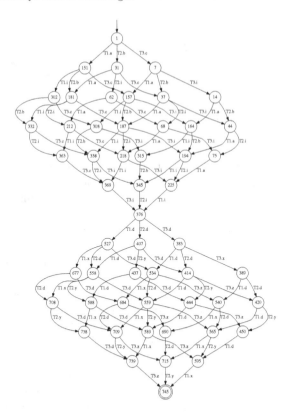

Fig. 5. CPG for the program consisting of T1, T2, and T3

Figure 6 presents an example program consisting of two tasks TL1 and TL2. Each task contains a loop and a `Wait_For_Release` inside the loop. If the number of loop iterations is the same in both tasks, the final node 61 is reached; otherwise, the program stalls at nodes 30 or 54. The number of loop iterations cannot be calculated by the Kronecker approach. For this purpose e.g. some sort of symbolic analysis [6] is needed. In the simplest case, only lower and upper bounds of for-loops have to be compared.

3.2 Comparison to a Barrier Implementation Using Semaphores

In the following, we compare our barrier construct with the barrier implementation on page 41 in [8]. The pseudo code of this example is as follows.

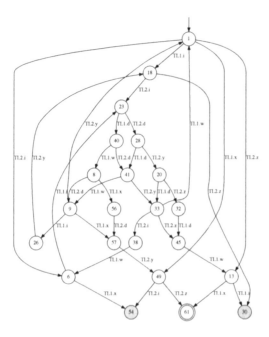

Fig. 6. CPG for the program consisting of TL1 and TL2

Listing 1.1. Reusable Barrier Solution using Semaphores

```
# rendezvous

mutex.wait()                              # ps
    count += 1                            # i
    if count == n:
        turnstile2.wait()                 # pb2, lock the second
        turnstile.signal()                # vb1, unlock the first
    else # empty                          # T1.a; T2.e
mutex.signal()                            # vs

turnstile.wait()                          # pb1, first turnstile
turnstile.signal()                        # vb1

# critical point                          # T1.b; T2.f

mutex.wait()                              # ps
    count -= 1                            # d
    if count == 0:
        turnstile.wait()                  # pb1, lock the first
        turnstile2.signal()               # vb2, unlock the second
    else # empty                          # T1.c; T2.g
mutex.signal()                            # vs

turnstile2.wait()                         # pb2, second turnstile
turnstile2.signal()                       # vb2
```

Three semaphores, namely `mutex`, `turnstile` and `turnstile2`, are used in order to implement the barrier functionality. Two of them, `mutex` and `turnstile2` are initially unlocked semaphores as shown in Fig. 1a. The semaphore `turnstile` is an initially locked one as depicted in Fig. 1b. We assume that the two threads T1 and T2 execute the code. Some lines are modeled by the same labels for both threads (e.g. both threads use ps in order to get access to the variable count). Other lines are modeled by different labels (e.g. T1 and T2 execute b and f, respectively, as their critical point). The CPG of the reusable barrier solution is depicted in Fig. 7. The graph contains the potential deadlock nodes 681, 761, 1774, 1790, 1961 and 2030. The dotted edges are dead paths which can be ruled out by a value-sensitive (e.g. symbolic) analysis (cf. [6]). Due to these edges some nodes are unreachable which are filled light gray. As an effect of this, it is easy to see, that all the potential deadlock nodes are unreachable. We can conclude that the implementation using three semaphores is correct but it is obviously more complex than our solution (cf. Fig. 4) and thus it is harder to prove its correctness. In addition, to exclude the dead paths in Fig. 7, advanced approaches like symbolic analysis are needed.

Similar to the reusable barrier solution above, we discuss the non-reusable barrier solution, which can be found on page 29 in [8], in the following.

Listing 1.2. Non-reusable Barrier Solution using Semaphores

```
# rendezvous

mutex.wait()                         # ps
    count = count + 1                # c
mutex.signal()                       # vs

if count == n: barrier.signal() # T1.v, T1.a; T2.v, T2.x
else # empty                         # T1.b; T2.y

barrier.wait()                       # p
barrier.signal()                     # v

# critical point
```

Two semaphores, namely mutex and barrier, are used in order to implement the barrier's functionality. The first (i.e. mutex) is an initially unlocked semaphore as shown in Fig. 1a. The second semaphore (i.e. barrier) is an initially locked semaphore as depicted in Fig. 1b. The CPG of the non-reusable barrier solution is depicted in Fig. 8. Again there are dead paths (the corresponding edges are dotted) in the resulting CPG. This graph includes also a deadlock node (i.e. node 181). Again, the paths to this node can be revealed as dead paths by e.g. symbolic analysis. Thus the node 181 is filled light gray which states that this node is unreachable (as several other nodes). In contrast to that, our approach does not generate any deadlock nodes nor dead paths.

Theoretical results such as [21] state that synchronization-sensitive and context-sensitive analysis (similar to the halting problem) is undecidable even for the simplest analysis problems. Our system model differs in that it supports subprograms (e.g. procedures) only via inlining and recursions are not allowed. Given this restriction, we can state that our approach is sound i.e. it finds all possible deadlocks. Stated the other way round, our approach proves a program deadlock free when no deadlock nodes (i.e. nodes without successors which are no final nodes) are found. On the other hand, our static approach may find

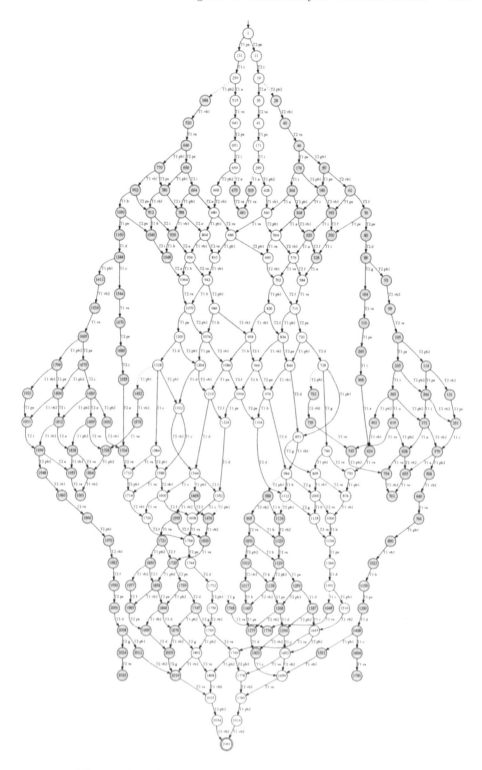

Fig. 7. CPG of the reusable barrier solution using semaphores

Fig. 8. CPG of the non-reusable barrier solution using semaphores

false positives. Advanced techniques may be used in order to reveal that the corresponding deadlock nodes are unreachable.

We can conclude this section by stating that we introduced a technique for formally and automatically analyze barrier implementations and programs using barriers. Thus, the informal proof of barriers, which is mentioned in [8], can be replaced by an automatic and a more reliable one.

4   Related Work

Barriers can be employed in various parallel programming models, such as single program multiple data (SPMD, e.g. OpenMP), fork/join, and shared memory interleaving semantics based models. In the following we compare some of the work done in these areas to our work.

In [1] the concept of structural correctness is defined to ensure that all threads execute the same number of barriers. Static analysis is used to determine if or not a program is structural correct. Combining this approach with ours, a large number of programs can be automatically verified.

In [13, 24] the focus is on determining which portions of the program may execute in parallel. However, such analyses do not verify the correctness of barrier synchronization. Our approach delivers whether or not a statement is concurrently executed via the structure of the CPG.

Paper [23] generalizes [1] by introducing barrier matching which allows to prove a larger set of barrier scenarios correct. Our approach combined with symbolic analysis [6], however, is capable to verify an even larger set of such scenarios.

In [15] a bounded permission system and a concurrent separation logic are presented for verifying fork/join programs with static and dynamic barriers. Since Ada supports static barriers only, our approach can only be compared to that part of [15]. We are sure, that our approach via symbolic analysis can verify the same set of scenarios.

In [16] several barrier scenarios are verified. It will be interesting future work to see whether these proofs have counterparts in our graph-based model.

Although not related directly, we note that our Kronecker algebra model is also used in the railway domain. The adaptations required for railway systems were done in [19] and it was extended in several publications (e.g. [22]).

5   Conclusions

We have shown how Kronecker algebra can be employed for static analysis of concurrent Ada programs that use reusable static barriers for synchronization. The implementation of our novel barrier synchronization primitive has to be provably correct. Otherwise, a proof could state correctness while abstracting away from a faulty implementation. This proof can be done independently from proving a barrier usage scenario correct.

In addition, we have compared our novel barrier synchronization primitive with a barrier implementation based on semaphores. As a byproduct we have shown how our CPG-based approach can be used as a basis for proving such implementations correct. In fact it is possible to use any implementation of a barrier based on semaphores to verify a barrier usage scenario together with the barrier's implementation.

Our barrier construct is better suited for program analysis because it fully can be analyzed by static analysis, while the implementations using semaphores, in order to omit dead paths, require advanced techniques (e.g. symbolic analysis). Anyway, programs using our barrier synchronization primitive from within loops or conditional statements will still require advanced techniques.

Since Kronecker algebra is based on the theory of finite automata, dynamically allocated tasks and dynamically allocated protected objects cannot be modeled by our approach. As our analysis targets safety related systems, we do not consider this a severe limitation.

The usefulness of our approach has been proved by a lazy implementation of extended Kronecker algebra done in Ada. The implementation is very memory efficient and has been parallelized to exploit modern many-core hardware architectures [17]. Generating CFGs for Ada programs is based on [9].

References

1. Aiken, A., Gay, D., Barrier inference. In: POPL, pp. 342–354 (1998)
2. Bellman, R.: Introduction to Matrix Analysis. Classics in Applied Mathematics, 2nd edn. Society for Industrial and Applied Mathematics, Philadelphia (1997)
3. Brukardt, R.L. (ed): Annotated Ada Reference Manual, ISO/IEC 8652:2012(E) with COR.1:2016 (2016). http://www.ada-auth.org/standards/aarm12_w_tcl/AA-Final.pdf
4. Buchholz, P., Kemper, P.: Efficient computation and representation of large reachability sets for composed automata. Discrete Event Dyn. Syst. **12**(3), 265–286 (2002)
5. Burgstaller, B., Blieberger, J.: Kronecker algebra for static analysis of Ada programs with protected objects. In: George, L., Vardanega, T. (eds.) Ada-Europe 2014. LNCS, vol. 8454, pp. 27–42. Springer, Heidelberg (2014)
6. Burgstaller, B., Scholz, B., Blieberger, J.: A symbolic analysis framework for static analysis of imperative programming languages. J. Syst. Softw. **85**(6), 1418–1439 (2012)
7. Davio, M.: Kronecker products and shuffle algebra. IEEE Trans. Comput. **30**(2), 116–125 (1981)
8. Downey, A.B.: The Little Book of Semaphores. Green Tea Press, Virginia (2005)
9. Fechete, R., Kienesberger, G., Blieberger, J.: A framework for CFG-based static program analysis of Ada programs. In: Kordon, F., Vardanega, T. (eds.) Ada-Europe 2008. LNCS, vol. 5026, pp. 130–143. Springer, Heidelberg (2008)
10. González, J.F.: Java 7 Concurrency Cookbook. Packt Publishing Ltd., Birmingham (2012)
11. Graham, A.: Kronecker Products and Matrix Calculus with Applications. Ellis Horwood Ltd., New York (1981)
12. Hill, J.M.D., Skillicorn, D.B.: Practical barrier synchronisation. In: PDP, pp. 438–444 (1998)
13. Kamil, A., Yelick, K.A.: Concurrency analysis for parallel programs with textually aligned barriers. In: Ayguadé, E., Baumgartner, G., Ramanujam, J., Sadayappan, P. (eds.) LCPC 2005. LNCS, vol. 4339, pp. 185–199. Springer, Heidelberg (2006)
14. Kuich, W., Salomaa, A.: Semirings, Automata, Languages. Springer, Heidelberg (1986)
15. Le, D.-K., Chin, W.-N., Teo, Y.-M.: Verification of static and dynamic barrier synchronization using bounded permissions. In: Groves, L., Sun, J. (eds.) ICFEM 2013. LNCS, vol. 8144, pp. 231–248. Springer, Heidelberg (2013)
16. Malkis, A., Banerjee, A.: Verification of software barriers. In: PPoPP (2012)
17. Mittermayr, R., Blieberger, J.: Shared memory concurrent system verification using Kronecker algebra. Technical report 183/1-155, Automation Systems Group, TU Vienna, September 2011. http://arxiv.org/abs/1109.5522
18. Mittermayr, R., Blieberger, J.: Timing analysis of concurrent programs. In: Vardanega, T. (ed) 12th WCET, vol. 23, pp. 59–68 (2012)

19. Mittermayr, R., Blieberger, J., Schöbel, A.: Kronecker algebra based deadlock analysis for railway systems. J. PROMET **2012**, 359–369 (2012)
20. Plateau, B.: On the stochastic structure of parallelism and synchronization models for distributed algorithms. In: SIGMETRICS 1985, vol. 13, pp. 147–154 (1985)
21. Ramalingam, G.: Context-sensitive synchronization-sensitive analysis is undecidable. ACM Trans. Program. Lang. Syst. **22**(2), 416–430 (2000)
22. Stefan, M., Blieberger, J., Schöbel, A.: Application of Kronecker algebra in railway operation. Tehnički vjesnik - Technical Gazette (2016, to appear)
23. Zhang, Y., Duesterwald, E.: Barriers matching for programs with textually unaligned barriers. In: PPoPP, pp. 194–204 (2007)
24. Zhang, Y., Duesterwald, E., Gao, G.R.: Concurrency analysis for shared memory programs with textually unaligned barriers. In: Adve, V., Garzarán, M.J., Petersen, P. (eds.) LCPC 2007. LNCS, vol. 5234, pp. 95–109. Springer, Heidelberg (2008)

Real-Time Systems

An Empirical Investigation of Eager and Lazy Preemption Approaches in Global Limited Preemptive Scheduling

Abhilash Thekkilakattil[1]([✉]), Kaiqian Zhu[1], Yonggao Nie[1], Radu Dobrin[1], and Sasikumar Punnekkat[2]

[1] Mälardalen Real-Time Research Center, Mälardalen University, Västerås, Sweden
abhilash.thekkilakattil@mdh.se
[2] Birla Institute of Technology and Science, Goa, India

Abstract. Global limited preemptive real-time scheduling in multi-processor systems using Fixed Preemption Points (FPP) brings in an additional challenge with respect to the choice of the task to be preempted in order to maximize schedulability. Two principal choices with respect to the preemption approach exist (1) the scheduler waits for the lowest priority job to become preemptible, (2) the scheduler preempts the first job, among the lower priority ones, that becomes preemptible. We refer to the former as the Lazy Preemption Approach (LPA) and the latter as the Eager Preemption Approach (EPA). Each of these choice has a different effect on the actual number of preemptions in the schedule, that in turn determine the runtime overheads.

In this paper, we perform an empirical comparison of the run-time preemptive behavior of Global Preemptive Scheduling and Global Limited Preemptive Scheduling with EPA and LPA, under both Earliest Deadline First (EDF) and Fixed Priority Scheduling (FPS) paradigms. Our experiments reveal interesting observations some of which are counter-intuitive. We then analyse the counter-intuitive observations and identify the associated reasons. The observations presented facilitate the choice of appropriate strategies when using limited preemptive schedulers on multiprocessor systems.

1 Introduction

Real-time computing systems are increasingly being used in modern mission and safety critical systems. In a real-time system, the events occurring in the environment are typically handled by a set of real-time tasks, with the requirement that the task executions must complete by their respective deadlines. A real-time scheduling algorithm ensures the timely execution of these real-time tasks. Real-time scheduling theory has traditionally focused on fully preemptive and fully non-preemptive scheduling of real-time tasks on uniprocessor [8] and multiprocessor platforms [1]. However, both these paradigms can become prohibitively expensive when considering the effects of preemption related overheads and

© Springer International Publishing Switzerland 2016
M. Bertogna et al. (Eds.): Ada-Europe 2016, LNCS 9695, pp. 163–178, 2016.
DOI: 10.1007/978-3-319-39083-3_11

blocking. Preemptively scheduling real-time tasks implies context switch overheads, cache related preemption and migration delays, increased bus contention and pipeline delays. Non-preemptive scheduling, on the other hand, can be infeasible at arbitrarily small utilizations [19].

The multi-core revolution has revived the interest among researchers and practitioners, particularly in the field of real-time embedded systems, to leverage on the ability of multiprocessing platforms to provide higher performance. In this paper, we focus on global scheduling on a multiprocessor platform that can be broadly classified into fixed task priority, fixed job priority and dynamic job priority scheduling algorithms. Note that preemptive scheduling on multiprocessor platforms using the global approach also implies that resuming tasks may be migrated to other processors. In this paper, we consider Global Preemptive Fixed Priority Scheduling (G-P-FPS) which is a fixed task priority scheduling paradigm, and Global Preemptive Earliest Deadline First (G-P-EDF) scheduling which is a fixed job priority scheduling paradigm. In general, EDF incurs less preemptions than FPS since EDF assigns priorities according to absolute deadlines, because of which preemptions occurring towards the end of the task executions, specifically due to higher priority tasks having later deadlines, are avoided (and no new ones occur) [9].

High preemption and migration related overheads are an emerging issue in many real-time applications [2]. Recent experiments show that, among the various operating system data structures, the stack is the most susceptible to faults [4], and that preemptive scheduling makes the system significantly susceptible to faults [19]. Moreover, there is a clear link between the run-time preemptions on higher criticality tasks and the associated actual execution times that in turn decide the scheduling of lower criticality tasks in mixed criticality systems (see [7] for an overview). The foundation of mixed-criticality systems is based on the premises that tasks have different levels of assurances on their WCETs depending on their criticality [7]. Higher criticality tasks which have/require high levels of assurances, typically have over-approximated WCETs to account for the different unpredictable overheads, a significant one being the overhead associated with preemptions. At any given time instant the system is assumed to be executing at a criticality level L, which is given by the criticality of the currently executing lowest criticality tasks. Every task in the system has a budgeted time for the criticality level L, the overrun of which triggers a *criticality switch* during which all tasks with criticality L or lower are discarded. It is clear that the schedulability of lower criticality tasks depends on the actual execution time of higher criticality tasks [7]. If the higher criticality tasks are preempted very often, the probability of the system switching to a higher criticality level is high since there is a greater chance for the higher criticality tasks to overrun their budgeted time for that criticality level because of the associated preemption related overheads.

One way of minimizing preemption overheads while controlling the effects of blocking is to limit preemptions to predefined locations in the tasks (see [10] for a survey). Among the different methods to limit preemptions, fixed preemption points [6] enable offline analysis since the points of preemptions are known before-hand. Limited preemptive scheduling on multiprocessor platforms presents an additional problem with respect to the choice of the running lower priority tasks to be preempted. The scheduler can choose to wait for the lowest priority task to become preemptible or preempt the first lower priority running task that becomes preemptible. The former is a Lazy Preemption Approach (LPA) and the later is an Eager Preemption Approach (EPA).

Each approach may have a different effect on the actual number of pre-emptions at run-time, that in turn determines the overheads in the schedule. Consequently, there is a need for a thorough study of the preemptive behavior of the different approaches. Note that we consider tasksets in which the optimal fixed preemption points are already known. Consequently, the overheads depend on whether or not a preemption actually occurs at these points. In other words, since preemptions are possible only at these optimal preemption points, the system performance will depend on the actual number of preemptions instead. In this paper, we investigate (1) Which approach among EPA and LPA gener-ates fewer number of preemptions at run-time? (2) Which scheduling paradigm among G-LP-FPS and G-LP-EDF generates fewer number of preemptions at run-time? We make several observations, and in particular show that limited preemptive scheduling on multiprocessors may generate more preemptions than fully preemptive scheduling.

The rest of the paper contains the system model in Sect. 2, some background in Sect. 3 experiments in Sect. 4, and analysis of results in Sect. 5. Finally, we present the conclusions in Sect. 6.

2   System Model

We consider a set of n sporadic real-time tasks $\Gamma = \{\tau_1, \tau_2, \ldots \tau_n\}$ scheduled on m identical processors. Each task τ_i is characterized by a minimum inter-arrival time T_i, and a relative deadline $D_i \leq T_i$, and is assumed to contain $q_i \geq 0$ optimal preemption points specified by the designer/programmer [18]. Let $b_{i,j}$, $j = 1 \ldots (q_i + 1)$ denote the worst case execution time of task τ_i between its $(j-1)^{th}$ and j^{th} preemption points. We use the notation $b_{i,j}$ to also refer to the corresponding Non-Preemptive Region (NPR). The Worst Case Execution Time (WCET) of each task τ_i can be calculated as $C_i = \sum_{j=1}^{q_i+1} b_{i,j}$.

3   Global Limited Preemptive Scheduling

In this section, we describe the two approaches to preemption under global LP scheduling viz. the eager and lazy preemption approaches. Please note that in all the figures in this paper an up arrow represents the release time and a down arrow represents the deadline of the associated task.

3.1   Lazy Preemption Approach

In the Lazy Preemption Approach (LPA), if a higher priority task is released and all lower priority jobs are executing their NPRs, the scheduler waits for the lowest priority job to complete its NPR (*i.e.*, to become *preemptible*) before allowing the higher priority job to preempt [3,5]. We illustrate this approach using the following example illustrated in Fig. 1.

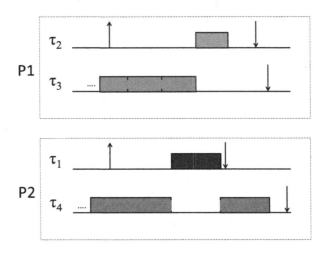

Fig. 1. Example for lazy preemption approach.

Example 1. Consider four tasks τ_1, τ_2, τ_3 and τ_4, where τ_1 has the highest priority and τ_4 has the lowest, scheduled on 2 processors P1 and P2. Consider the scenario in Fig. 1 in which τ_1 and τ_2 are released during the execution of NPRs of τ_3 and τ_4 as shown. If the scheduling algorithm used is G-LP-FPS with lazy preemptions, τ_1 and τ_2 will be blocked until τ_4 finishes executing its NPR, after which τ_1 is scheduled on P2. However, τ_2 cannot be scheduled because τ_3 has already started executing its NPR at this point. Once τ_3 completes execution of its NPR, τ_2 is allowed to execute on P1. Although we have considered tasks with fixed priorities, it can be easily seen from the example that the same conclusions can be made about the preemptive behavior under G-LP-EDF with lazy preemption.

3.2   Eager Preemption Approach

Under the Eager Preemption Approach (EPA), if a higher priority task is released and all lower priority executing jobs are executing their NPRs, the scheduler preempts the first lower priority that becomes *preemptible*. We illustrate this approach using the following example that is illustrated in Fig. 2.

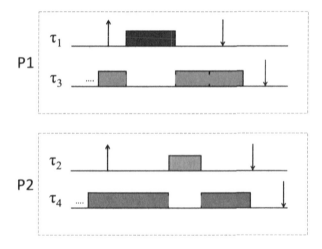

Fig. 2. Example for eager preemption approach.

Example 2. Consider the same four tasks τ_1, τ_2, τ_3 and τ_4 presented in Example 1, and the same scenario in which τ_1 and τ_2 are released during the execution of NPRs of τ_3 and τ_4. If the scheduling algorithm used is G-LP-FPS with eager preemptions, the scheduler will allow τ_1 to preempt τ_3 rather than wait for τ_4 since it is the first available opportunity to preempt (see Fig. 2). Once τ_4 completes its NPR, τ_2 is scheduled on P2.

Although we have considered tasks with fixed priorities, the same conclusions can be made about the preemptive behavior under G-LP-EDF with lazy preemption.

3.3 Related Works

All of the major works on *multiprocessor* limited preemptive scheduling [3,11, 12,14,16,20,21] focused on schedulability and not the preemptive behavior. We clarify that in our previous work [21] we considered schedulability under (only) limited preemptive FPS with Fixed Preemption Points (FPP). In this paper, we instead consider the "preemptive behavior" of both limited preemptive EDF and FPS under FPP. Marinho [15] presented some observations regarding the preemptive behavior under EPA and LPA; however he did not present detailed empirical comparisons. Previously, a preliminary study of the preemptive behavior of G-LP-FPS [17] and that of G-LP-EDF [23] was conducted with respect to the number of preemptions under both EPA and LPA. In this paper, we perform a comprehensive comparison of the preemptive behavior using a weighted metric similar to weighted schedulability [2] and vary different parameters that may have an impact on the number of preemptions. To our knowledge, this is the first such effort towards investigating the runtime preemptive behavior of limited preemptive scheduling on multiprocessors.

4   Empirical Investigation of the Preemptive Behavior

In this paper, we investigate how the decision of choosing a scheduling paradigm *viz.* EDF and FPS, and the preemption approach *viz.* EPA and LPA affect the number of preemptions at run-time. The number of run-time preemptions influence the preemption overheads in the schedule, which in turn influence, among others, schedulability of lower criticality tasks in mixed criticality systems and resource contention. Note that the performance of different combinations of schedulers and the approaches to preemption differ based on the underlying hardware and the specific application (task parameters, cache access patterns etc.). As an exhaustive study on real cases that allows us to sufficiently generalize our results is resource and time demanding, we had to restrict the current experiments to the use of synthetic tasksets. A more detailed version of this paper can be found online at [22].

Method for the Experimental Design: The experimental methodology is similar to the one adopted by Buttazzo [9]. In order to perform the experiments, due to the very limited availability of simulators implementing limited preemptive scheduling under eager and lazy preemption approaches, we developed a simulator that takes as input the task parameters and generate the different schedules for a user defined time duration. The task parameters were generated using well accepted techniques and is described in the following: We used the UUnifast-discard algorithm [13] to generate individual task utilizations that were varied between U_{min} and U_{max}. For the case of FPS, we adopted the deadline-monotonic priority assignment – note that we are interested in the number of preemptions and not deadline misses. The scheduling algorithms, whose preemption behaviors we want to compare are in fact incomparable with respect to schedulability [14]. Therefore, to investigate the preemptive behavior, building on the speed-up bounds [1] and schedulability experiments, *e.g.*, [5], that indicate high schedulability for tasksets that utilize up to 50 % of the platform under both preemptive EDF and FPS, we set, $U_{max} = \frac{m}{2}$. Note that a fully preemptive schedule can be obtained using a limited preemptive scheduler by enabling preemptions after every unit of execution, therefore, if a taskset is preemptively schedulable, it is also LP schedulable. However, in one set of the experiments, we consider tasksets with utilization up to 100 % of the processing platform in order to investigate the preemptive behavior for high utilization tasksets. The task periods were randomly generated between $T_{min} = 5$ and $T_{max} = 500$ (this represents tasks with periods 5-500 ms as found in many typical real-time systems), and execution times were computed using the generated utilizations. We assumed deadlines to be equal to periods; note that this assumption does not affect the generality of the results since we consider the preemptive behavior and not schedulability. The largest NPR of each task was generated as a percentage of its execution time, with the ceiling function applied to obtain integer values (*i.e.*, in case of a decimal NPR we approximate it to the smallest integer greater than the decimal number)– in our experiments, this was set to 10 % (*i.e.*, each task has no more than 9 preemption points). Note that we also vary the NPR lengths in one of the experiments. We counted the number of preemptions generated for one hundred tasksets under each of the following paradigms: (1) G-P-FPS (2) G-P-EDF (3) G-LP-FPS with eager preemptions (EPA-FPS) (4) G-LP-FPS with lazy preemptions (LPA-FPS) (5) G-LP-EDF with eager preemptions (EPA-EDF) (6) G-LP-EDF with lazy preemptions (LPA-EDF), by simulating the respective schedules for a duration of 10000 time units.

Weighted Metric: In order to understand how the number of preemptions vary with a second parameter, *e.g.*, number of tasks, in addition to utilization, we adopted a weighted measure similar to weighted schedulability [2]. We weighted the number of preemptions N_i, for a taskset Γ_i with respect to a parameter p over a simulation run for Δ time units, with the taskset utilization U_i as follows:

$$W_p = \frac{\sum_{\forall \Gamma_i} U_i N_i}{\sum_{\forall \Gamma_i} U_i}$$

We investigated how the number of preemptions in the actual schedule varies with (1) total utilization (2) number of processors (3) number of tasks and (4) length of the NPR.

4.1 Varying the Total Utilization

In this set of experiments, we investigated the preemptive behavior of the scheduling algorithms for increasing utilizations. We considered a 4 processor platform and generated tasksets with 25 tasks and utilizations ranging from 1 to 4. We calculated the average number of preemptions per 100 time units, after simulating the schedule for a duration of 10000 time units – the results are reported in Fig. 3. We observe that G-LP-EDF with EPA generates the maximum number of preemptions that is greater than G-LP-FPS with eager preemptions. Perhaps surprisingly, G-P-EDF and G-P-FPS generate fewer preemptions than their limited preemptive counterparts with eager preemptions. Moreover, we observed that the uniprocessor behavior of EDF with respect to generating fewer number of preemptions than FPS [9] generalizes to the multiprocessor case; G-P-EDF generated less preemptions than G-P-FPS. The least number of preemptions is generated by G-LP-FPS with LPA that generated slightly fewer number of preemptions even when compared to G-LP-EDF with LPA.

In the following, we conduct experiments with varying number of processors after adopting the weighted metric described above.

4.2 Varying Number of Processors

We generated tasksets with 25 tasks having utilizations ranging from 1 to $U_{max} = m/2$ for $m = 4$ to $m = 20$ in steps of 2. The results of the experiments are reported in Fig. 4. We can see that the number of preemptions, in general,

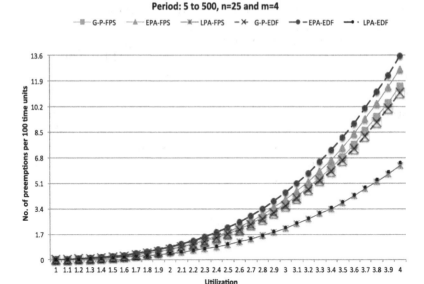

Fig. 3. Average number of preemptions per 100 time units under varying utilizations for NPR length=10 % of WCET.

decreases with increasing number of processors (since more processors for the same number of tasks imply a reduced need for preemption). The interesting observation here is that G-LP-EDF with EPA generated more preemptions than G-LP-FPS with EPA. The fully preemptive variants of EDF and FPS generated fewer preemptions than their limited preemptive counterparts with EPA. The least number of preemptions are generated by G-LP-EDF and G-LP-FPS; both under LPA. Here again, G-LP-FPS with LPA generates slightly fewer number of preemptions compared to G-LP-EDF with LPA. The use of the weighted metric described above makes it less visible from the graph (note: G-LP-EDF with EPA generates significantly more preemptions than G-LP-FPS with EPA).

4.3   Varying Number of Tasks

We varied the number of tasks per taskset from $n = 6$ to $n = 26$ in steps of 2 and counted the number of preemptions for tasksets with utilizations between 1 and $U_{max} = m/2$. The results are reported in Fig. 5. We observed a similar trend observed by Buttazzo [9]. The fully preemptive variant of EDF generated fewer preemptions than G-P-FPS. Moreover, the number of preemptions increased with increasing number of tasks. We expect that increasing the number of tasks further will lead to a decrease in the number of preemptions because individual task execution times will decrease to keep the utilization constant as noted by

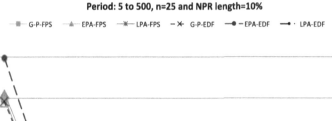

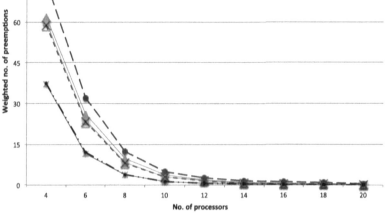

Fig. 4. Weighted number of preemptions under varying number of processors.

Buttazzo [9]— the decreasing trend is observable when number of tasks change from 22 to 26.

We can see trends that are similar to the one observed in the previous experiments reported in this paper: G-LP-EDF with EPA generated most preemptions while G-LP-FPS (together with G-LP-EDF) with LPA generated the least. Here again G-LP-FPS with LPA generated slightly fewer number of preemptions than G-LP-EDF with LPA (not visible due to scaling issues— see appendix of [22]). Also, note that G-LP-FPS with EPA generated significantly fewer preemptions than G-LP-EDF with EPA.

4.4 Varying Length of Non-preemptive Regions

Lastly, we wanted to investigate if the preemption behavior would be any different if we had chosen a different size for the non-preemptive regions. We considered a 4 processor platform and counted the number of preemptions generated when the NPR lengths changed from 5 % to 100 % of the task WCETs (no. of tasks per taskset = 25). The experimental results are reported in Fig. 6. The graph indicates that when using EPA (under EDF or FPS), the number of preemptions increases if the length of the NPRs increase without decreasing the number of preemptions points. This is observed by the increased number of preemptions when the NPR lengths increase from 35 % to 40 % (the number of preemptions remains unchanged at 2) and from 50 % to 80 % (when the number

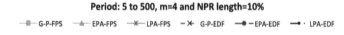

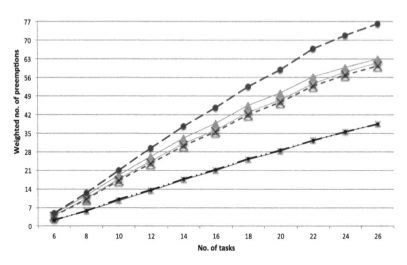

Fig. 5. Weighted number of preemptions under varying number of tasks.

of preemptions remains unchanged at 1). Once past 80 %, most of the tasks become non-preemptive since we apply the ceiling function, and hence there is a decrease in the number of preemptions. Similar trends are also observed in the case of EPA although less pronounced.

In all the cases, LPA outperformed all the other variants of the scheduling algorithms. Moreover, G-LP-EDF with EPA continued to have the highest number of preemptions for shorter NPR lengths, but showed similar performance as G-LP-FPS with EPA for larger NPR lengths (from around 45 % as seen from Fig. 6). Notably, for NPR lengths larger than 20 %, EPA (under both EDF and FPS) generated fewer preemptions than the fully preemptive counterparts. An enlarged version of the above graph available in the Appendix of [22] illustrates that for shorter NPR lengths, G-LP-FPS generated fewer preemptions than G-LP-EDF with both EPA and LPA, while for larger NPR lengths EDF fares better. However, we would like to clarify that this is observed only for NPR lengths larger than 50 % (*i.e.,* for tasks with a single preemption point). If there are more preemption points, then clearly FPS outperforms EDF. Moreover, note that very large NPR lengths may imply unschedulability due to the "long task problem" [19].

Note that graphs Figs. 4, 5 and 6 shows the *weighted number of preemptions* as described above, instead of directly showing the number of preemptions.

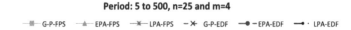

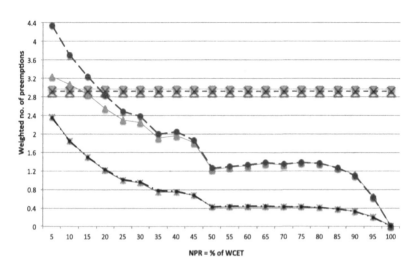

Fig. 6. Weighted number of preemptions under varying NPRs.

5 Analysis of the Experimental Results

In this section, we discuss the (counter-intuitive) experimental results in detail and identify reasons behind the observed behaviors.

5.1 Preemptive Scheduling Vs. Limited Preemptive Scheduling with EPA and LPA

As seen from the evaluations presented in Sect. 4, global LP scheduling with eager preemptions generates more preemptions than global fully preemptive scheduling. This is because more preemptions are required to resolve the priority inversions occurring due to the eager preemption of the lower priority executing task (not necessarily the lowest) that first completes executing its NPR. This is detailed in the following.

When using the eager preemption approach, if the first executing lower priority task that becomes preemptible is preempted by a higher priority job, what essentially happens is that the higher priority task *transfers* the priority inversion to the preempted task if it is not the lowest priority one (since there are lower priority tasks still executing on other processors). The preempted task, which is in the ready queue, may preempt another lower priority task that first completes its NPR (again not necessarily the lowest priority one) thereby transferring priority inversion. This could potentially continue like a domino effect until no more priority inversion exists in the system. In order to resolve priority inversion for each task, there is a need for preemption, consequently increasing

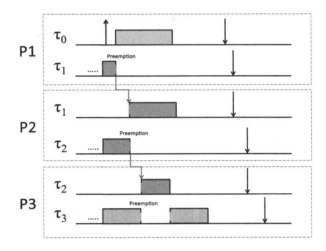

Fig. 7. Preemptions under eager preemption approach.

the number of preemptions. The absence of the above described domino effect explains the better performance of global LP scheduling with lazy preemptions when compared to eager preemptions. These are clarified in the following using a simple example.

Example 3. Consider the scenario presented in Fig. 7 in which 3 tasks τ_1, τ_2 and τ_3, with priorities in the order $\tau_1 > \tau_2 > \tau_3$, are executing on 3 processors. Suppose a higher priority task τ_0 is released. If the scheduler used is a fully preemptive scheduler, τ_0 will preempt τ_3 resulting in only a single preemption. On the other hand, under LP scheduling with eager preemptions, τ_0 will preempt the first task that becomes preemptible, in this case τ_1 (as seen from Fig. 7). Note that τ_1, has the highest priority among the executing ones. Consequently, there is a priority inversion on τ_1 since the other processors are executing lower priority tasks. The task τ_1 will wait for one of the lower priority tasks to become preemptible. In our scenario, τ_2 is the next task that becomes preemptible first. Consequently, τ_2 will be preempted by τ_1. However, the priority inversion persists because τ_2, which was preempted, has a higher priority than τ_3 that is still executing on P3, and hence there is one more preemption. Note that the number of preemptions in this case is 3 instead of 1 under fully preemptive scheduling. In the same scenario, under global LP scheduling with lazy preemption, the scheduler will preempt the lowest priority job τ_3 and hence the domino effect described earlier will not occur (as seen from Fig. 8). Global LP scheduling with lazy preemption performs better than fully preemptive scheduling since the upper-bound on the number of preemptions in a task is determined by the number of preemption points instead of the number of higher priority task releases (that can be significantly larger).

The consequences of such a domino effect under EPA on the total number of observed preemptions can be severe on platforms with large number of

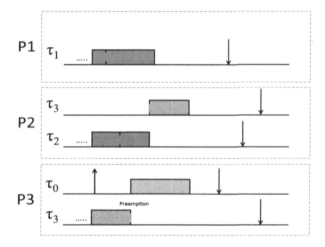

Fig. 8. Preemptions under lazy preemption approach.

processors since in the worst case m such priority inversions need to be resolved per high priority release which can be potentially very large especially in many-core systems.

5.2   Global Limited Preemptive FPS Vs. EDF

In general, preemptive EDF generates fewer number of preemptions than preemptive FPS [9]. This is because, many of the preemptions necessitated by the fixed priority task assignment, do not occur under EDF. The preemptions required by task releases that may have a higher priority under an FPS scheme, towards the end of the execution of tasks, that may have a lower priority under an FPS scheme, are avoided under EDF because of the deadline based priority ordering. On the other hand, in this scenario under FPS, a preemption occurs. Similarly, it is easily seen that uniprocessor limited preemptive EDF generates fewer preemptions than limited preemptive FPS. As seen from the experiments, similar to the uniprocessor case, G-P-EDF performs better in reducing the actual number of preemptions at run-time when compared to G-P-FPS.

However, under *limited preemptive scheduling on multiprocessors*, G-LP-EDF generates more preemptions than G-LP-FPS (under both EPA and LPA). The reason is that, EDF priority ordering generates more priority inversions consequently "forcing" eager preemptions. For example, under G-LP-FPS with LPA, higher priority tasks released during the execution of the final NPR of the lowest priority task wait for it to complete. This does not happen under EDF since at least one of the executing jobs may have a larger absolute deadline and hence can be preempted. We clarify the reason for the relatively poor performance of G-LP-EDF using the following example.

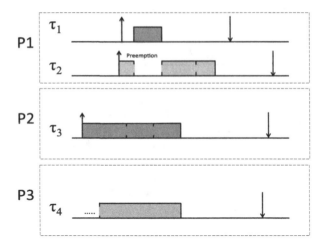

Fig. 9. Preemptive behavior of G-LP-EDF.

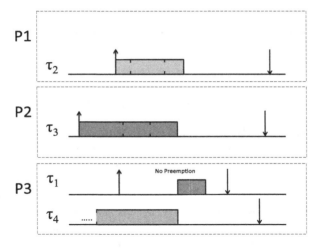

Fig. 10. Preemptive behavior of G-LP-FPS.

Example 4. In this example, consider three tasks τ_2, τ_3 and τ_4 that are currently executing on 3 processors and another task τ_1 that is released during their execution as illustrated in Fig. 9. Assume that τ_4 has started executing its final NPR and the tasks have time periods $T_1 < T_2 < T_3 < T_4$. Under G-LP-EDF using lazy preemptions, when τ_1 is released, τ_2 is the task with the latest deadline and hence has the lowest priority; therefore τ_1 preempts τ_2. On the other hand under G-LP-FPS with lazy preemptions (as shown in Fig. 10), assuming rate monotonic priority ordering, τ_4 has the lowest priority and hence the scheduler waits for the final NPR of τ_4 to complete instead of preempting τ_2 (and hence requiring no preemption). When considering EPA, under G-LP-EDF with EPA, τ_1 will preempt τ_3 since it is the first preemption point available. Now since τ_3 has an earlier *absolute deadline than τ_2, τ_3 will preempt τ_2 at the next preemption point of τ_2. On the other hand, under G-LP-FPS with EPA, τ_1 preempts τ_3, but τ_3 does not preempt τ_2 due to its fixed (higher) priority when compared to τ_3.*

Therefore, for applications in which run-time preemptions are directly or indirectly harmful, such as in the case of safety-critical system or energy constrained systems, it is best to use G-LP-FPS since it generates fewer number of preemptions than G-LP-EDF at runtime.

6   Conclusions and Future Work

In this paper, we empirically investigated the preemptive behavior of G-LP-EDF and G-LP-FPS under eager and lazy preemption approaches, along with G-P-FPS and G-P-EDF, varying a wide range of parameters. Our investigations reveal a number of interesting observations with respect to the observed number of preemptions under the different paradigms. In particular:

1. Limited preemptive scheduling on multiprocessors does not necessarily reduce the number of preemptions; in fact with an eager preemption approach, the number of preemptions could be larger than in the case of fully preemptive scheduling, as well as global LP scheduling with LPA.
2. We show that the well known observation regarding the preemptive behavior of EDF on uniprocessors generalizes to multiprocessors; G-P-EDF generates fewer preemptions than G-P-FPS.
3. We also show that the reduction in preemptions observed with EDF on uni- and multiprocessors, however, does not generalize to global limited preemptive scheduling; G-LP-EDF suffers from more preemptions than G-LP-FPS.
4. Our experiments show that G-LP-FPS with LPA suffers from the least number of preemptions.

Future work include studies on a real hardware and trade-offs involving preemption point placement, schedulability and approach to preemption *viz.* EPA and LPA.

References

1. Baruah, S., Bertogna, M., Buttazzo, G.: Multiprocessor Scheduling for Real-Time Systems. Embedded Systems. Springer International Publishing, Switzerland (2015)
2. Bastoni, A., Brandenburg, B.B., Anderson, J.H.: Cache-related preemption, migration delays: empirical approximation and impact on schedulability. In: The International Workshop OSPERT (2010)
3. Block, A., Leontyev, H., Brandenburg, B.B., Anderson, J.H.: A flexible real-time locking protocol for multiprocessors. In: The 13th IEEE International Conference on Embedded and Real-Time Computing Systems and Applications (2007)
4. Borchert, C., Schirmeier, H., Spinczyk, O.: Generative software-based memory error detection and correction for operating system data structures. In: The 43rd International Conference on Dependable Systems and Networks, June 2013

5. Brandenburg, B.B.: Scheduling and locking in multiprocessor real-time operating systems. Ph.D. thesis, University of North Carolina at Chapel Hill (2011)
6. Bril, R.J., Lukkien, J.J., Verhaegh, W.F.J.: Worst-case response time analysis of real-time tasks under fixed-priority scheduling with deferred preemption. Real-Time Syst. **42**, 63–119 (2009)
7. Burns, A., Davis, R.: Mixed criticality systems - a review. http://www-users.cs.york.ac.uk/burns/review.pdf. Accessed 31 July 2015
8. Buttazzo, G.: Hard Real-time Computing Systems: Predictable Scheduling Algorithms and Applications. Real-Time Systems Series, vol. 24. Springer, Heidelberg (2004)
9. Buttazzo, G.: Rate monotonic vs. EDF: judgment day. Real-Time Syst. **29**, 5–26 (2005)
10. Buttazzo, G.C., Bertogna, M., Yao, G.: Limited preemptive scheduling for real-time systems: a survey. IEEE Trans. Ind. Inform. **9**, 3–15 (2012)
11. Chattopadhyay, B., Baruah, S.: Limited-preemption scheduling on multiprocessors. In: The 22nd International Conference on Real-Time Networks and Systems. ACM (2014)
12. Davis, R., Burns, A., Marinho, J., Nelis, V., Petters, S., Bertogna, M.: Global fixed priority scheduling with deferred pre-emption. In: The International Conference on Embedded and Real-Time Computing Systems and Applications (2013)
13. Davis, R.I., Burns, A.: Improved priority assignment for global fixed priority preemptive scheduling in multiprocessor real-time systems. Real-Time Syst. **47**, 1–40 (2011)
14. Davis, R.I., Burns, A., Marinho, J., Nelis, V., Petters, S.M., Bertogna, M.: Global and partitioned multiprocessor fixed priority scheduling with deferred preemption. ACM Trans. Embed. Comput. Syst. **14**, 47 (2015)
15. dos Santos Marinho, J. M.S.: Real-time limited preemptive scheduling. In Ph.D. thesis, FEUP Porto (2015)
16. Marinho, J., Nelis, V., Petters, S., Bertogna, M., Davis, R.: Limited pre-emptive global fixed task priority. In: The Real-time Systems Symposium (2013)
17. Nie, Y.: Limited-preemptive fixed priority scheduling of real-time tasks on multiprocessors. Master thesis, Malardalen University (2015)
18. Peng, B., Fisher, N., Bertogna, M.: Explicit preemption placement for real-timeconditional code. In: The Euromicro Conference on Real-Time Systems, July 2014
19. Short, M.: The case for non-preemptive, deadline-driven scheduling in real-time embedded systems. In: Lecture Notes in Engineering and Computer Science: Proceedings of the World Congress on Engineering (2010)
20. Thekkilakattil, A., Baruah, S., Dobrin, R., Punnekkat, S.: The global limited preemptive earliest deadline first feasibility of sporadic real-time tasks. In: The 26th Euromicro Conference on Real-Time Systems, July 2014
21. Thekkilakattil, A., Davis, R., Dobrin, R., Punnekkat, S., Bertogna, M.: Multiprocessor fixed priority scheduling with limited preemptions. In: The 23rd International Conference on Real-Time Networks and Systems (2015)
22. Thekkilakattil, A., Zhu, K., Nie, Y., Dobrin, R., Punnekkat, S.: An empirical investigation of eager and lazy preemption approaches in global limited preemptive scheduling. Technical report, September 2015. http://www.es.mdh.se/publications/4057-
23. Zhu, K.: Limited-preemptive EDF scheduling of real-time tasks on multiprocessors. Master thesis, Malardalen University (2015)

The Polling Effect on the Schedulability of Distributed Real-Time Systems

Héctor Pérez, J. Javier Gutiérrez$^{(\boxtimes)}$, Michael González Harbour, and J. Carlos Palencia

Software Engineering and Real-Time Group, Universidad de Cantabria, 39005 Santander, Spain
{perezh, gutierjj, mgh, palencij}@unican.es
http://www.istr.unican.es/

Abstract. The usage of polling tasks continues to be quite common in today's distributed real-time systems, despite the availability of event-driven software mechanisms and response time analysis techniques that can be applied to this kind of systems. This paper proposes a model for polling tasks that allows current response time analysis techniques for event-driven distributed systems to be applied, and it also studies the impact that polling has in the schedulability of a distributed system, using analytic results. A performance evaluation on an Ada-based platform is also provided. As expected, polling produces response times much higher than a pure event-driven alternative. The analysis techniques and the evaluation presented in the paper allows engineers to assess the negative effect of polling on the schedulability of distributed real-time systems.

Keywords: Distributed systems · Real-time · Schedulability analysis · Embedded systems · Polling

1 Introduction

Schedulability analysis techniques for fixed-priority distributed systems have notably evolved in the last three decades [1]. However, in real systems engineers continue to use periodic polling to check for the arrival of events that trigger activities such as the execution of tasks or the transmission of messages through real-time networks. An example can be found in the aerial vehicle tracking system proposed in [2]. In the context of our work, a polling task is defined as a task that periodically polls for the arrival of its triggering event, thus executing its regular code only when detecting that the event had arrived. When the event is not present the detection code is executed anyhow, therefore causing overhead.

In some cases the use of polling may be justified, such as when using data coming from a sensor where there may be no concept of event that must be managed, and it is enough to deal with the latest available data. However, in many other cases what is

---

This work has been funded in part by the Spanish Government and FEDER funds under grant numbers TIN2011-28567-C03-02 (HI-PARTES) and TIN2014-56158-C4-2-P (M2C2).

M. Bertogna et al. (Eds.): Ada-Europe 2016, LNCS 9695, pp. 179–194, 2016.
DOI: 10.1007/978-3-319-39083-3_12

sought with the use of polling is to decouple different subsystems avoiding the dependencies implied by handling events. This is the case of multi-rate real-time systems in the automotive industry [3, 4]. Under this decoupling technique it is possible to apply schedulability analysis to each processor or network separately. Such simplification practices are commonly used in industry, with the consequence that the real capabilities of the systems are wasted.

Generally, distributed systems provide communication primitives with blocking or non-blocking services for the reception of messages that allow tasks both to poll for the arrival of a message, or to wait until a message arrives at the reception queue. This behavior can also be found in distribution middleware, e.g., the DDS (Data Distribution Service for Real-Time Systems) standard [5] allows subscribers to receive data from a topic through (1) polling, (2) listeners to asynchronously access the data, or (3) wait-sets for synchronous access to the data. There are other standards for specific domains like ARINC 653 [6] on avionics, which establishes the communication between processes throughout special ports: (1) sampling ports where the arriving message overwrites the current message stored in the buffer with a freshness indication, thus allowing recipients to be designed to cope with intermittent loss of data; and (2) queuing ports where the arriving message is appended to a FIFO queue, and a process can be blocked on a receiving process queue. These concepts in ARINC 653 are also extended to the communications among processors using the AFDX network [7].

As we have shown, it is easy to find software in different domains that allows blocking on communications or data events, and thus a pure event-driven behavior in a distributed system can be conceived. In this work, we want to quantify the effect of polling tasks on the performance of real-time distributed systems when they are used in an event-driven architecture. To analyze polling tasks, we will propose an equivalent model based on periodic tasks that allows using current response time analysis techniques. We will quantify the effects of polling in two ways: (1) by applying the proposed analysis technique to a representative example looking at the worst-case response times, and (2) by the implementation of the example in a real platform to evaluate whether the average response times follow the same behavior or not. This work is focused on polling tasks that are used in event-driven distributed systems where clock synchronization is not required.

The document is organized as follows. Section 2 presents the event-driven model for the distributed system and the response time analysis techniques that can be applied to this model. In Sect. 3, a motivating example as well as the representative scenarios for evaluation are introduced. A new method for modeling and analyzing polling tasks is presented in Sect. 4. Section 5 deals with the application of the new analysis technique to the proposed scenarios, under different conditions. An experimental evaluation of average performance is presented in Sect. 6 using an Ada-based platform that implements some of the scenarios with synthetic workloads. Finally, Sect. 7 draws the conclusions.

2 The System Model and Current Schedulability Analysis Techniques

Our system model assumes a real-time distributed system with multiple processing resources, i.e., CPUs and communication networks, scheduled by a fixed-priority preemptive policy. We will use the system model called MAST (Modeling and Analysis Suite for Real Time Applications) [8], which is aligned with the MARTE (Modeling and Analysis of Real-Time Embedded systems) standard [9]. The MAST model considers a system composed of distributed end-to-end flows with periodic or sporadic activations. Sporadic activations are treated as periodics, using a period equal to the minimum interarrival time. Each end-to-end flow Γ_i is released by a periodic sequence of external events with period T_i, and contains a set of steps that model tasks and messages. We assume that all event sequences that arrive at the system and their worst-case rates are known in advance, and we also assume that tasks and messages are statically assigned to processors and networks respectively (migration is not allowed). The relative phasing of the activations of different end-to-end flows is assumed to be arbitrary.

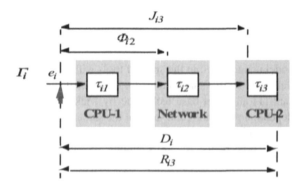

Fig. 1. System model

When schedulability analysis techniques for distributed systems are applied to this model, it is assumed that each periodic release of an end-to-end flow causes the execution of the set of steps, each step being released when the preceding one finishes its execution. This behavior represents a coupled execution of the steps in which all the events have to be processed assuming the existence of buffers between steps with enough size to ensure that events are not lost. However, as we mentioned in the introduction, real applications and standards for middleware, runtimes, or networks, can follow other communication paradigms that decouple the execution of the steps, allowing the loss of events. A classification in different scenarios according to the activation of steps and the kind of buffer used will be discussed in Sect. 3.

Figure 1 shows an example of one of these end-to-end flows, with just three steps, each executing in a different processing resource (two CPUs and one network in this case).

The arrival of the external event that releases the end-to-end flow is represented by a vertical arrow and has a period of T_i. The horizontal arrows represent the release of the following step in the end-to-end flow. The j-th step of end-to-end flow Γ_i, is identified as τ_{ij}. It has a worst-case execution time (WCET) or worst-case transmission time of C_{ij}. The non-preemptability of a network packet causing a delay for the transmission of a step is modeled through a blocking time which alternatively accommodates blocking due to mutual exclusion synchronization in the processors.

The timing requirements that we consider are end-to-end deadlines, D_i, that start at the end-to-end flow instance's period, and must be met by the final step. We allow deadlines to be larger than the periods, and thus at each time there may be several instances of the same end-to-end flow pending. For each step τ_{ij} we define its response time as the difference between its completion time and the instant at which the period of the end-to-end flow instance started. The worst-case response time, WCRT, or an estimation of an upper bound on it, will be called R_{ij}.

We allow the external event that triggers an end-to-end flow to have a maximum release jitter J_{i1} in relation to the nominal start of the instance's period. Other steps τ_{ij} may also have an initial release jitter J_{ij} causing the actual release to have an arbitrary delay between zero and J_{ij}, relative to the nominal release. Despite this jitter, global deadlines and response times always refer to the nominal start of the instance's period, not to the actual release of the end-to-end flow. Each step τ_{ij} may also have an associated initial offset, Φ_{ij}, which is the minimum release time for the step, relative to the nominal start of the instance's period. We assume that J_{ij} and Φ_{ij} may be larger than the period of their end-to-end flow, T_i.

The MAST model is integrated in the suite of tools with the same name [10], which implements schedulability analysis techniques for distributed systems. In particular, the main techniques are (1) an offset-base technique by Mäki-Turja and Nolin [11] that exploits the interdependencies among the steps of the same end-to-end flow through the use of task offsets; and (2) another offset-based technique by Palencia and González [12] that exploits the precedence relations among the steps. The former is called *Offset_Based_Slanted* in MAST and it is the one used in this work.

3   Motivating Example and Definition of Evaluation Scenarios

In order to illustrate the evaluation of the polling mechanism we have selected the architecture of an interesting example presented by Di Natale et al. in Sect. 3 of [13]. This simple example illustrates the drawbacks associated with the two activation models present in common automotive systems. Figure 2 shows an adaptation of this example in which 3 end-to-end flows composed by 8 tasks and 5 messages are allocated to three CPUs and one packet-based network (like the CAN bus in [13]). According to the model defined in Sect. 2, horizontal arrows represent the precedence relations of the steps in the end-to-end flow. We initially assume the same priority assignment than in [13], i.e., the priorities are assigned to steps in deadline monotonic order according to the end-to-end deadline of the end-to-end flow, and they are assigned in decreasing order from each external event to its subsequent steps located in the same processing resource.

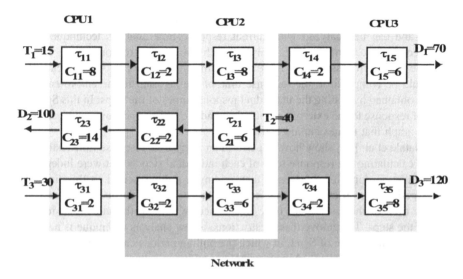

Fig. 2. Reference example of a distributed system (times in ms)

We will consider the following scenarios, taking into account the different ways in which the steps can be activated by the previous ones in the end-to-end flow:

- Scenario 1 (Scn1): independent task model. All the steps are activated periodically as if they were independent. The first step in the end-to-end-flow is activated by an external event, and the subsequent steps execute always the same code independently of whether the triggering event has arrived or not. This is the scenario implied by sampling ports in ARINC 653 where tasks always work with the last available data. The notion of processing a particular event is lost, as it is not possible to determine which data is being processed.
- Scenario 2 (Scn2): polling model. All the steps poll periodically for the arrival of an event, except the first step in the end-to-end-flow which is activated by the external event. In this case, the notion of processing a particular event is still valid, as the event is only processed when it arrives. This behavior occurs in a polling task implementing a data reader in DDS.
- Scenario 3 (Scn3): event-driven model. Each step in the end-to-end-flow is triggered by the completion of the previous one, except the first one that is activated by an external event. This is a common behavior of tasks sending messages asynchronously to the network, and tasks waiting for incoming data, e.g., in the context of Ada a task executing the remote part of an RPC can wait for the reception of the call directly in the network driver.
- Scenario 4 (Scn4): polling tasks and asynchronous messages. A different behavior is considered for task and messages. All the tasks poll periodically for the arrival of the event, except the first one in the end-to-end-flow that is activated by an external event, and all the messages are triggered by the completion of the previous task.

The scenarios presented here are representative of different architectures of real systems and can be analyzed with current response time analysis techniques under certain conditions. Scn1 can be analyzed with the classic response time analysis technique for uniprocessors with arbitrary deadlines and jitter [14]. End-to-end deadlines could be compared to the response time of the last step in the end-to-end flow, which is obtained by adding the individual response times of the steps. In this Scn1, the notion of response to the external event is lost and the end-to-end flow can be seen as a directed graph that relates certain activities.

Di Natale et al. [13] show how to perform an alternative response time analysis for Scn2 by calculating the response time of each individual step as if it were independent (as it would be done for Scn1) and then adding a polling period to this time. The polling period is restricted to being equal to the period of the external event. The response time of the end-to-end flow is obtained by adding the individual response times of the steps. To remove these restrictions, a new analysis technique is needed to analyze the general case of Scn2, in which the polling periods can be different than the period of the external event. A new technique addressing these requirements is presented in the next section.

Any of the response time analysis techniques available for event-driven end-to-end flows can be applied to Scn3, and a combination of these techniques with the new one for polling steps introduced in the next section will allow the analysis of Scn4.

4   Modelling and Analysis Technique for Polling Tasks

When a task is scheduled under the polling policy it is activated periodically to test for the arrival of its triggering event. When this triggering event is periodic itself, obviously the polling period (T_{poll}) must be less than or equal to the event period (T); otherwise the task would not be able to catch up with the workload that it is servicing and response times would be unbounded.

The selection of the polling period has an important impact on both the response times and the overhead. In the worst case it is possible that a triggering event arrives just after the polling task has negatively tested for its arrival. The polling mechanism will therefore introduce a delay that is up to T_{poll} in the worst case, thus making the task's worst-case response time (WCRT) larger than in the case of direct event processing. One would be tempted to use a small T_{poll} to minimize this delay, but it is necessary to balance it with the overhead introduced by the polling mechanism. Each time the task tests for the arrival of an event that has not yet arrived there is an execution using the computing resource for some time: C_{over} in the worst case. Obviously this overhead is incurred more frequently as T_{poll} becomes smaller. A compromise between response times and overhead has to be made at design time by tuning the polling period [2].

In this section we will show that an upper bound to the effects of executing the polling task and its overhead can be modeled as two separate periodic tasks with jitter. This model is very convenient because it allows us to analyze a system with polling tasks using the regular schedulability analysis techniques for periodic tasks. We pay attention to three main issues that can influence the analysis: the analysis of the own

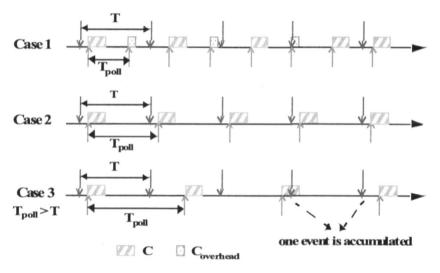

Fig. 3. Cases in the analysis of polling for periodic events

polling task, the effect of polling on the analysis of lower priority tasks, and the overhead effects. We distinguish three cases as a function of the relation between T and T_{poll}. Figure 3 shows the three cases considered for analysis.

Case 1: Tpoll < T

Analysis of the own task: The response time is calculated using the selected analysis technique, but an additional value of T_{poll} should be added to account for the delay introduced by polling in the worst case.

$$R_{poll} = R_{periodic} + T_{poll} \qquad (1)$$

Analysis of lower priority tasks: An equivalent task is created to model the task execution using the parameters described in Lemma 1.

Lemma 1: Assume a task with WCET C, period T and release jitter J executed under the polling policy with a polling period $T_{poll} < T$ and no overhead. Its interference on lower priority tasks is no larger than the interference of an equivalent periodic task with the same WCET and period as the original task, but using an additional jitter of

$$J_{additional} = T_{poll} \qquad (2)$$

Proof: In the analysis of periodic tasks with jitter the interference of a task on lower priority tasks in the time interval [0,t] is [15]:

$$I(t) = \left\lceil \frac{t + J}{T} \right\rceil C \qquad (3)$$

We now need to add the effects of the polling policy. The number of whole polling periods that are found in the interval [0, t] is $\lfloor t/T_{poll} \rfloor$. In the worst case we must accumulate the most work at the beginning of the busy period [15] which can be accomplished if the first event arrived at time -T_{poll} and just missed the execution by the polling mechanism. The interval during which events that are processed inside the busy period may arrive is therefore [-T_{poll}, t]. The interference on lower priority tasks is the number of events arriving in that interval multiplied by the WCET:

$$I(t) = \left\lceil \frac{t + T_{poll} + J}{T} \right\rceil C \tag{4}$$

Therefore, an additional jitter value of T_{poll} must be added to the original jitter of the event.   □

This equivalent task is pessimistic, as it introduces additional interference specially for short response times. However it approaches the exact case as response times increase.

In addition to modeling the effects of the execution of events, we need to model the overhead with the inclusion of a new independent periodic task.

Lemma 2: Assume a task with WCET C, period T and release jitter J executed under the polling policy with a polling period $T_{poll} < T$. The interference of its overhead (i.e., the execution when no event is processed) on lower priority tasks is no larger than the interference of an equivalent periodic task with WCET=C_{over}, period T_{over} and release jitter J_{over} according to:

$$T_{over} = \frac{(T \cdot T_{poll})}{T - T_{poll}} \qquad J_{over} = T_{over} \tag{5}$$

Proof: Since $C_{over} < C$ we assume the worst case scenario in which the polling task executes an event just at the beginning of the busy period. The number of activations of the polling task between 0 and t, either to execute the full task to service an incoming event or just to execute the overhead, is $\lceil t/T_{poll} \rceil$. From these executions we need to subtract the minimum number of arrivals of the event, because these will result in the execution of the full task and not the overhead. A lower bound on the number of arrivals of the event between 0 and t is $\lfloor t/T \rfloor$. Under the conditions used for the worst-case analysis presented in Lemma 1 the release jitter has no influence on this lower bound, because it is used to concentrate the most work at the beginning of the critical instant, not to distribute it during a longer time.

The number of releases of the polling overhead is therefore not less than

$$\left\lceil \frac{t}{T_{poll}} \right\rceil - \left\lfloor \frac{t}{T} \right\rfloor = \left\lceil \frac{t}{T_{poll}} \right\rceil + \left\lceil \frac{-t}{T} \right\rceil \tag{6}$$

and then we get

$$\left\lceil \frac{t}{T_{poll}} \right\rceil + \left\lceil \frac{-t}{T} \right\rceil \le \left\lceil \frac{t}{T_{poll}} - \frac{t}{T} \right\rceil + 1 = \left\lceil \frac{t}{T_{poll}} - \frac{t}{T} + 1 \right\rceil = \left\lceil t \left(\frac{1}{T_{poll}} - \frac{1}{T} \right) + 1 \right\rceil =$$

$$\left\lceil \frac{t + 1/(1/T_{poll} - 1/T)}{1/(1/T_{poll} - 1/T)} \right\rceil = \left\lceil \frac{t + (T \cdot T_{poll})/(T - T_{poll})}{(T \cdot T_{poll})/(T - T_{poll})} \right\rceil = \left\lceil \frac{t + T_{over}}{T_{over}} \right\rceil \tag{7}$$

where we have used the following properties of ceiling and floor functions [16]: $\lfloor x \rfloor = -\lceil -x \rceil$ and $\lceil x \rceil + \lceil y \rceil - 1 \le \lceil x + y \rceil \le \lceil x \rceil + \lceil y \rceil$. The last expression in Eq. (7) is the number of releases of the proposed equivalent task with period T_{over} and the same release jitter. ☐

This equivalent model allows us to obtain an upper bound on the overhead. It is pessimistic as it could add an extra C_{over}, but this pessimism remains constant with time so that as response times become larger its relative effect is smaller.

Case 2: Tpoll = Ti

Analysis of the own task: as in case 1 the response time is calculated by using the selected analysis technique and then T_{poll} should be added to account for the delay introduced by the polling mechanism.

Analysis of lower priority tasks: The polling task executes periodically with period T, and therefore the equivalent task has WCET = C and period = T without any additional jitter. There is no overhead caused by polling.

Case 3: Tpoll > Ti

Analysis of the own task: As mentioned above, the response time is unbounded in this case.

Analysis of lower priority tasks: The polling task executes periodically with WCET = C and period = T_{poll} without additional jitter. There is no overhead caused by polling as the polling task always has events to process.

5   Analytic Evaluation of Different Scenarios

This section provides the evaluation of the example with the architecture presented in Fig. 2 under the four scenarios defined in Sect. 3. The objective of this section is to quantify the effect of polling in the worst-case response times of steps, by applying the analysis technique proposed in Sect. 4. We have implemented the analysis technique for polling tasks in the MAST tools. The effect of polling is modeled in MAST as a priority-based scheduling policy with extra attributes: the polling period, and the minimum, average and maximum overheads. We apply the schedulability analysis techniques to the different scenarios as follows:

- The technique called *Offset_Based_Slanted* [11] in MAST is applied to all scenarios.
- For Scn1, the response time reported for the last step in the end-to-end flow is the sum of the response times of all the steps.
- The scenarios with polling steps (Scn2 and Scn4) are evaluated for different values of the polling period, in particular for ratios T_{poll}/T equal to 1, 3/4, 1/2, and 1/4. We denote these cases with the name of the scenario followed by the corresponding ratio in brackets.

Table 1 shows the worst-case response times of the end-to-end flows and the system slack for the different scenarios and conditions tested using the priorities specified in [13]. The system slack is an estimation of the sensitivity of the system and is defined in MAST as the percentage by which the execution times of all the steps in the system may be increased while still keeping the system schedulable, if positive, and the percentage by which they have to be decreased to make the system schedulable, if negative. Slack cannot be calculated for Scn1 as task and messages are modelled as independent steps and there are no individual deadlines associated to them. Bold face is used for numbers representing schedulable end-to-end flows, and shaded columns for schedulable systems, i.e., those in which all end-to-end flows are schedulable.

Table 1. Response times for the reference example with the priorities proposed in [13] (times in ms), and system slack (%)

E2E FLOW	SCN1	SCN2 (1)	SCN2 (3/4)	SCN2 (1/2)	SCN2 (1/4)	SCN3	SCN4 (1)	SCN4 (3/4)	SCN4 (1/2)	SCN4 (1/4)
Γ_1	**32**	92	77	**64**	47	32	**62**	**54.5**	**47**	**38.75**
Γ_2	**52**	152	164	132	102	72	112	120	102	**92**
Γ_3	**104**	452	820	654	490	332	392	545	486	425
SLACK		-100.00	-78.91	-59.77	-39.45	-16.80	-37.50	-45.70	-35.16	-28.13

In Table 1, we can see that only Scn1 in which all the steps are independent can be scheduled. However, in this scenario there may be loss of events, which means that its results cannot be compared to those of the other three scenarios where no events are lost. In any case this is a possible implementation and therefore we leave this scenario as a reference. In this case none of the other scenarios are schedulable, although the following conclusions can be drawn:

- Polling adversely affects system schedulability. Scn2, in which all steps do polling, is the one with higher response times and thus it is more distant in general from schedulability (lower values of slack). In Scn4, with less polling steps, lower response times and systems closer to schedulability are obtained. Scn3, the pure event-driven scenario, is the one with the best real-time performance.
- Schedulability is improved by reducing the polling period, as expected. This can be seen in the slacks obtained for Scn2 and Scn4. It is also noted that this improved schedulability produces lower response times for the higher priority tasks to the detriment of those with lower priority.

The disadvantage of polling had been observed for a system like Scn2(1) in [13]. That work proposed mixing polling and event-driven activation to improve the system schedulability. Another work [17], noted that the periodic activation of messages (called polling-based output management) is not the right choice for real-time systems.

The priorities specified in [13] may be optimal considering the system as a set of uniprocessors with independent steps (such as in Scn1), but they can be optimized for an event-driven distributed system [18]. In order to better assess the impact of polling on distributed systems, we repeat the experiments in Table 1 optimizing the priority assignment with the HOSPA algorithm [19] available in MAST. The priorities assigned to the steps for the different scenarios are depicted in the Appendix. From the results shown in Table 2, we can draw the following conclusions[1]:

Table 2. Response times for the reference example with the priorities assigned by MAST (times in ms), and system slack (%)

E2E FLOW	SCN1	SCN2 (1)	SCN2 (3/4)	SCN2 (1/2)	SCN2 (1/4)	SCN3	SCN4 (1)	SCN4 (3/4)	SCN4 (1/2)	SCN4 (1/4)
Γ_1	32	110	128	102	77	58	84	84.5	79	67.5
Γ_2	52	148	154	124	82	52	98	104	72	62
Γ_3	104	200	219	168	119	96	138	133	122	111
SLACK		-100.00	-59.77	-35.55	-9.77	4.69	-23.44	-21.09	-11.33	2.73

- All scenarios can be better scheduled, except Scn1 that cannot be optimized because it is treated as a set of uniprocessor systems, as we already mentioned.
- Polling continues to show a negative effect on schedulability, although response times are closer to deadlines and slacks are higher with optimized priorities.
- Again, improved response times are observed when reducing polling periods. A scenario using polling is now schedulable.
- Scn3 with pure event-driven activation remains the one with the best response times and slacks.

As we can see, the availability of response time analysis techniques allows us to assess the schedulability under different conditions. We have seen that reducing the polling period can decrease response times, but this reduction may take an associated overhead. Our final test is devoted to studying the effects of overhead in Scn4, as it is a scenario using polling where a schedulable solution has been found when optimizing priorities. Table 3 shows the response times assuming that the polling overhead is a realistic value of 0.2 ms for any of the polling tasks. Results for the priority assignment proposed in [13], and for the priority assignment obtained with MAST are shown (details for the assignments can be found in the Appendix). The increases in the utilization of the processing resources due to the polling overhead are shown in Table 4 for Scn4. These results show that polling overhead should be also taken into account as it could have a serious impact on the system schedulability.

---

[1] In the application of the HOSPA algorithm the following configurations parameters have been used in the MAST tool 1.5.1.0: (1) Ka = (0.25, 2.00, 3.00) and Kr = (1.50, 2.00, 3.00) for Scn3, and (2) Ka = (1.50, 2.00, 3.00) and Kr = (0.50, 2.00, 3.00) for Scn2 and Scn4.

Table 3. Response times for Scn4 with polling overheads (times in ms), and system slack (%)

E2E FLOW	PRIORITIES SPECIFIED IN [13]			PRIORITIES ASSIGNED BY MAST		
	SCN4 (3/4)	SCN4 (1/2)	SCN4 (1/4)	SCN4 (3/4)	SCN4 (1/2)	SCN4 (1/4)
Γ_1	**55.30**	**47.8**	**39.35**	88.9	78.4	**66.3**
Γ_2	129.0	111.2	102.6	104.8	**95**	**81.6**
Γ_3	589.8	491.4	458.4	140.4	122.4	**113.6**
SLACK	-47.27	-36.72	-31.64	-23.05	-10.94	0.00

Table 4. Processing resource utilizations for Scn4 with polling overhead (in %)

Processing resource	Scn4 (1)	Scn4 (3/4)	Scn4 (1/2)	Scn4 (1/4)
CPU1	95.00	95.17	95.50	96.50
CPU2	88.33	89.00	90.33	94.33
CPU3	66.67	67.33	68.67	72.67
Network	45.00	45.00	45.00	45.00
System (AVG.)	73.74	74.13	74.88	77.13

6   Average Performance Evaluation on an Ada-Based Distributed Platform

The implementation and evaluation of the whole set of scenarios previously described in Sect. 3 would be too extensive to be included in this paper. Instead, this section presents the most representative scenarios to evaluate the performance impact of using polling in a distributed real-time platform. In particular, scenarios Scn3 and Scn4 with ratios T_{poll}/T equal to 1 and 1/4 will be implemented in a real distributed system, evaluated for the two priority assignments analysed, and then discussed. Our objective is to quantify the effect of polling on the average response times by implementing some of the scenarios in a real platform.

The hardware platform used for this evaluation consists of three single core 800 MHz embedded nodes that are interconnected through a CAN bus. For the CAN messages we have used 11-bit identifiers with a bit rate of 62.5 Kbit/s, and messages with 7 bytes of data. According to this configuration, the maximum transmission time of each message is 2 ms, assuming worst-case bit stuffing [20]. The message identifiers also determine the CAN bus transmission priorities.

The software platform consists of a distributed Ada application running on top of MaRTE OS v1.9 [21], a real-time kernel for embedded systems that follows the Minimal Real-Time POSIX.13 subset. The task workloads are synthetic and take random values in the range [C/5, C]. They are implemented using execution-time clocks in Ada. Furthermore, polling tasks have been implemented using an Ada conditional entry call in a protected object.

The Phillips SJA1000 CAN controller chip has been used in this evaluation. As part of the development, we have implemented a set of Ada functions to configure the bus speed and the acceptance filter associated with each chip. Furthermore, the SJA1000 chip presents a transmission buffer with capacity to store a single CAN message for transmission over the network. This feature can lead to unbounded priority inversion problem, as messages with higher priority can be waiting while a low-priority message is taking part of the bus arbitration process. To address this issue, the implemented driver replaces the message stored in the transmission buffer whenever a message with higher priority is ready to be transmitted, except when the transmission of the message currently in the buffer is already in progress.

There is a lack of a common clock to make temporal measurements in this distributed system. To address this issue, the response times have been obtained using an oscilloscope to measure the delay between two digital signals that are set/cleared in different nodes. Then, the samples obtained are sent and processed in a PC. The oscilloscope provides a sampling rate of 50 kHz and each simulation has been run enough time to allow a minimum of 2000 activations for the end-to-end flow under evaluation.

From the results shown in Table 5, it can be observed that the measured results are far from reaching the worst-case response time computed by the schedulability analysis tool. This is expected as real execution for a limited time does not guarantee hitting worst-case activation and execution patterns. In any case, the results provide a glimpse of the tendency of the evaluated scenarios. Hence, the average response times obtained in Scn3 are lower than in Scn4 for both priority assignments. Regarding Scn3, the priorities obtained with MAST cause a higher response time for the first end-to-end flow, whereas the two remaining end-to-end flows present lower response times than with the priorities specified in [13]. The results obtained in Scn4 for both priority assignments show how reducing the polling period can also decrease the average response times. Again, the priorities obtained with MAST cause a higher response time for the first end-to-end flow as a trade-off to decreasing the response time of the remaining end-to-end flows, thus increasing the system slack. The general behavior is consistent with the analytic results presented in Sect. 5, showing that polling has a negative effect on the schedulability of the system, thus producing higher response times than the event-driven approach.

Table 5. Average response times measured in the distributed platform (times in ms)

E2E flow	Priorities proposed in [13]			Priorities assigned by MAST		
	Scn3	Scn4 (1)	Scn4 (1/4)	Scn3	Scn4 (1)	Scn4 (1/4)
Γ_1	16.9	34.9	20.5	19.9	51.5	22.8
Γ_2	20.5	41.8	23.8	19.2	37.6	21.9
Γ_3	27.3	90.8	33.4	22.0	79.7	26.3

7   Conclusions

Polling on the arrival of events or messages coming from a network is a common practice followed by engineers in the development of distributed real-time systems. We can find mechanisms in software that allow waiting directly on events or messages, thus allowing us to avoid polling. In this paper we have shown the negative effects of using polling. We have also shown that optimizing the assignment of priorities significantly enhances the real-time performance of the system when polling cannot be avoided.

This paper also provides a modeling and analysis technique that allows calculating worst-case response times for polling tasks, by using the current response time analysis techniques for distributed systems. The analysis technique takes into account overheads in those cases when the polling period is lower than the period of the event. We have implemented this new technique in the MAST tools and we have also evaluated its analytical results, which are completed with an average performance evaluation on a real distributed platform with synthetic workloads. As expected, waiting directly on events, which is supported by standard programming languages, distribution middleware, communication software, and operating systems, should be the preferred option in order to increase the schedulability of distributed real-time systems, thus advising the use of polling only for imperative cases. Even in those cases the analysis techniques presented in this paper allow engineers to assess the schedulability of their designs.

Appendix

The priority assignments used in the different scenarios are depicted in Tables 6 and 7. A priority range between 1 and 13 has been used for the assignment in each processing resource. The higher the number the higher the priority.

Table 6. Priorities assigned in [13] used in all scenarios, and priorities assigned by MAST for Scn1, Scn2 and Scn3

Step	Priorities in [13]	Scn1	Scn2 (1)	Scn2 (3/4)	Scn2 (1/2)	Scn2 (1/4)	Scn3
τ_{11}	13	9	5	5	5	5	9
τ_{12}	12	11	8	8	8	8	6
τ_{13}	11	9	1	1	1	1	1
τ_{14}	10	8	6	3	3	1	3
τ_{15}	9	7	7	7	7	7	7
τ_{21}	8	5	9	9	9	9	9
τ_{22}	7	6	1	1	1	3	11
τ_{23}	6	5	1	1	1	1	1

(*Continued*)

Table 6. (*Continued*)

Step	Priorities in [13]	Scn1	Scn2 (1)	Scn2 (3/4)	Scn2 (1/2)	Scn2 (1/4)	Scn3
τ_{31}	5	1	9	9	9	9	5
τ_{32}	4	3	11	11	11	11	8
τ_{33}	3	1	5	5	5	5	5
τ_{34}	2	1	3	6	6	6	1
τ_{35}	1	1	1	1	1	1	1

Table 7. Priorities assigned by MAST for Scn4 with and without polling overhead

Step	Without polling overhead				With polling overhead		
	Scn4 (1)	Scn4 (3/4)	Scn4 (1/2)	Scn4 (1/4)	Scn4 (3/4)	Scn4 (1/2)	Scn4 (1/4)
τ_{11}	5	5	5	5	5	5	5
τ_{12}	8	8	6	6	8	8	8
τ_{13}	1	1	1	1	1	1	1
τ_{14}	1	1	1	3	1	1	6
τ_{15}	7	7	7	7	7	7	7
τ_{21}	9	5	9	9	5	5	9
τ_{22}	6	3	11	11	3	3	1
τ_{23}	1	1	1	1	1	1	1
τ_{31}	9	9	9	9	9	9	9
τ_{32}	11	11	8	8	11	11	11
τ_{33}	5	9	5	5	9	9	5
τ_{34}	3	6	3	1	6	6	3
τ_{35}	1	1	1	1	1	1	1

References

1. Sha, L., Abdelzaher, T., Årzén, K.-E., Cervin, A., Baker, T., Burns, A., Buttazzo, G., Caccamo, M., Lehoczky, J., Mok, A.K.: Real time scheduling theory: a historical perspective. Real-Time Syst. J. **28**(2–3), 101–155 (2004)
2. Henia, R., Rioux, L.: FMTV challenge 2015. In: 6th International Workshop on Analysis Tools and Methodologies for Embedded and Real-time Systems (WATERS), Lund, Sweden (2015). https://waters2015.inria.fr/files/2014/11/FMTV-2015-Challenge.pdf
3. Feiertag, N., Richter, K., Nordlander, J., Jonsson, J.: A compositional framework for end-to-end path delay calculation of automotive systems under different path semantics. In: Proceedings of the Workshop on Compositional Theory and Technology for Real-Time Embedded Systems (co-located with RTSS), Barcelona, Spain (2008)

4. Mubeen, S., Mäki-Turja, J., Sjödin, M.: Implementation of end-to-end latency analysis for component-based multi-rate real-time systems in Rubus-ICE. In: Proceedings of the 9th IEEE International Workshop on Factory Communication Systems (WFCS), Lemgo, Germany, pp. 165–168 (2012)

5. Object Management Group: Data distribution service for real-time systems. OMG Document, v1.4, formal/15-04-10 (2015)

6. Airlines Electronic Engineering Committee, Aeronautical Radio INC.: ARINC Specification 653-1: Avionics Application Software Interface, Required Services, November 2010

7. Airlines Electronic Engineering Committee, Aeronautical Radio INC.: ARINC Specification 664 P7-1: Aircraft Data Network, Part 7 - Avionics Full Duplex Switched Ethernet Network, 23 September 2009

8. González Harbour, M., Gutiérrez, J.J., Palencia, J.C., Drake, J.M.: MAST: modeling and analysis suite for real-time applications. In: Proceedings of the 13th Euromicro Conference on Real-Time Systems, Delft, The Netherlands, pp. 125–134 (2001)

9. Object Management Group: UML profile for MARTE: modeling and analysis of real-time embedded systems. OMG Document, v1.1 formal/2011-06-02 (2011)

10. MAST. http://mast.unican.es/

11. Mäki-Turja, J., Nolin, M.: Efficient implementation of tight response-times for tasks with offsets. Real-Time Syst. J. 40(1), 77–116 (2008)

12. Palencia, J.C., González Harbour, M.: Exploiting precedence relations in the schedulability analysis of distributed real-time systems. In: Proceedings of the 20th Real-Time Systems Symposium, pp. 328–339. IEEE, Phoenix, AZ, USA (1999)

13. Di Natale, M., Pinello, C., Giusto, P., Sangiovanni, A.: Optimizing end-to-end latencies by adaptation of the activation events in distributed automotive systems. Proceedings of the 13th IEEE Real Time and Embedded Technology and Applications Symposium, Bellevue, Washington, USA, pp. 293–302 (2007)

14. Tindell, K., Burns, A., Wellings, A.: An extendible approach for analysing fixed priority hard real-time tasks. Real-Time Syst. J. 6(2), 133–151 (1994)

15. Palencia, J.C., Gutiérrez, J.J., González Harbour, M.: On the schedulability analysis for distributed hard real-time systems. In: Proceedings of 9th Euromicro Workshop on Real-Time Systems, pp. 136–143 (1997)

16. Graham, R.L., Knuth, D.E., Patashnik, O.: Concrete Mathematics, 2nd edn. Addison-Wesley Publishing Company, Boston (1994). ISBN 0-201-55802-5

17. Di Natale, M., Zeng, H.: Practical issues with the timing analysis of the controller area network. In: Proceedings of the 18th IEEE International Conference on Emerging Technologies and Factory Automation, Cagliari, Italy, pp. 293–302 (2013)

18. Gutiérrez, J.J., González Harbour, M.: Prioritizing remote procedure calls in Ada distributed systems. In: 9th International Real-Time Ada Workshop, Tallahassee, USA, vol. XIX, no. 2, pp. 67–72. ACM Ada-Letters (1999)

19. Rivas, J.M., Gutierrez, J.J., Palencia, J.C., González Harbour, M.: Schedulability analysis and optimization of heterogeneous EDF and FP distributed real-time systems. In: Proceedings of the 23rd Euromicro Conference on Real-Time Systems, Porto, Portugal, pp. 195–204 (2011)

20. Davis, R.I., Burns, A., Bril, R.J., Lukkien, J.J.: Controller area network (CAN) schedulability analysis: refuted, revisited and revised. Real-Time Syst. J. 35(3), 239–272 (2007)

21. Aldea Rivas, M., González Harbour, M.: MaRTE OS: an Ada kernel for real-time embedded applications. In: Strohmeier, A., Craeynest, D. (eds.) Ada-Europe 2001. LNCS, vol. 2043, pp. 305–316. Springer, Heidelberg (2001)

Combining Time-Triggered Plans with Priority Scheduled Task Sets

Jorge Real[1]([⊠]), Sergio Sáez[2], and Alfons Crespo[1]

[1] Instituto de Automática e Informática Industrial,
Universitat Politècnica de València, Camino de Vera, S/n, 46022 Valencia, Spain
{jorge,alfons}@disca.upv.es
[2] Instituto Tecnológico de Informática, Universitat Politècnica de València,
Camino de Vera, S/n, 46022 Valencia, Spain
ssaez@disca.upv.es

Abstract. Time-triggered and concurrent priority-based scheduling are the two major approaches in use for real-time and embedded systems. Both approaches have their own advantages and drawbacks. On the one hand, priority-based systems facilitate separation of concerns between functional and timing requirements by relying on an underlying real-time operating system that takes all scheduling decisions at run time. But this is at the cost of indeterminism in the exact timing pattern of execution of activities, namely variable release jitter. On the other hand, time-triggered schedules are more intricate to design since all scheduling decisions must be taken beforehand in the design phase, but their advantage is determinism and more chances for minimisation of release jitter. In this paper we propose a software architecture that enables the combined and controlled execution of time-triggered plans and priority-scheduled tasks. We also describe the implementation of an Ada library supporting it. Our aim is to take advantage of the best of both approaches by providing jitter-controlled execution of time-triggered tasks (e.g., control tasks), coexisting with a set of priority-scheduled tasks, with less demanding jitter requirements.

Keywords: Real-time systems · Jitter · Time-triggered scheduling · Ada

1 Introduction

Using concurrent tasks in real-time systems software allows designers to clearly separate functional from timing requirements, letting them focus on functionality and delegating the scheduling of activities on the underlying real-time operating system (RTOS). The RTOS uses a priority scheme to select which task (or tasks,

This work has been partly supported by the Spanish Government's project M2C2 (TIN2014-56158-C4-1-P-AR) and the European Commission's project EMC2 (ARTEMIS-JU Call 2013 AIPP-5, Contract 621429).

© Springer International Publishing Switzerland 2016
M. Bertogna et al. (Eds.): Ada-Europe 2016, LNCS 9695, pp. 195–212, 2016.
DOI: 10.1007/978-3-319-39083-3_13

in multiprocessor systems) can execute at a given time [1]. This approach is backed by extensive research results that define the conditions under which this type of systems can be guaranteed to comply with their deadlines at run time.

However, priority scheduling introduces a fundamental issue in tasks with strict release jitter requirements. Release jitter is the difference in time between the theoretical and actual release time of a task. In major application areas, such as automatic control or synchronised distributed communications, excessive release jitter causes performance degradation that needs be avoided. Some amount of jitter is in practice unavoidable, since scheduling decisions take time and that translates into scheduler's overhead that ultimately interferes the whole task set. But in priority scheduled systems, all but the highest-priority task may be additionally interfered by other higher-priority tasks. When this interference straddles a task's theoretical release time, then the task will suffer release jitter until all higher-priority levels become idle.

On the other hand, time-triggered scheduling is based on an offline predefined schedule (a plan) in which the designer identifies the exact points in time when every planned activity must start. From that release time, the activity is granted a time slot to execute, whose duration is, by design, sufficiently large to accommodate its computational needs. No other activity is scheduled until the end of the previous slot. This property translates into small and bounded jitter, because time-triggered activities do not interfere each other and they are solely affected by the scheduler's overhead. In addition, a time-triggered scheduler is comparatively simple, since all scheduling decisions are taken at well-defined points dictated by the static plan. This means small overhead, and therefore, less jitter. The main drawback attributed to time-triggered scheduling is that plans may become difficult to design, specially when they are large and involve a large number of activities.

In this paper we explore an alternative that combines both schemes for the same application. Activities imposing strict jitter requirements are scheduled according to a time-triggered plan, whereas the rest of tasks are scheduled by a priority-based scheduler. The whole set of tasks (time-triggered and priority-scheduled tasks) will be running under the same preemptive, priority scheduler, but time-triggered activities will do it at the highest priority of the whole set. This is in order to ensure minimal latency in their activations, given that they don't suffer interference from (non-existent) higher-priority tasks, and hence their release jitter can be kept controlled and short. The rest of tasks execute at lower priority levels under the same dispatching policy (preemptive, non-preemptive, EDF) or under a combination of several dispatching policies, e.g. by making use of Ada's priority specific dispatching. The Ada programming language is very well suited for our purpose and we will be using it to illustrate our proposal.

Our approach also pays attention to providing temporal isolation to time-triggered activities. A well-designed time-triggered plan guarantees, by construction, temporal isolation among activities. However, run-time guarantees must be provided to cater for potential overruns (execution of an activity could take longer than assumed due to underestimation of its actual worst-case execution time). We want to guarantee that an overrunning time-triggered activity will not jeopardise temporal isolation by executing beyond its allocated slot. This would increase its interference on priority-scheduled tasks and could even make it enter the slot of another time-triggered task and delay its release. There are several ways to handle overruns, their appropriateness being dependent on the application. One possibility is to abort the offending activity, although this may not be an option for some applications. Another way is to take the system to a degraded mode. Our proposed model and implementation support mode changes at the time-triggered level, hence this is always a possibility. But more specific to the overrun issue, our proposal also supports handling overruns by allowing the offending activity to continue executing at a harmless, lower priority level. At that priority level, they may find time to complete by the start of their next allocated time slot, without interfering higher-priority levels. Our approach therefore supports these three models. Which option to take is not imposed by our proposed scheduler, but enforced by the particular pattern implementing the activity. We propose several such patterns in this paper.

Although we confine most of our discussion to uniprocessor platforms, nothing prevents our model to be applied on multiprocessors. This paper, however, focuses on showing how the approach performs in terms of granting a reduced upper bound to the release jitter of time-triggered activities, limiting our study to a uniprocessor example. General considerations for application on multiprocessor systems are given in Sect. 8.

The rest of this paper is organised as follows. Section 2 presents related work. Section 3 explains our system model for the time-triggered plan. Section 4 describes an interface for the time-triggered scheduler and in Sect. 5 we propose several patterns for time-triggered activities that make use of the scheduler functionalities. Implementation details are discussed in Sect. 6. We have conducted several experiments and obtained jitter measurements that are presented and discussed in Sect. 7. Finally, in Sect. 8 we give our conclusions and pointers to further work.

2   Related Work

The issue of jitter in control and communication systems has been tackled from different angles. From a Control Engineering perspective, the work in [2] proposes to dynamically adjust the controller's parameters to compensate for the presence of jitter. Our perspective is different, albeit complementary, since our focus is on the minimisation of jitter at run time (while preserving the benefits of priority scheduling for tasks that are more tolerant to variable jitter).

From a scheduling perspective, [3] proposes methods to transform an off-line schedule into an equivalent fixed-priority task set that matches its runtime behaviour. This transformation is however not always possible, in which case the original task set needs be modified by splitting tasks into instances, hence generating a new task set. Our approach does not impose any transformations to the original task set, hence avoiding the need for scheduling artefacts. In [4], the focus is on the control-scheduling co-design of the system. A so called Control Server uses feedback from execution-time measurements and dynamically modifies the sampling periods to optimise control performance. In our proposal, the workload does not need to go through period modifications. Instead, control tasks preserve their timing parameters because they always run at the highest priority, irrespective of lower-priority events, hence experiencing minimal release jitter. Changes to the workload are however possible in our approach by dynamically changing the whole time-triggered plan. In [5], the authors propose to decompose control tasks in three parts: initial, mandatory and final (the IMF model). This decomposition is then used to assign higher priority to the parts that are most sensitive to jitter (initial and final) which in turn reduces the amount of interference they suffer and therefore contributes to reducing their jitter and improving the control performance. In [6], a method is proposed to reduce delay variations caused by overload perturbations. Their task model includes both IMF and non decomposed tasks and their method is to adjust their deadlines dynamically, according to a heuristic algorithm, so that tasks incur less delay. The algorithm is however non trivial and it introduces additional runtime overhead. In our proposed approach, control tasks are scheduled according to a time-triggered plan, hence their release times are clearly identified and deviation from the planned release points can only be caused by the scheduler's overhead, but not from higher-priority interference.

In summary, existing methods that tackle the jitter issue from a scheduling perspective, assume the system uses a priority scheduler and try to minimise the release jitter of selected tasks by finding clever priority assignments and timing parameters for them and by decomposing them into smaller parts. To the best of our knowledge, there is no previous work that tackles this issue by combining the predictability and controlled jitter of time-triggered schedules for jitter-sensitive tasks, with the flexibility of priority scheduling for the rest of tasks, all running under the same priority scheduler but granting the highest priority to the time-triggered plan.

3   System Model

In our system model, an offline, static time-triggered plan coexists with a set of concurrent, priority scheduled tasks. The priority scheme for these tasks can be either fixed per task (e.g., deadline monotonic, DM) or dynamic per task, fixed per job (e.g., earliest deadline first, EDF). These priority-based models have been extensively described in the literature and are fully supported in Ada [7]. Ada also supports the concept of priority-specific dispatching, which makes it possible to have a combination of dispatching policies conveniently spread over priority bands. In the following subsections we describe the system model for the static time-triggered plan, both in regard to what defines a plan and what are the actions taken by the time-triggered scheduler, and when those actions are executed. By assigning the time-triggered plan the highest priority, the set of priority scheduled tasks does not interfere the execution of the plan.

3.1   The Time-Triggered Plan

A time-triggered plan is described by an ordered sequence of *time slots*. Figure 1 shows a 6-slot example plan. Each slot has its own sequence number (a natural number), and is characterised by two parameters: a **work identifier**, (*Work_Id*), an integer value ultimately referring to either a piece of user-provided application code or a predefined scheduler action; the **slot duration**, a time interval after which the next slot starts. All scheduling decisions are made exclusively at the beginning of each slot. When designing the plan, the slot duration should be made large enough to accommodate the execution of the work denoted by the slot's work identifier

For example, *Slot 2* in Fig. 1 allocates 300 time units for the execution of *Work 3*. The whole plan sequence starts at a given time (identified here as time 0) and each slot starts right after the end of its predecessor in the plan. In the absence of mode changes (see later), the plan is repeated cyclically. In some cases, and for some types of slot, the slot duration may be zero. We consider three types of slots, depending on the kind of activity that must be executed during the slot duration:

- A **regular slot** defines a time interval for the execution of an application-specific activity. It is denoted by a *regular Work_Id* and a strictly positive slot duration. For *regular Work_Id* we mean a positive integer corresponding to a regular work identifier, i.e. one that ultimately refers to a piece of user-supplied application code. The duration of a regular slot must be, by design, sufficient to accommodate the worst-case execution time of that work – we will consider overrun handling in Subsect. 3.2. In Fig. 1, slots 0, 1, 2 and 4 are regular.

The following two types of slots correspond to scheduler actions exclusively and they have no associated application-specific activity.

- An **empty slot** defines a time interval during which no user activity is planned. This is useful for inserting gaps in the plan where they are needed, making the CPU available to priority scheduled tasks. Note that, even though there is no application-specific activity to execute during an empty slot, there will be scheduler actions executed at the beginning of the slot, as described in Subsect. 3.2. Empty slots use the special value zero as *Work_Id*. Slot 5 in Fig. 1 is an empty slot.
- A **mode-change slot** defines a point in time where it is possible to substitute the current plan with a new one. This polling approach is consistent with the nature of time-triggered scheduling, although the definition of mode-change slot provides an extra degree of flexibility, since the designer can place these polling points wherever the system can admit a mode change. At the start of a mode-change slot, the scheduler will check whether there is a pending mode-change request to process. If there is one, then the new plan will start executing at the end of the mode-change slot. The change will be immediate if the mode-change slot duration is defined to be zero. The ability to change

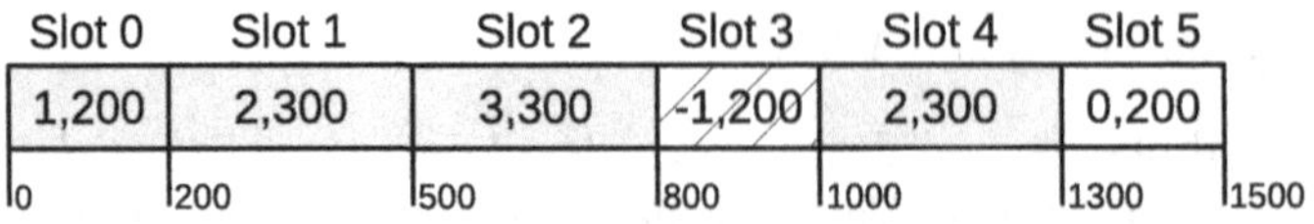

Slot 0	Slot 1	Slot 2	Slot 3	Slot 4	Slot 5
1,200	2,300	3,300	-1,200	2,300	0,200

0   200   500   800   1000   1300   1500

Fig. 1. A time-triggered plan. For each slot, the first number is the work identifier and the second is the slot duration. Slot 3 is a mode change slot. Slot 5 is an empty slot.

mode (substitute the current plan with a new one at run time) introduces a degree of flexibility that off-line, static schedules do not possess by nature. The inclusion of mode change slots provides a flexible means to specify in which points of the plan a mode change can be enforced. Mode change slots (such as Slot 3 in Fig. 1) are identified by $Work\_Id = -1$.

Note that each slot can accommodate at most *one* application-specific activity, as opposed to the classic *cyclic executive* [8,9]. This has several advantages: one is that we want to have the highest possible control over release jitter, which cannot be accomplished if several activities of varying execution times share the same slot; another reason is that, with only one activity per slot, the scheduler only needs to check one activity at a time for potential overrun (see next subsection), which helps keep the scheduler simple, and consequently helps keep release jitter small. Another substantial difference is that each slot may have a different duration, as opposed to the fixed duration of minor frames in the classic cyclic executive.

3.2   The Time-Triggered Scheduler

The time-triggered scheduler is the element of the system that enforces the timely execution of the time-triggered plan. This includes not only releasing the activities at their predefined release times, but also controlling that all activities behave as per the plan's design. In particular, the scheduler must check and take correcting actions for possible overruns, i.e., activities whose actual execution time may exceed their allocated slot duration. The scheduler must also give support to mode changes, as described in the previous subsection. Contrary to the case of priority-based schedulers, where scheduling decisions are taken at arbitrary points in time, all the decisions and actions of the time-triggered scheduler must be taken and executed at predefined points in time; in our case, at the start of each slot. Note that this is not necessarily a periodic event, since slots may have different durations.

At the start of **any slot**, the scheduler checks whether there is still pending work from the previous slot. Since the slot duration must accommodate, by design, the worst-case execution time of its work, continued execution of an activity from the previous slot constitutes an overrun. There are several possible ways to treat this situation. One possibility is to lead the system to a fail-safe state (as in [10]), which can be achieved by means of a mode change as we will show later. For the rest of this paper, we take a *less drastic* approach and allow the offending activity to continue executing at a lower priority, so that it only affects a particular set of tasks in the system (including an empty set, if the overrunning activity is set to *background* priority). The particular *demoted priority* can be specified for each activity as will be shown in the following sections. After this overrun check, the scheduler takes different actions depending on the type of slot:

Regular slot: The scheduler releases the execution of the slot's activity, denoted by its regular *Work_Id*, and assigns it the time-triggered level priority.

Empty slot: No time-triggered activity needs be executed until the arrival of the next slot. During an empty slot, time is fully available for priority scheduled tasks.

Mode change slot: The scheduler checks whether there is a pending mode change request. If there is one, then the current plan is substituted with the new mode plan (which may be totally different) and the next slot will be the first slot of the new plan. Otherwise, the slot duration is also available for priority scheduled tasks.

The actual implementation details of mode changes depend on the concrete platform. Ideally, the hardware includes enough memory resources to allocate all the required time-triggered tasks for all modes. On platforms with scarce resources however, it may be necessary to delete old-mode tasks and load new-mode tasks to memory. The time needed for these operations, as well as any additional overhead incurred to enforce the mode change, can be absorbed by the mode-change slot duration.

4   API for Time-Triggered Plans

We propose an Application Program Interface (API) for Ada programs to use time-triggered plans, possibly in combination with other concurrent, priority scheduled tasks. The API for time-triggered plans is provided via the Ada package Time_Triggered_Scheduling. Listing 1 shows the most relevant aspects of its specification.

The type Any_Work_Id refers to work identifiers in general, including regular and *special* work identifiers (such as empty slots and mode change slots, as described in Subsect. 3.1). Subtype Special_Work_Id covers the negative range of Any_Work_Id, plus the value zero, whereas subtype Regular_Work_Id refers to strictly positive numbers that correspond to regular work identifiers. Constants Empty_Slot and Mode_Change_Slot (assigned in the private part of the package) identify their corresponding special work identifiers.

The record type Time_Slot encapsulates the two defining elements of time slots: their duration and the work identifier for that slot. Additionally, we include the record field Next_Slot_Separation, whose value is to be supplied at design time, indicating the time separation between the start of the current slot and the next slot in the plan allocated to the same work. The use of this piece of information is further explained in Sect. 5.

A time-triggered plan is an ordered sequence of time slots, as represented by the array type Time-Triggered-Plan. Additionally, the access type Time-Triggered-Plan-Access provides access to time-triggered plans, so that plans can be efficiently passed as parameters to subprograms.

Listing 1. Time-triggered API (incomplete)

```
-- Context clauses omitted
package Time_Triggered_Scheduling is
    type Any_Work_Id is new Integer;
    subtype Special_Work_Id is Any_Work_Id range Any_Work_Id'First .. 0;
    subtype Regular_Work_Id is Any_Work_Id range 1 .. Any_Work_Id'Last;
    Empty_Slot      : constant Special_Work_Id;
    Mode_Change_Slot : constant Special_Work_Id;

    type Time_Slot is record
        Slot_Duration       : Time_Span;
        Work_Id             : Any_Work_Id;
        Next_Slot_Separation : Time_Span; -- Distance to next slot of same Work_Id
    end record;
    type Time_Triggered_Plan is array (Natural range <>) of Time_Slot;
    type Time_Triggered_Plan_Access is access all Time_Triggered_Plan;

    protected type Time_Triggered_Scheduler (Nr_Of_Work_Ids: Regular_Work_Id)
        with Priority => System.Interrupt_Priority'Last is
        -- Setting a new time-triggered plan
        procedure Set_Plan (TTP : in Time_Triggered_Plan_Access; At_Time : in Time);
        procedure Set_Plan (TTP : in Time_Triggered_Plan_Access; In_Time : in Time_Span);
        -- Time-triggered tasks wait here for their activation
        entry Wait_For_Activation (Work_Id : Regular_Work_Id);

        -- Features for composed task patterns
        -- Continue TT task at default or given demoted priority
        procedure Leave_TT_Level (Work_Id : Regular_Work_Id);
        procedure Leave_TT_Level (Work_Id : Regular_Work_Id; Prio: System.Priority );
        -- Release time of the last slot of a given Work_Id
        function Get_Last_Release (Work_Id : Regular_Work_Id) return Time;
        -- Duration of the last slot of a given Work_Id
        function Get_Last_Slot_Duration (Work_Id : Regular_Work_Id) return Time_Span;
        -- Separation between the start of the last slot and the next slot of a given Work_Id
        function Get_Next_Slot_Separation (Work_Id : Regular_Work_Id) return Time_Span;
    private
        -- ... Further details in listing 4
    end Time_Triggered_Scheduler;

private
    Empty_Slot      : constant Special_Work_Id := 0;
    Mode_Change_Slot : constant Special_Work_Id := -1;
    -- ... Further details in listing 4
end Time_Triggered_Scheduling;
```

Listing 1 continues with the definition of protected type Time-Triggered-Scheduler, which encapsulates all data and subprograms used to implement the time-triggered scheduler. The type has a discriminant (Nr-Of-Work-Ids) to specify the number of regular work identifiers used by all plans in all modes. Based on this number, we define bounded data structures (in the private part of the protected type, not shown here) that are needed for the scheduler's operation. The priority of the time-triggered scheduler is set to the maximum to prevent interference from other parts of the system with its operations. Care has been taken to implement all the provided operations using constant cost subprograms. The protected procedure Set-Plan sets a new plan (given by parameter TTP) to be started after a given point in time – the two versions of Set_Plan differ only in using a relative or an absolute value for that starting time. A plan set by means of Set_Plan will start executing immediately after that starting time if there was no plan running (it was the first plan to be set) or at the end of the next mode change slot otherwise. The entry Wait_For_Activation suspends the calling task until the work corresponding to its Work_Id must be released, according to the current plan.

The rest of protected subprograms are useful for composed task patterns such as those described in Sect. 5. With Leave_TT_Level, a time-triggered work requests to continue executing at a default demoted priority, or a particular priority for each invocation. This is useful for works with an optional part that cannot be granted by the plan due to an excessive or unbounded worst-case execution time. The optional part can continue executing in competition with priority scheduled task and calculate the best possible response in the available time, without interfering other planned activities. The three getter functions provide the indicated values: the time when the calling work was last released (Get_Last_Release); the duration of the slot in which the work was last released (Get_Last_Slot_Duration); and the time distance between the work's current slot and the next slot in the plan that is allocated to that work (Get_Next_Slot_Separation). The following Section shows how different patterns can take advantage of these functions.

5   Patterns for Time-Triggered Tasks

Common practice in time-triggered systems is to have all activities implemented by subprograms that are directly called from the scheduler. We have taken a different approach, whereby every activity (work) is executed by its own associated Ada task: there is one task behind each work. Before we justify this implementation decision, note that we are considering time-triggered schedules as part of a more complex system that includes also other priority-scheduled tasks. Hence we are not imposing here a special requirement on the operating system or runtime support: a priority-based, preemptive scheduler is given for granted. Our approach is to implement each time-triggered work with a high-priority task and let the RTOS decide which task to execute at a given time, be it a time-triggered task or a priority-scheduled task. In addition, the implementation must also be prepared for demoting overrunning time-triggered tasks, as explained in Sect. 3. This feature alone requires that works must be executed by tasks whose priorities can be changed by the scheduler at run time. Hence we use task types to define patterns. We observe however that communication between works requires protected objects (not just shared memory) if we allow overrunning time-triggered tasks to continue executing at a demoted priority beyond their allocated slot, concurrently with other tasks. Using protected objects ensures that priority demotion of overrunning tasks occurs only when data integrity is not compromised ([7], D.5.1).

The API described in Sect. 4 may be used for implementing time-triggered works of different complexity. Listing 2 shows the simplest pattern for time-triggered tasks we can think of, implemented by task type Simple_Worker. The task first calls the scheduler's entry Wait_For_Activation. The scheduler will then keep the calling task blocked until a slot arrives in which its work identifier is planned to execute. Upon completion of the call to Wait_For_Activation, the task then executes its specific work actions. This is repeated in an infinite loop. Worker tasks are created by instantiation of this task type.[1] Each instance must use a different value for the discriminant Work_Id – this is checked at runtime by the scheduler and the exception Program_Error is raised if a task tries to use another task's work identifier. The discriminant Prio specifies the default demoted priority, i.e., the priority to which the task will be demoted in case of overrun or when it calls Leave_TT_Level without specifying a demoted priority value. We use the CPU aspect here to set the affinity of all time-triggered tasks to the same processor, although this is not compulsory. On a multiprocessor platform, each processor may be running a different plan and each work task must be confined to its respective CPU.

Listing 2. Simple pattern for time-triggered tasks

```
TTS: Time_Triggered_Scheduler(3); –– A scheduler for 3 different works ( arbitrary )

task type Simple_Worker (Work_Id: Regular_Work_Id; Prio: System. Priority )
  with Priority => Prio, –– Demoted priority in case of overrun
       CPU      => 1;    –– Set task's affinity
task body Simple_Worker is
begin
  loop
      TTS.Wait_For_Activation (Work_Id); –– Block here until my slot arrives
      Do_My_Work (...);                   –– Specific work actions
  end loop;
end Simple_Worker;
```

More elaborated task patterns are also supported by the scheduler described in Sect. 4. In particular, we propose the following additional patterns:

Worker_With_Cancellation. Before causing an overrun, a task following this pattern will cancel its activity, instead of following the default behaviour of continuing its execution at a demoted priority level. This pattern is intended for tasks that cannot contribute any value after their allocated slot duration, for example because their result must be applied to a system output immediately.

The pattern modifies the Simpe_Worker by enclosing the Do_My_Work sentence in the abortable part of an Ada asynchronous transfer of control statement. The triggering alternative is an absolute delay until the end of the current slot, hence the work will be aborted before incurring overrun.[2] This time is obtained by adding the slot duration to its corresponding start time (Get_Last_Slot_Duration + Get_Last_Release).

---

[1] Note that, for general application of the pattern, the actions represented by Do_My_Work are different for each work. We have kept the patterns simple, but in actual systems the task's actions should be determined more flexibly (e.g. by using access to subprogram or generic packages for task patterns).

[2] To be on the safe side, we should subtract the worst-case duration of abort-deferred operations in the work's code. This would avoid the work to cross a slot barrier while executing an abort-deferred operation.

Worker_With_Initial_Final. This pattern is conceived for works that require controlled and short jitter both at the beginning and towards the end of their activity. The work is said to have an *initial* part (e.g., sensing a physical environment variable) and a *final* part (e.g., the actuation phase of a control algorithm).

This pattern is a simple duplication of the loop actions of Simple_Pattern: there are two calls to Wait_For_Activation, one preceding the initial part and one preceding the final part of the work. Note that the same effect can in principle be obtained by two works, one for the initial part and one for the final. Using this pattern, however, the advantage is that all communication between the initial and the final part is immediate since both parts share the common task's stack (no inter-task communication is needed).

Worker_With_Initial_Optional_Final. This pattern is for activities with initial and final parts with strict jitter restrictions, plus an optional part between them. The optional part may implement an optimisation algorithm for improving a *quick and dirty* result obtained during the time allocated to the initial part. The execution time of optimisation algorithms may be quite disperse, and hence it is not easy to define their required slot duration: too large a duration would impose delays to other activities; too short and the potential for run-rime overruns increases.

This pattern executes first the initial part until completion. After calling procedure Leave_TT_Level, the task continues with the optional part at a demoted priority. When the optional part is completed, the task will wait again for activation until the arrival of the next slot corresponding to its work identifier. In that slot, the work's task executes the final part using the best result obtained during the optional part. If the optional part has not finished by the time when starting the final part is due, then the optional part is aborted (as in the Worker_With_Cancellation pattern). Listing 3 gives the implementation of pattern Worker_With_Initial_Optional_Final .

Listing 3. Pattern for works with initial, optional and final parts

```
task body Worker_With_Initial_Optional_Final is
   -- Common data to all parts goes here
begin
   loop
      TTS.Wait_For_Activation(Work_Id);
      Initial_Work ;  -- Do initial part
      TTS.Leave_TT_Level(Work_Id,Optional_Part_Prio); -- Prepare to start optional part
      select
         delay until TTS.Get_Last_Release(Work_Id) + TTS.Get_Next_Slot_Separation(Work_Id);
      then abort
         Optional_Work; -- Do optional part
      end select ;
      TTS.Wait_For_Activation(Work_Id);
      Final_Work;      -- Do final part
   end loop;
end Worker_With_Initial_Optional_Final ;
```

Figure 2 shows the execution of an example plan with three time-triggered tasks (work tasks 1, 2 and 3) and two priority-based tasks (T4 and T5). Work 1 is a Simple_Worker, work 2 is a Worker_With_Initial_Final and work 3 uses the more elaborated Worker_With_Initial_Optional_Final pattern. T4 and T5 execute at their lower priorities, using the time made available by empty slots and early completion of work tasks. Work 3 starts executing the initial part (marked 3_I), which gets completed before the end of the allocated slot duration. It then calls Leave_TT_Level to continue the execution of the optional part (marked 3_O) at a given priority, in competition with the rest of priority- or time-triggered-scheduled tasks. In this case, the demoted priority is half way between the priorities of T4 and T5. When the optional part completes, it calls Wait_For_Activation to wait for the arrival of the final part slot (marked 3_F). Note that the optional part is abortable, hence it can be forced to not cause overrun. All we need to do is set the delay of the triggering statement to the right value: by the arrival of the next slot allocated to this work. We obtain our last activation time by using the above mentioned extension Get_Last_Release. To this time, we need to add the duration of all slots in between the current slot and the next slot for the current *Work_Id*. This imposes a time cost (traversing the plan) that we do not want to charge on the scheduler at run time. To avoid this overhead on the scheduler, we use the Next_Slot_Separation field of Slot_Type record. The separation to my next slot can be easily calculated at design time and stored in the plan using this field, where the scheduler can read it immediately. The API function Get_Next_Slot_Separation returns precisely this value for a given *Work_Id*.

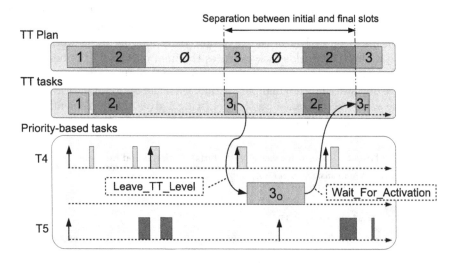

Fig. 2. Execution of a **Worker_With_Initial_Optional_Final** pattern.

6   Implementation Details

A thorough description of all implementation details is not possible here due to space limitations. We will limit ourselves to the most relevant details in terms of their impact on jitter, i.e., the actions taken by the scheduler to timely enforce the plan. We will omit discussing the implementation details of (much less frequent) mode changes.

As shown in Sect. 4, a time-triggered scheduler is enclosed in a protected object with the highest priority. This grants mutually exclusive access to it. Listing 4 shows the private parts of package Time_Triggered_Scheduling and protected type Time_Triggered_Scheduler, which were omitted in Listing 1. They include all required types and state variables needed for the time-triggered scheduler to enforce the execution of the plan according to the model described so far.

Listing 4 shows the private details of the time-triggered scheduler. The private part of the protected type includes the entry family Wait_Until_Released, with as many members as work identifiers used in the system (across all modes). When a worker task calls the scheduler's entry Wait_For_Activation, it is ultimately requeued to its corresponding entry family member, where it waits until its specific barrier is open by the scheduler. All barriers are simple Booleans stored in Work_Control, one per work identifier – more specifically, the field Allow_Release of the record type Work_Info.

Registration of work tasks in the plan is automatically handled by the scheduler the first time a task calls Wait_For_Activation. Registration consists in taking note of the caller's Task_Id and its default demoted priority, taken from the caller's base priority. Additional checks are enforced by the scheduler to make sure the calling task is the one that registered for the specified work identifier. Program error is raised otherwise.

Listing 4. Private parts of scheduler package and protected type

```
package Time_Triggered_Scheduling is
    ... -- Types for storing runtime information
    type Work_Info is private;
    type Work_Info_Array is array (Regular_Work_Id range <>) of Work_Info;

    protected type Time_Triggered_Scheduler (Nr_Of_Work_Ids: Regular_Work_Id)  ...  is
        -- See full spec in Listing 1
    private  -- Of protected type
        entry Wait_Until_Released (1 .. Nr_Of_Work_Ids);      -- Entry family: one entry per work
        procedure MC_Handler (Event : in out Timing_Event);  -- Handler for mode change timing event
        procedure NS_Handler (Event : in out Timing_Event);  -- Handler for new slot timing event
        procedure Change_Plan (At_Time : Time);              -- Enforce plan change
        procedure Update_Slot_Info;                          -- Update indexes and times to new slot
        Current_Plan, Next_Plan : Time_Triggered_Plan_Access := null;  -- Current and next plans
        NS_Event, MC_Event     : Timing_Event;               -- New Slot and Mode Change TEs
        Current_Slot_Index , Next_Slot_Index  : Natural:= 0;  -- Relevant indexes and times
        Next_Mode_Release, Next_Slot_Release : Time := Time_Last;
        Work_Control : Work_Info_Array (1.. Nr_Of_Work_Ids);  -- Runtime work info
    end Time_Triggered_Scheduler;
private  -- Of package
    ...
    type Work_Info is record
        Is_Running: Boolean:= False;                  Demoted_Priority: System. Priority := System. Priority ' First ;
        Work_Task_Id: Task_Id:= Null_Task_Id ;  Allow_Release: Boolean:= False;
        Last_Release : Time:= Time_Last;              Last_Slot_Index : Natural:= 0;
    end record;
end Time_Triggered_Scheduling;
```

Listing 5. Handler for the new slot timing event

```
procedure NS_Handler (Event : in out Timing_Event) is
    Current_Work_Id : Any_Work_Id;    Now : Time;
begin
    -- Check for overrun (Current_Slot_Index refers to the just expired slot)
    if Current_Slot_Index in Current_Plan'Range then
        Current_Work_Id := Current_Plan ( Current_Slot_Index ).Work_Id;
        if Current_Work_Id in Regular_Work_Id and then  -- Regular work
            Work_Control(Current_Work_Id).Is_Running then  -- Still running => demote
            Set_Priority (Work_Control(Current_Work_Id).Demoted_Priority,
                          Work_Control(Current_Work_Id).Work_Task_Id);
        end if ;
    end if ;
    -- Prepare to process current slot
    Now := Next_Slot_Release;            -- Start time of current slot
    Update_Slot_Info ;                   -- Update Current_Slot_Index and Next_Slot_Release
    Current_Work_Id := Current_Plan( Current_Slot_Index ).Work_Id; -- Obtain current Work_Id
    case Current_Work_Id is    -- Process current slot actions
        when Mode_Change_Slot =>
            if Next_Plan /= null and then Next_Mode_Release <= Now then
                Change_Plan (Next_Slot_Release); -- Enforce new plan at the end of MC slot
            else
                NS_Event.Set_Handler (Next_Slot_Release, NS_Handler'Access); -- Reprogram NS_Event
            end if ;
        when Empty_Slot =>
            NS_Event.Set_Handler (Next_Slot_Release, NS_Handler'Access); -- Reprogram NS_Event
        when Regular_Work_Id'Range => -- It's a regular slot
            Work_Control(Current_Work_Id).Allow_Release := True;      -- Release the work's task
            NS_Event.Set_Handler (Next_Slot_Release, NS_Handler'Access); -- Reprogram NS_Event
        when others =>
            raise Program_Error with "Undefined Work Id";
    end case;
end NS_Handler;
```

The scheduler may be triggered by two possible timing events: NS_Event, which signals the arrival of a new slot, and MC_Event for mode change events. Their handlers are, respectively, NS_Handler and MC_Handler. As justified above, here we describe only the handling of the new slot event, implemented by protected procedure NS_Handler.

Other objects declared in the private part of protected object Time_Triggered_Scheduler include Change_Plan, which assigns control variables and programs the NS_Event timing event for the first slot of the next plan to switch to; Update_Slot_Info, also a simple procedure that updates control variables when a new slot starts; eight control variables used by the scheduler; and Work_Control, the array of work control blocks.

Listing 5 shows the handler for the timing event signalling the arrival of a new slot (NS_Handler). According to the model described in Sect. 3, there are different checks to make at the start of every slot. The first one is to detect overrunning work from the just expired slot. The two nested *if* statements check that the task associated to the previous slot is still running, in which case it is demoted to its Demoted_Priority, which is retrieved from its corresponding work control block. The task will continue at a non-disturbing priority level, where its interference is bounded to what is acceptable by the rest of application tasks.

The handler then goes on with processing the just started slot. After updating some indexes and times, the new slot is processed in a *case* statement. If it is a mode change slot and there is a pending mode change request (a revious call to Set_Plan has set a non null value for the Next_Plan control variable), then the new mode is enforced at the end of the current slot if the starting time of the new plan is not in the future – if it happens to be in the future, then the mode change handler (not described here) will take care of changing the plan. If there is no pending plan change to process, then the new slot timing event is reprogrammed for the start time of next slot. In the case of an empty slot, we just need to reprogram the next slot timing event. If it is a regular slot, then the scheduler opens the barrier for the work task, which will be released at the highest priority immediately after completion of the handler, and reprograms the new slot timing event. In the body of each member of Wait_Until_Released, where works wait to be released by the scheduler, the task's priority is set to the time-triggered level (it could have been demoted due to a previous overrun, or a call to Leave_TT_Level, or it could be the first activation of the task). The other two simple operations in Wait_Until_Released are to close again its barrier and to mark the work as *running* in its work control block.

We note that all the required scheduler functionality can be implemented using three types of sentences: simple assignments, setting one task's priority, and setting one timing event. How efficiently these two last operations operations are supported by the runtime is of crucial importance to keep the scheduler's overhead small and hence to cause minimal jitter to work tasks. The time needed to release a work task contributes also to the scheduler's overhead; but that would be the only blocked task in its corresponding Wait_Until_Released member, which contributes to shorten the completion of that protected action.

7   Experimental Results and Discussion

In order to evaluate the performance of the proposed approach, we have conducted experiments to measure release jitter of a combined set of tasks: three time-triggered tasks plus two deadline monotonic tasks. The system matches the one depicted in Fig. 2.

The two deadline monotonic tasks, T4 and T5, execute at lower priorities 6 and 4, and have periods of 325 and 500 ms, respectively. The total plan duration is 1200 ms and it contains the following sequence of 7 slots: 100 ms for W1; 200 ms for WI2; an empty slot of 300 ms; 100 ms for WI3; an empty slot of 200 ms; another 200 ms for WF2; and finally 100 ms for WF3.

We compiled this system for MaRTE OS [11] in bare machine configuration and executed it on two hardware platforms, one using a Celeron CPU at 1.8 GHz and the other using an older Pentium III at 800 MHz. Figure 3 shows cumulative frequency histograms of release jitter measured on both platforms for all tasks in the system. Note that the X axes are pseudo-logarithmic and cover the range from 0 to 1 second.

On both platforms the results are comparable in terms of trend. Priority scheduled tasks T4 and T5 experience a wide range of jitter values. In 50 to 60 % of the cases, jitter is comparable to that of time triggered tasks, but then there is a slowly growing trend with release jitters up to 140 ms of T5 on the Celeron

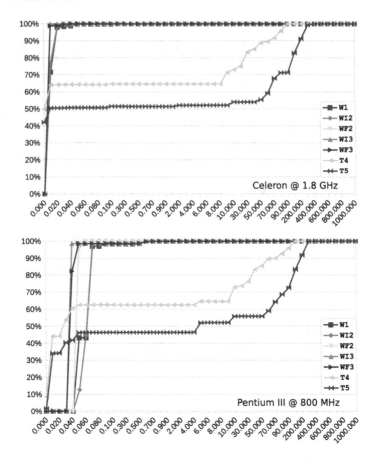

Fig. 3. Cumulative frequency histograms of jitter, measured in ms.

and 395 ms on the slower Pentium III. This makes T4 and T5 inappropriate for implementing control algorithms or precisely synchronised communications. Time-triggered tasks experience a maximum jitter of 272 μs on the Celeron and 702 μs on Pentium III. Furthermore, in 98.5 % of the cases, jitter on time-triggered tasks was below 30 μs on the Celeron and 80 μs on the Pentium III. Even considering the totality of cases, the results on maximum jitter are 3 orders of magnitude apart between time-triggered and priority-scheduled tasks.

Looking at minimum jitter values, we observe (more clearly in the Pentium case) that priority-scheduled tasks experience shorter minimum jitter than time-triggered tasks. This occurs when they are released at idle times, when they are free from higher-priority interference. This was expected because releasing a time-triggered task has the additional overhead of the timing event, plus priority promotion, plus completing the protected action implemented by the Wait_Until_Released entry.

8   Conclusions and Future Work

This paper has proposed and explored an approach that allows a time-triggered plan to run under the same priority scheduler where other priority-scheduled tasks are running. By using the highest priority level for the time-triggered schedule, and controlling the scheduler by means of a timing event, the effect is a two-level scheduler that ensures precedence of time-triggered activities over priority-scheduled tasks, which is essential to keep release jitter low for time-triggered activities.

We have also proposed several programming patterns for task time-triggered activities, from the simplest cyclic pattern, to patterns accommodating the structure of decomposed tasks, an approach proposed for control tasks that can also be used for other purposes such as handling communications in networks requiring strict synchronisation (e.g., the CAN bus).

Experimental data indicate that all time-triggered tasks are subject to similar interference, bounded to values that are, in the vast majority of cases, orders of magnitude lower than the release jitter experienced by priority-scheduled tasks. Our approach naturally accepts previously designed time-triggered plans, and facilitates the extension of those plans with additional priority-scheduled tasks. There are other aspects of the proposal, not covered in this paper, that are the subject of current and future work. They include:

Use on multiprocessor platforms: Although we have limited our experiments to a single CPU, the approach presented in this paper is applicable to multiprocessor platforms. In a fully partitioned system, each processor executes its own plan and work tasks have their affinity statically assigned. A certain amount of migration is also possible, whereby work tasks can alternate slots of plans supported by different processors, to balance the overall time-triggered workload. Global scheduling of work tasks (i.e. allowing them to migrate at arbitrary points in time) seems not appropriate in this case, since plans assign slots to one and only one work task.

Schedulability analysis: A schedulability analysis is needed to assess the feasibility of the full task set, including both the time-triggered plan and the priority-based scheduling levels. The plan can be guaranteed by construction, since it executes at the highest priority level and suffers no interference from priority-based tasks. But the analysis of priority-based tasks needs to take into account the interference caused by the execution of the higher-priority plan. One possibility is to consider the whole plan as a real-time transaction, as defined in the computational model of [12]. The period of the transaction would be the length of the plan and each time slot can be considered as a task of the transaction with a static offset equal to its release time. Adjacent time slots can be considered as a single task in the equivalent transaction. This transaction has the highest priority and the interference introduced in lower priority levels can be computed as described in [12].

Tools and integration with real-time framework: Designing a plan can be a difficult task, especially for multiprocessors and with a certain degree of migration. Development of software tools to ease building and analysing these combined systems would be of great value. Additionally, the integration of this approach with existing real-time frameworks (such as those proposed in [13–15]) would facilitate the use of pre-designed periodic tasks patterns, and the independent handling of modes at the two different levels, priority-based and time-triggered. We want to explore the feasibility and properties derived from such integration effort.

References

1. Liu, C., Layland, J.: Scheduling algorithms for multiprogramming in a hard real-time environment. J. ACM **20**(1), 46–61 (1973)
2. Martí, P., Fuertes, J., Fohler, G.: Jitter compensation for real-time control systems. In: Real-Time Systems Symposium (2001)
3. Dobrin, R.: Combining off-line schedule construction and fixed priority scheduling in real-time computer systems. Ph.D. thesis. Mälardalen University (2005)
4. Cervin, A.: Integrated control and real-time scheduling. Ph.D. thesis. Lund Institute of Technology, April 2003
5. Balbastre, P., Ripoll, I., Vidal, J., Crespo, A.: A task model to reduce control delays. Real-Time Syst. **27**(3), 215–236 (2004)
6. Hong, S., Hu, X., Lemmon, M.: Reducing delay jitter of real-time control tasks through adaptive deadline adjustments. In: 22nd Euromicro Conference on Real-Time Systems - ECRTS, pp. 229–238. IEEE Computer Society (2010)
7. ISO/IEC-JTC1-SC22-WG9: Ada Reference Manual ISO/IEC 8652:2012(E) (2012). http://www.ada-europe.org/manuals/LRM-2012.pdf
8. Baker, T.P., Shaw, A.: The cyclic executive model and Ada. In: Proceedings IEEE Real Time Systems Symposium 1988, Huntsville, Alabama, pp. 120–129 (1988)
9. Liu, J.W.S.: Real-Time Systems. Prentice-Hall Inc., Upper Saddle River (2000)
10. Pont, M.J.: The Engineering of Reliable Embedded Systems: LPC1769. SafeTTy Systems Limited, Skelmersdale (2014). ISBN: 978-0-9930355-0-0
11. Aldea Rivas, M., González Harbour, M.: MaRTE OS: an Ada kernel for real-time embedded applications. In: Strohmeier, A., Craeynest, D. (eds.) Ada-Europe 2001. LNCS, vol. 2043, pp. 305–316. Springer, Heidelberg (2001)
12. Palencia, J., González-Harbour, M.: Schedulability analysis for tasks with static and dynamic offsets. In: 9th IEEE Real-Time Systems Symposium (1998)
13. Wellings, A.J., Burns, A.: A framework for real-time utilities for Ada 2005. Ada Lett. XXVI **XXVII**(2), 41–47 (2007)
14. Real, J., Crespo, A.: Incorporating operating modes to an Ada real-time framework. Ada Lett. **30**(1), 73–85 (2010)
15. Sáez, S., Terrasa, S., Crespo, A.: A real-time framework for multiprocessor platforms using Ada 2012. In: Romanovsky, A., Vardanega, T. (eds.) Ada-Europe 2011. LNCS, vol. 6652, pp. 46–60. Springer, Heidelberg (2011)

Author Index

Printed in the United States
By Bookmasters